《《《《《《《《《《《《《《《《《《《《《〈〉》》》》》》》》》》》》》》》》》》》》

THE PHILOSOPHY
OF LANGUAGE

«««««««««««««‹›»»»»»»»»»»»»»»

THE PHILOSOPHY

«««««««««««««‹›»»»»»»»»»»»»»»

STUDIES IN LANGUAGE
Noam Chomsky and Morris Halle, Editors

HARPER & ROW, *Publishers*   *New York and London*

《《《《《《《《《《《《《《《《《《《《《《《《《《《《《《《《《《《《》》》》》》》》》》》》》》》》》》》》》》》》

OF LANGUAGE

《《《《《《《《《《《《《《《《《《《《《《《《《《《《《《《《《《《《》》》》》》》》》》》》》》》》》》》》》》》》

JERROLD J. KATZ

Department of Humanities
and Research Laboratory of Electronics
Massachusetts Institute of Technology

THE PHILOSOPHY OF LANGUAGE

Copyright © 1966 by Jerrold J. Katz

C-1

Library of Congress Catalog Card Number: 66-11265

To my sons,

Seth and Jesse

CONTENTS

PREFACE

This book is an attempt to develop a new approach to the philosophy of language and to justify it by showing its superiority over other approaches in solving significant philosophical problems. What is new about this approach is that it asks what the theory of language —that theory in empirical linguistics that concerns the nature of language—can say about philosophical problems. That is, this approach to the philosophy of language deals with philosophical problems that can be represented as questions in empirical linguistics about the nature of language in general, and it provides solutions on the basis of theoretical constructions from a theory of language. It seeks to understand conceptual knowledge on the basis of discoveries in empirical linguistics about the manner in which such knowledge is expressed and communicated in natural languages. Thus, the aim of the philosophy of language, as conceived here, is the same as that of other branches of philosophy, but the means for achieving this common aim are different. The justification for going outside the boundaries of philosophy proper for solutions of philosophical problems, in the cases concerned, is that the solutions are there.

The theory of language is a statement of linguistic universals, i.e., of features that all natural languages have in common. It formulates the principles that determine the necessary form and content of natural languages and defines the notion 'natural language.' From the viewpoint of linguistics, the theoretical constructions in a theory of language are devised to provide the apparatus for representing features that are invariant from natural language to natural language. From the viewpoint of my approach to the philosophy of language, on the other hand, these theoretical constructions provide the apparatus for constructing solutions to philosophical problems. Accordingly, unlike the linguist who asks only whether these constructions are adequate to serve the scientific function for which they were intended, the philosopher of language must also ask whether they meet the conditions for solutions to philosophical problems. Hence, if there are theoretical constructions in the theory of language that do meet the conditions for the solution to some philosophical problem, and if their empirical support in terms of linguistic evidence is strong enough, then these constructions must be an acceptable solution to the philosophical problem.

This approach to the philosophy of language is not intended as a reconstruction or reformulation of any approach that traditional or contemporary philosophers have taken. Consequently, no effort will be made to justify it by appealing to the words or deeds of any philosophers. For one thing, it is quite doubtful whether any philosophers, past or present, take the same approach, or even one sufficiently similar. For another thing, such an appeal would be beside the point because, rather than justifying the adoption of my approach, it could at best establish its historical antecedents. Hence, the only attempt at justification will be to try to show that this approach yields important philosophical results concerning the nature of conceptual knowledge, results that are not forthcoming on the basis of alternative approaches. If this attempt proves successful, there is strong reason to hold that this approach to the philosophy of language is the best framework within which to pursue the aims of the philosophy of language.

In Chapter 1, I have discussed the place of philosophizing about and from language—construed broadly to include all approaches to the philosophy of language—in the context of philosophy proper. Chapter 2 presents my approach and differentiates it from other approaches to the philosophy of language. Chapter 3 considers the two approaches that have dominated the philosophy of language thus far in this century: logical empiricism and ordinary language philosophy. It tries to show that both have failed to establish any conclusive solutions to significant philosophical problems, and that neither is capable of doing so, principally because neither bases itself on an adequate theory of linguistic structure. In Chapter 4, I have given a fairly detailed, introductory account of the theory of language as currently developed in empirical linguistics. And, in Chapter 5, I try to show that a number of outstanding philosophical problems (falling in the areas of analyticity, categories, innate ideas, and philosophical method) can be naturally handled within the theory of language described in Chapter 4. The selection of these particular problems implies no intended limitation on the philosophical applications of the theory of language. Indeed, no such limitation can be reasonably foreseen until a far more thorough study of both the theory of language and its philosophical applications has been made.

I am happy to take this opportunity to express my gratitude to Professor George Miller of Harvard University who made it possible for me to finish this book by enabling me to spend a year's leave of absence at the Center for Cognitive Studies, Harvard University. I wish to thank Mr. David Perlmutter and Mr. Richard Carter for their help in reading proofs and for the numerous improvements they suggested to me.

This work was supported in part by the Joint Services Electronics Program (Contract DA36-039-AMC-03200[E]); in part by the National Science Foundation (Grant GP-2495); the National Institute of Health (Grant MH-04737-04); the National Aeronautics and Space Administration (Grant NsG-496); and the United

States Air Force (ESD Contract AF 19[628]-2487). This work was also supported in part by a grant from the National Institute of Health (No. MH-05120-04) to Harvard University, Center for Cognitive Studies.

J. J. K.

December, 1965

Je croye veritablement, que les langues sont le mielleur miroir de l'esprit humain, et qu'une analyse exacte de la signification des mots feroit mieux connoitre que toute autre chose, les operations l'entendement.

LEIBNIZ

It is astonishing what language can do. With a few syllables it can express an incalculable number of thoughts, so that even a thought grasped by a human being for the first time can be put into a form of words which will be understood by someone to whom the thought is entirely new. This would be impossible, were we not able to distinguish parts in the thought corresponding to the parts of a sentence, so that the structure of the sentence serves as an image of the structure of the thought.

GOTTLOB FREGE

THE PHILOSOPHY
OF LANGUAGE

THE PHILOSOPHY
OF LANGUAGE

It is a somewhat paradoxical fact that the conceptual systems that give man an understanding of himself and his world are themselves not adequately understood by him. Everyone will readily agree that Copernican astronomy, atomic physics, the kinetic theory of heat, relativity theory, and other comparable scientific systems have made our universe a far more comprehensible place to live in than it was before their construction. Such conceptual systems successfully explain large ranges of complex natural phenomena; yet they stand in need of much explanation themselves. Indeed, it is not too much to say that, as things are presently, there is need for clarification

1

on almost every point concerning the nature of such systems and that even the most elementary questions about them still remain unanswered. For example, we are still unable to say exactly what a scientific theory is, what sorts of explanations are obtained from empirically successful theories, how theories differ from laws, what laws are, or how laws and theories are confirmed by evidence. Thus, we are very far from a full understanding of these conceptual systems taken as objects of theoretical investigation, even though they are understood in the straightforward sense in which an understanding of them is essential to gaining the understanding they afford of their subject matter.[1] Paradoxically, we lack an understanding of what they are, even though, in the straightforward sense, we understand them well enough to say quite a lot about other things.

It is with this need to understand the nature of conceptual systems that philosophical inquiry begins. Philosophy takes the conceptual systems developed by scientists, mathematicians, art critics, moralists, theologians, et al., as its subject matter and seeks to explain and clarify what has to be explained and clarified about such systems in order to render them fully comprehensible. Philosophers pursue this task by describing the structure of these conceptual systems, analyzing the methods by which such systems are arrived at, and evaluating the validity of the claims made for them. Today such description, analysis, and evaluation of particular

---

[1] I am not denying that they are understood in the sense in which we say, "Jones understands atomic physics."

conceptual systems within various academic disciplines is carried on within the several branches of philosophy: philosophy of science, philosophy of mathematics, philosophy of art (aesthetics), philosophy of morality (ethics), philosophy of religion, and so forth.

But the particular conceptual systems considered in each of these special branches of philosophy are far from independent of one another. Rather, not only do such particular conceptual systems overlap—so that one system in one discipline utilizes the insights of and poses problems for others in different disciplines—but together the particular conceptual systems from every discipline form an integrated fabric of conceptual knowledge. Thus, philosophy, in its most embracing concern, studies this over-all fabric of conceptual knowledge, seeking to articulate the general structure of conceptual knowledge, to determine the intellectual and empirical methods common to all forms of conceptual construction, and to reveal the principles by which genuine cognitive claims can be distinguished from spurious or insubstantial ones. Consequently, although the philosophical investigation of the over-all system of conceptual knowledge and the philosophical investigation of particular conceptual systems are distinguishable, and this distinction is quite important to the division of philosophical labor, they are strongly dependent on each other. The results of each investigation must perforce contribute significantly to those of the other, with the former providing organization and research focus for the latter and the latter providing findings that serve as evidence for the former. Without such interconnections and interaction the former's achievements would lack substantiation, while the latter's would lose much of their intellectual significance.

Philosophy of language is an area in the philosophical investigation of conceptual knowledge, rather than one of the several branches of contemporary philosophy, such as philosophy of science, philosophy of mathematics, philosophy of art, and so forth. It is that area which seeks to learn what can be learned about conceptual knowledge from the manner in which such knowledge is expressed and communicated in language. Accordingly, the basic premise of the philosophy of language is that there is a strong relation between the form and content of language and the form and content of conceptualization. The special task of the philosophy of language is, therefore, to explore this relation and make whatever inferences about the structure of conceptual knowledge can be made on the basis of what is known about the structure of language.

Thus, the philosophy of language is a distinct field from the philosophy of linguistics,[2] which is that division of the philosophy of science whose major concern is the examination of the theories, methodology, and practice

[2] In our paper, "What's Wrong with the Philosophy of Language?" *Inquiry*, vol. 5, 1962, J. A. Fodor and I took the view that is here explicitly rejected. We wrote, "Insofar as current linguistics provides an empirical theory of language, the philosophy of language should be construed as nothing other than the philosophy of linguistics: a discipline analogous in every respect to the philosophy of psychology, the philosophy of mathematics, the philosophy of physics, etc." Thus, my present view is that Fodor and I were quite wrong in construing the philosophy of language as a branch of the philosophy of science.

of the descriptive linguist. There may, of course, be considerable interpenetration between these two fields; but, nonetheless, they have fundamentally different research aims and proceed at different levels of abstraction.

This conception of the philosophy of language is broad enough to encompass the work of the most diverse philosophers who have occupied themselves with language. It covers Plato's work on language as well as Aristotle's; it covers the work of rationalists such as Descartes, Cordemoy, Arnauld, and Leibniz as well as that of empiricists such as Locke, Berkeley, Hume, and Mill; and it covers the work of such modern philosophers as Frege, Husserl, Russell, Wittgenstein, Carnap, Ryle, Austin, and others. Moreover, it represents what is certainly the philosopher's unique concern with language: the desire to acquire information about language that will help him deal with the basic problems of philosophy. Thus, this conception distinguishes the philosopher's concern with language from that of scholars in other disciplines whose concern with language stems from an interest in things other than an understanding of conceptual knowledge per se, that is, from the linguist's concern with language for its own sake, the sociologist's concern for the light it sheds on society, the psychologist's concern for the insight it can give about the development and character of mental processes, the anthropologist's concern for the clarification it can afford about the nature of culture, etc.

Finally, note that this conception does not place the linguistic questions with which philosophers have often dealt outside the sphere of the philosophy of language;

but it does mean that the task of the philosopher of language is not completed once he has obtained the answers to purely linguistic questions, for then the implications of such answers for the solutions to questions about the structure of conceptual knowledge still remain to be drawn. Information about language is thus his starting point only. His goal is to utilize such information to contribute to the solutions of those traditional philosophical problems that stand in the way of a full understanding of conceptual knowledge.

AN APPROACH
TO THE PHILOSOPHY
OF LANGUAGE

The characterization of the philosophy of language given in Chapter 1 is a definition of a field in philosophy, not a definition of an approach to achieving the goals of that field. Accordingly, it had to be made very broad to allow for the full variety of alternative approaches that can be taken to the philosophy of language. This characterization thus places no constraints (1) on the kind of linguistic information that might be considered relevant to obtaining an understanding of conceptual knowledge, (2) on the source of such information, (3) on the sort of justification that has to be given for linguistic statements on which putative claims about conceptual knowledge or putative solutions to philosophical problems rest, (4) on the form in which linguistic information must be organized, or (5) on the manner in which a philosopher of language may argue from language to philosophy. Therefore, to delineate clearly one's own approach to the philosophy of language and to defend it against other possible approaches, it is necessary to indicate how one's approach differs in terms of (1)–(5) from others that fall under this broad characterization and to offer acceptable reasons for differing with other approaches in these respects.

My own approach to the philosophy of language is that the philosopher of language should begin with and draw his linguistic information from the theory of language as developed in descriptive linguistics. Thus, the theory of language is the first step toward an account of conceptual knowledge in terms of its mode of expression and communication in natural languages. It supplies the philosopher with generalizations about the form and content of languages upon which he can base inferences to revealing truths about the form and content of conceptual knowledge. But it is only the first step. This theory does not tell him which generalizations to use, how to use them, or what philosophical problems will yield to solution if he uses such generalizations.

The theory of language is the theory in descriptive linguistics that represents the facts about linguistic structure common to all natural languages. Accordingly, it must be distinguished from descriptions of particular languages that represent the facts that are idiosyncratic to those languages. In short, while a description of a particular language, say of English, must specify those features that the language has by virtue of which it is the language it is, rather than some other language, the theory of language must specify those features of every natural language by virtue of which they are all natural languages. Thus, in the study of particular natural languages we examine the details of these languages in order to uncover the extent of diversity in linguistic communication, whereas in the study of language we examine the features natural languages share in order to uncover the limits of such diversity.

These studies are interdependent. On the one hand, the study of particular natural languages provides us with descriptions—of English, Chinese, French, etc.—from which we may abstract in order to arrive at generalizations about language. On the other hand, the study of language in general provides us with generalizations expressing the invariant features of language which we may particularize as the requirement that an empirically correct description of a natural language represents such invariants. Since these invariants have to do with the form of the generalizations in particular languages, and the linguistic elements between which linguistic generalizations hold, the theory of language can be conceived of as a model that prescribes the form of the rules that express linguistic generalizations in descriptions of particular natural languages and a vocabulary of theoretical constructs from which those constructs employed in the formulation of such rules may be drawn. Thus, the study of language in general provides a model that tells us how to systematize the facts about each particular natural language.

There is no circularity here. Descriptions of particular languages are empirically confirmed if the linguistic evidence shows that the descriptions correctly differentiate one language from another, i.e., if the evidence supports the claim that each description provides a necessary and sufficient condition for a distinct natural language. Alternatively, the theory of language receives its empirical support from empirically successful descriptions of particular languages that conform to its prescriptions. A theory of language is justified to the extent that the rules of every correct description of a natural language have the form it prescribes and employ the constructs to which it accords the status of universals of language. Hence, the very same body of linguistic facts that provide empirical substantiation for linguistic descriptions provides empirical substantiation for the cross-language generalizations that constitute the theory of language.

Suppose that the theory of language contains generalizations about natural languages such as the following. Every sentence of a natural language contains both a verb and a noun phrase subject of that verb; there exists a very small number of fixed, universal, phonetic features, such as nasality, consonantality, etc., that suffice to describe fully the sound system of any natural language; the concepts of an object, event, state, action, process, etc., are components of the meanings of some words in every natural language. The truth of such generalizations does not imply that there is a point-for-point correspondence between natural languages, but only that, in some as yet undetermined sense, each natural language is built up out of the same phonological, syntactic, and semantic elements. Furthermore, the existence of generalizations in the theory of language that say that phonological, syntactic, and semantic regularities in each natural language have a certain definite formal structure does not imply isomorphic formal structure between languages, but only that, again, in some as yet undetermined sense, each natural language is organized on the same formal pattern.

Such generalizations are confirmed *for a particular language* if the evidence accumulated about the pronunciation, syntax, and meaning of its sentences conforms to what they predict—that is, if the best description we can write of the particular language is one whose phonological, syntactic, and semantic rules have the prescribed formal structure and are formulated in terms of the prescribed constructs. Obviously, no body of evidence about a language, no matter how large, can conclusively prove a set of generalizations about that language. As in other sciences, the evidence underdetermines a generalization. Thus, the generalization inductively extrapolates the regularity exhibited in the evidence to an open set of equivalent cases. If further evidence continues to confirm the generalization, we have sound reason to keep the generalization; but if the generalization is not confirmed by further evidence, it may have to be replaced. Likewise, generalizations about the form and content of all languages cannot be conclusively proved either. Generalizations such as those mentioned above are confirmed *for all languages* if evidence validating their predictions about universal formal and substantive features is found in the case of each particular language that has been carefully studied. Just as we cannot obtain all the evidence about any single natural language, we cannot obtain reasonably complete descriptions of every possible natural language. Hence, the cross-language generalizations in the theory of language have to be regarded as inductive extrapolations from the lower-level generalizations about the languages studied to those languages that have not been studied. Again, acquiring further evidence—this time in the form of sound generalizations about newly examined languages—confirms the generalizations if such evidence accords with their predictions. Otherwise, these second-level generalizations have to be replaced with better ones.

With respect to a theory of language in this sense, we can distinguish our approach to the philosophy of language from other possible approaches in terms of each of the relevant respects (1)–(5). First, the kind of linguistic information that can be utilized by a philosopher of language who follows this approach is the sort that is expressed in the theory of language, i.e., the general facts about the nature of language that are forthcoming from empirical investigations of natural languages. Second, the source of this information is the judgments that fluent speakers can make about their language on the basis of their own linguistic competence. How such judgments are obtained and evaluated for adequacy is a matter that must be settled by developments in the methodology of field work in linguistics. The philosopher can no more decide such matters for himself than he can dictate the character of experiments in physics. Third, the justification to which the philosopher can appeal in support of some claim about conceptual knowledge or some putative solution to a philosophical problem is the same as that offered in the theory of language for the linguistic generalizations upon which his claim or putative solution rests. Fourth, the form in which he can use linguistic information will be the particular organization that that information is given as generalizations in the theory of language. Fifth, and finally, he must formulate his arguments from language to philosophy as inferences from premises about the nature of language found in the theory of language to conclusions about the nature of conceptual knowledge.

Before considering the disadvantages of certain current approaches to the philosophy of language and the manner in which our approach avoids them, we may mention one general advantage of our approach. This is the power of justifications for philosophical applications of linguistic principles that our approach has by virtue of the fact that the validation of such principles as truths about *all* natural languages can be introduced as part of the justification of a solution to a philosophical problem or the clarification of a philosophically significant concept. Solutions to philosophical problems and clarifications of philosophically significant concepts that are ob-

concerned themselves with what they call 'linguistic analysis' would strengthen the expectation that they are able to offer some philosophically relevant account of language. Unfortunately, however, this expectation is sadly mistaken.

The chief reason for this failure on the part of *logical empiricism* (or *logical positivism* as it was once called) and *ordinary language philosophy,* the two dominant movements in twentieth-century philosophy to concern themselves with language, was that both were governed in their inferences from language to philosophy by an assumption about the nature of language that kept them from developing philosophically fruitful insights into the structure of natural languages. The self-defeating assumption, which went wholly unchallenged within each of these movements, was that natural languages are highly unstructured and unsystematic conglomerations of verbal constructions. Thus, fluency is thought of as habit or disposition to respond verbally to situations of the appropriate sort, with particular verbal constructions elicited as responses being under only very weak linguistic constraints due to the unstructured and unsystematic character of language.

This assumption provided the logical empiricist and the ordinary language philosopher with an explanation of the origin of metaphysical speculation. Relative to this assumption, both philosophical movements explain that metaphysical speculation arises from this relatively unrestrained linguistic freedom enjoyed by speakers of natural languages, due to the excesses of those who fail to curb their exercise of this freedom in the interests of clarity and intelligibility. Moreover, this assumption provided both philosophical movements with a direction in which to look for a means of controlling this freedom and thus eliminating metaphysical speculation. Logical empiricists tried to construct artificial languages with sufficient constraints to prevent the expression of metaphysics in them. Ordinary language philosophers tried to explicate the standards of usage underlying the linguistic behavior of those who do not abuse this freedom. The former philosophers sought to create standards on the basis of an examination of and extrapolation from those that they thought were fashioned in the development of mathematics and physical science. The latter sought to reveal existing standards on the basis of an examination and description of those details of the ordinary use of particular linguistic constructions that might indicate how the metaphysician had gotten into bad linguistic habits and how he may learn good habits. Perhaps, the reason neither movement critically examined this assumption about the alleged unstructured and unsystematic character of natural language was that it occupied so central a place in their philosophical position.

In this chapter, we consider these two movements with respect to their doctrines on language and try to explain why neither was able to achieve sufficiently powerful insights into language to produce substantial results for the theory of conceptual knowledge.

LOGICAL EMPIRICISM

The logical empiricists, those philosophers who followed Carnap, Schlick, and Reichenbach, among others, wanted to cure philosophy of the disease of metaphysical speculation. For them, metaphysical speculation was a disease of the intellectual faculties whose crippling effects could be unmistakably seen in such works as Hegel's *Phenomenology of Mind* or Heidegger's *Being and Time*. Their aim was both therapeutic and preventive. In this respect, they were true descendants of earlier forms of empiricism and positivism, especially British Empiricism and the positivism of Comte and Mach. The most influential of the British Empiricists, David Hume, concluded his *Inquiry Concerning Human Understanding* with a statement, which has ever since stood as the most emphatic and concise formulation of the empiricist principle, that all our knowledge of the world comes to us from our experience. He wrote: "When we run over libraries, persuaded of these principles, what havoc must we make? If we take in hand any volume—of divinity or school metaphysics, for instance,—let us ask, *Does it contain any abstract reasoning concerning quantity or number?* No. *Does it contain any experimental reasoning concerning matters of fact and existence?* No. Commit it then to the flames, for it can contain nothing but sophistry and illusion."[1] The logical empiricists agreed

---

[1] D. Hume, *An Inquiry Concerning Human Understanding*, Bobbs-Merrill Company, 1955.

with the spirit, if not the letter, of this formulation. Knowledge claims, they held, are about either the abstract realm of mathematics or the concrete world we experience or else they are about nothing at all. The mainspring of their empiricism is the view that the assertions of speculative metaphysics, such as 'The Absolute is perfect' or 'Nothing Nothings,' though seeming to inform us about a spiritual realm beyond sensory experience, are, in fact, literally devoid of cognitive meaning. According to the logical empiricists, such assertions cannot, in principle, be either true or false, for unlike mathematical assertions they claim to do more than express conceptual relations systematized in the postulates of a mathematical system and unlike the factual assertions in science and everyday life cannot be confirmed or disconfirmed by what is found in experience.

The logical empiricists justified their revival of empiricism on the grounds that earlier versions of empiricism lacked a firm enough basis for the critique of speculative metaphysics. Traditional empiricism, the logical empiricists contended, did not have the analytic tools at its disposal to establish adequate criteria for deciding when a nonmathematical statement formulated in a natural language is confirmable by appealing to experience and when such a statement is strict nonsense. Their advantage, they thought, lay in their being able to utilize formal logic, especially the work of Frege, Hilbert, and Russell and Whitehead, as the analytic tool required to fashion a conclusive empiricist critique of metaphysics. Modern formal logic would give them the technical apparatus to accomplish the following necessary three things. First, it would enable them to say what mathematical truth is,[2] and in so doing, distinguish metaphysical claims to knowledge from genuine claims to knowledge in mathematics. Second, it would make it possible to formulate the relation that holds between a statement S and statements expressing the results of direct observations of the world if S is cognitively meaningful. Third, it would provide the conceptual apparatus needed for constructing the linguistic conventions to prevent certain metaphysical statements from escaping the charge of violating the restrictions on meaningful communication. The hopes that logical empiricists held for such fruitful applications of modern formal logic to philosophy explain the qualification 'logical' in the name they gave to their philosophical position.

The logical empiricists pursued all three of these applications of formal logic. Since the first two are not of direct concern here, they will not be discussed. The first is best regarded as a program in the philosophy of mathematics, while the second, the attempt to formulate a verifiability criterion that says how a statement must be related to possible sensory experience for it to count as cognitively significant, is best regarded as an investigation in the philosophy of science concerned with providing an analysis of the scientific concept 'testability in principle.'[3]

[2] A particularly good treatment of the logical empiricist's conception of mathematical truth can be found in C. G. Hempel, "On the Nature of Mathematical Truth," *American Mathematical Monthly*, vol. 52, 1945; reprinted in *Readings in Philosophical Analysis* by H. Feigl and W. Sellars (eds.) Appleton-Century-Crofts, New York, 1949.

[3] For a critical survey of the literature on the concept of testability

The third of these programs, the attempt to construct an ideal, artificial language whose principles of sentence formation and semantic interpretation would exclude metaphysical statements as violations of proper linguistic relations, will be our primary concern in discussing logical empiricism.

Carnap, who was always the main spokesman for logical empiricism, thought that metaphysical speculation arose, not from a departure from the linguistic conventions that define correct usage in natural language, but from the absence of such conventions at just those places where they are most needed. He thought that the conceptual confusions which engender metaphysics come about because we tend to assume that something counts as sensible so long as it does not violate the conventions that exist in natural language, even though natural languages lack the conventions to always guide us in sensible usage. In his famous paper, "The Elimination of Metaphysics through the Logical Analysis of Language,"[4] Carnap admitted that there are syntactic conventions in natural languages whose violation produces such counter-syntactic sequences of words as "Caesar is and" but he held that there are no semantic conventions to

in principle, the reader is referred to C. G. Hempel, "Problems and Changes in the Empiricist Criterion of Meaning," *Revue internationale de Philosophie*, vol. 11, 1950; reprinted in L. Linsky, (ed.), *Semantics and the Philosophy of Language*, University of Illinois Press, 1952. Also C. G. Hempel, "The Concept of Cognitive Significance: A Reconsideration," *Contributions to the Analysis and Synthesis of Knowledge, Proceedings of the American Academy of Arts and Sciences*, vol. 80, 1951.

[4] R. Carnap, "The Elimination of Metaphysics through the Logical Analysis of Language," in A. J. Ayer (ed.), *Logical Positivism*, Macmillan Company, 1959.

which the meaninglessness of "Caesar is a prime number" and similar cases can be referred and in terms of which they can be explained as linguistic deviations resulting from their violation. In that paper, he wrote: "The fact that natural languages allow the formation of meaningless sequences of words without violating the rules of grammar, indicates that grammatical syntax is, from the logical point of view, inadequate. If grammatical syntax corresponds exactly to logical syntax, pseudo-statements (statements having an apparently acceptable grammatical form but conveying no cognitive meaning) could not arise. . . . It follows that if our thesis that the statements of metaphysics are pseudo-statements is justifiable, then metaphysics could not even be expressed in a logically constructed language. This is the great philosophical importance of the task, which at present occupies the logicians, of building a logical syntax."[5]

Clearly, this program of building a system of logical syntax presupposes finding out just how much metaphysics the actual conventions of a natural language exclude and how much they allow to pass as linguistically well-formed. But neither Carnap nor any logical empiricist who sought to construct such an ideal, artificial language actually went to the trouble to examine natural languages to determine how much of the elimination of metaphysics was left unaccomplished and thus what needed to be done in the construction of an ideal, artificial language. Rather, Carnap and those who followed him, guided by their assumption about the relatively un-

[5] *Ibid.*

structured and unsystematic character of natural languages, ignored the examination of natural languages and tried to build their artificial language to contain conventions to deal with every case of meaninglessness that could not be accounted for as violations of good grammar. They made no attempt to look beyond the most obvious cases of correct and incorrect grammar to discover if the rules that cover these cases might not, when they are explicitly formulated, also decide the well-formedness of those that are not so obvious. Theirs was, curiously enough for empiricists, a wholly a priori decision about natural languages.

Carnap's first step toward the construction of such an ideal language was his attempt to develop a system of logical syntax as a supplement to grammatical syntax. In his highly influential book, *The Logical Syntax of Language*,[6] he tried to sketch the basic outlines of an ideal language formulated entirely in syntactic terms and supplied the linguistic conventions he thought were philosophically desirable and missing in natural language. Thus, this book attempts to formulate a metatheory dealing with the nature of such an ideal language. To appreciate the character of this enterprise, it is necessary to consider the conception of metamathematics developed by the German mathematician David Hilbert. It was Hilbert's metamathematics that served as Carnap's model for his construction of a metatheory about systems of logical syntax.

[6] R. Carnap, *The Logical Syntax of Language*, Routledge & Kegan Paul, London, 1937.

Toward the end of the nineteenth century, the foundations of classical mathematics were put on a rigorous basis. Whereas real numbers were formerly thought of in terms of geometrical intuitions, now they were defined as certain objects constructed out of natural numbers. Their properties were thereby reduced to the properties of sets of natural numbers. The objects of analysis were thus regarded as infinite sets of objects in arithmetic, and the whole arithmetization was carried out within the general theory of sets. However, the validity of this entire reduction became doubtful when paradoxes were discovered in the general theory of sets.[7] The response of many mathematicians to the discovery of these paradoxes, notably those mathematicians who subscribed to what is called 'the intuitionist philosophy of mathematics,'[8] was to repudiate those portions of classical mathematics that presuppose the completed infinite. Hilbert rejected this way of avoiding the paradoxes, and, instead, sought a proof of the consistency of classical mathematics.

Hilbert's approach to proving the consistency of classical mathematics consisted in first casting classical mathematics in the form of a formal axiomatic system and then proving this system free of internal contradiction by establishing a generalization about all possible proofs in this formal axiomatic system. An axiomatic system is given by the specification of four things: a *vocabulary*

[7] For a discussion, cf. S. C. Kleene, *Introduction to Metamathematics*, D. Van Nostrand Company, 1952.
[8] Cf. A. Heting, *Intuitionism*, North-Holland Publishing Company, Amsterdam, 1956.

that lists the symbols to be employed in the system, a set of *formation rules* that determine which strings of symbols in the vocabulary are syntactically acceptable as formulas of the system, i.e., as well-formed formulas, a set of *axioms* that comprise the unproven true well-formed formulas of the system, and a set of *inference rules* that determine the set of theorems with respect to the set of axioms. The function of an axiomatic system is to finitely specify all and only the infinitely many truths about a certain (in this case mathematical) domain. If the formation rules are adequate, the set of well-formed formulas expresses every possible assertion about the objects in the domain of the system. If the axioms are each true of the objects in this domain and if the inference rules preserve truth, i.e., they never permit us to infer a false formula from true ones, then the set of provable formulas, or theorems, contains only true assertions about the domain. If every truth about the domain can be proved as a theorem of the system, then the system is complete. An axiomatic system is formal just in case the rules of the system apply to a string of symbols on the basis of the form (or shape) of the symbols in the string and their arrangement and the instructions for converting one string into another embodied in the rule can be carried out by elementary operations of adding, deleting, substituting, and permutating symbols, themselves defined solely in terms of the form and arrangement of symbols in strings. Thus, from the viewpoint of a formal system, the symbols and strings of symbols are just meaningless marks classified into various syntactic categories. The virtue of thus excluding all features of the intended interpretation from playing a role in the construction of proofs is that decisions about the provability of a formula can be made mechanically. Elaborate and often inconclusive discussions of meaning are replaced by computation in the process of settling the questions that arise about the set of theorems.

The concept of a proof is itself purely formal. A proof is any finite sequence of well-formed formulas such that each member is either an axiom or inferred from preceding members by one of the inference rules. Such a sequence is a proof of the formula that is its last member. Since the concept of proof is formal, the notions of consistency and inconsistency are formal notions, too. A system is consistent if and only if the set of proofs in the system does not contain two members one of which is a proof of a formula F and the other is a proof of a formula not-F. If a system is inconsistent, then all the well-formed formulas of the system are provable in the system,[9] and thus the set of well-formed formulas and the set of theorems are identical. Given an adequate set of formation rules, this means that the whole system is useless since it makes no distinction between the true and false assertions about its domain. This, then, is the tragedy in the discovery of contradiction in a mathematical system and what Hilbert sought to show was not the fate of classical mathematics.

[9] If a contradiction F and not-F is provable, then we can deduce the formula F from it by simplification. If F is thus provable, so is F or P, where P is any formula, since F or P asserts the truth of at least one of the two formulas F and P. By the same argument that lets us infer F, we can deduce not-F. But F or P and not-F permits us to deduce P.

Hilbert invented metamathematics, which was to be the general theory about the structure of formal axiomatic mathematical systems, to serve as the theory within which it would be possible to prove the consistency of any complete axiomatic formalization of classical mathematics. Since the concepts of consistency and inconsistency refer only to formal properties of an axiomatic system, Hilbert thought that an adequate metamathematical theory of the formal structure of axiomatizations of classical mathematics would be capable of revealing the absence of those formal properties that make it possible to derive contradictory formulas in a system.

At the time Carnap was working out the ideas underlying his book *The Logical Syntax of Language*, Hilbert's metamathematical program was one of the most highly influential and promising lines of intellectual investigation. Moreover, metamathematics, as the general theory of the formal structure of the language of mathematics, was closely parallel to Carnap's idea of logical syntax, as the general theory of the formal structure of scientific and factual discourse. No wonder, then, that metamathematics appealed to Carnap as a model for his theory of logical syntax. In terms of this parallelism in conceptual status as metatheories, Carnap's fundamental aim of proving the ideal language of empirical science and ordinary factual discourse free of sentences expressing metaphysical speculations occupied essentially the same central place in his conception of logical syntax that Hilbert's fundamental aim of proving axiomatizations of classical mathematics free from contradiction occupied in metamathematics. With success in the latter case, classical mathematics would be validated, whereas, with success in the former case, speculative metaphysics would be invalidated. Further, this parallel encouraged Carnap to adopt a purely formal approach to the construction of an ideal, artificial language. Thus, the metatheory within which this construction was to be carried out, was conceived of as a theory of logical syntax.

Using metamathematics as his model, Carnap's first task in the development of such a metatheory for artificial languages that are free of sentences expressing metaphysical speculations was to find some formal basis for distinguishing metaphysical sentences from non-metaphysical sentences, on analogy to the formal basis for distinguishing contradictions from noncontradictions. Then, he could go on to try to show that an ideal, artificial language formally represents only sentences of empirical science and factual discourse. The final step in Carnap's program would be to show that the principles of logical syntax provide us with good reasons to exclude metaphysical sentences from such an ideal language.

It should be mentioned that this antimetaphysical motivation was not the only one that provided an incentive to develop a theory of logical syntax. Carnap also wished to provide a syntactic analysis of concepts in formal deductive logic such as provability, derivability from premises, etc. But the philosophical motive was dominant. In his intellectual autobiography, Carnap wrote, "The chief motivation for my development of the syntactical method, however, was the following. In our discussions in the Vienna Circle it had turned out that any attempt at formulating more precisely the philosophical problems in which we were interested ended up with problems of the logical analysis of language. Since in our view the issue in philosophical problems concerned the language, not the world, these problems should be formulated, not in the object language, but in the metalanguage. Therefore, it seemed to me that the development of a suitable metalanguage would essentially contribute toward greater clarity in the formulation of philosophical problems and greater fruitfulness in their discussions."[10]

Carnap's starting point and guiding principle was that most, if not all, genuine philosophical problems are controversies about what linguistic framework is best for some scientific or descriptive investigation, not controversies about the facts with which such investigations deal. The confusions that arise in the attempt to solve philosophical problems arise because philosophers have failed clearly to perceive that philosophical problems are purely linguistic in this sense. Natural languages, within which philosophical investigations are pursued, have, according to Carnap, two modes of speech. One, which he called the "material mode," is used when a sentence is formulated as an assertion about actual things or events rather than about linguistic constructions. The other, which he called the "formal mode" is used when a sentence is formulated as an assertion about linguistic constructions, their properties and relations. For

[10] Carnap, "Carnap's Intellectual Autobiography," *The Philosophy of Rudolf Carnap*, P. A. Schlipp (ed.). Open Court, La Salle, 1963.

example, the sentence "Roses are things" is in the material mode of speech because it appears to attribute a physical property to objects, but the sentence " 'roses' has five letters" is assigned formal mode status because it attributes a syntactic property to a linguistic construction. Accordingly, sentences that are framed as material mode sentences do not actually attribute nonlinguistic properties to objects in the world, but instead attribute a syntactical property to a term that designates the object(s) that such sentences appear to be about. These sentences are not true "object sentences" like "Five is a number," "Babylon was a big town," and "Lions are mammals," which are about the objects in the universe of discourse of the language. Rather, they are "pseudo-object sentences," sentences which are about the syntactical structure of linguistic constructions but which in grammatical form masquerade as object sentences. "Five is not a thing but a number" is a case in point. This sentence appears to be about some object called 'five' and to be asserting that it is not a thing much in the way we might assert of a shadow that it is not a thing, when, in reality, the sentence assigns the term 'five' to the syntactic category of numerical expressions. To each such sentence, there corresponds a "syntactical sentence" of the formal mode that explicates the real character of the pseudo-object sentence. In the case of our example, the corresponding syntactical sentence is " 'Five' is not a thing-word, but a number word." According to Carnap, most, if not all, genuine philosophical problems have to do with pseudo-object sentences. The confusions that have attended attempts to solve such problems is thus a consequence of the philosopher's failure to recognize them as "quasi-syntactical sentences" and their treatment of these sentences as genuine object sentences. Natural languages, according to Carnap, employ the material mode predominately both because of the speaker's concern with things rather than mere words and because natural languages do not have a sufficiently rich stock of syntactical concepts to make speech in the formal mode feasible. But this predominant use of the material mode leads speakers to employ pseudo-object sentences without realizing that they are not assertions about objects but just ascriptions of syntactic properties to words and expressions. That is, speakers become so accustomed to interpreting sentences in accord with the material mode that the relatively few pseudo-object sentences they encounter are, by force of habit, also interpreted in this manner. This failure to interpret pseudo-object sentences as syntactical sentences, where this is possible, is, Carnap claimed, what stands in the way of solutions to those traditional philosophical problems that are amenable to solution, i.e., those that are not merely the result of some conceptual muddle.[11]

In a particularly succinct statement of his position, Carnap writes, ". . . the object-questions which occur in the logic of science (for example, questions concerning

[11] Some traditional philosophical problems were taken to be conceptual muddles produced by the same sort of misinterpretation of pseudo-object sentences in cases where the pseudo-object sentences are not disguised versions of syntactical sentences, but express some thesis of speculative metaphysics.

numbers, things, time and space, relations between the psychical and the physical, etc.) are only pseudo-object questions,—i.e. questions which, because of a misleading formulation, appear to refer to objects while they actually refer to sentences, terms, theories, and the like—and are, accordingly, in reality, logical questions. . . . all logical questions are capable of formal presentation, and can, consequently, be formulated as syntactical questions. According to the usual view, all logical investigation comprises two parts: a formal inquiry which is concerned only with the order and syntactical kind of the linguistic expressions, and an inquiry of a material character, which has to do not merely with the formal design but, over and above that, with questions of meaning and sense. Thus the general opinion is that the formal problems constitute, at the most, only a small section of the domain of logical problems. As opposed to this, our discussion of general syntax has already shown that the formal method, if carried far enough, embraces all logical problems, even the so-called problems of content and sense. Accordingly, when we say that the logic of science is nothing more than the syntax of the language of science, we do not mean to suggest that only a certain number of the problems of what has hitherto been called the logic of science . . . should be regarded as true problems of the logic of science (but) rather that all problems of the current logic of science, as soon as they are exactly formulated, are seen to be syntactical problems."[12] Thus, pseudo-object sentences expressing substantive philo-

[12] Carnap, *The Logical Syntax of Language*.

sophical theses, such as "Numbers are classes of classes of things," "Identity is not a relation," "A thing is a complex of sense-data," "Time is continuous," etc., are to be translated, within the framework of the theory of logical syntax, into syntactical sentences in the formal mode, such as, respectively, "Numerical expressions are class-expressions of the second level," "The symbol of identity is not a descriptive symbol," "Every sentence in which a thing-designation occurs is equipollent to a class of sentences in which no thing-designations but sense-data designations occur," "The real-number expressions are used as time coordinates," etc. Without these translations, we are led "easily to self deception as regards the object under discussion: one believes one is investigating certain objects and facts, whereas one is, in reality, investigating their designations, i.e., words and sentences."[13]

Therefore, it is clear that Carnap's theory of the logical syntax of the language of empirical science and factual discourse should contain a general scheme for translating pseudo-object sentences from a natural language into syntactical sentences of an ideal, artificial language. But this scheme must also serve as the criterion to decide what sentences from a natural language make sense and what sentences do not. It thus is the means by which Carnap will attempt to show that the sentences that express principles of speculative metaphysics are devoid of cognitive meaning. As Carnap put it, "Sentences which do not give a slight indication to determine their transla-

[13] Ibid.

tion are outside the realm of the language of science and therefore are incapable of discussion, no matter what depths or heights of feeling they may stir."[14] We may, accordingly, formulate Carnap's antimetaphysical principle as follows: any sentence in a natural language that is not a genuine object-sentence and that cannot be translated into a syntactical sentence within the framework of the theory of logical syntax has no cognitive meaning. Since genuine object-sentences are the sentences we use to express matters of fact, and syntactical sentences are those we ought to use to express mathematical, logical, and other conceptual relations, Carnap's antimetaphysical principle can be regarded as tantamont to Hume's empiricist principle that whatever can neither be confirmed in experience nor established as a necessary relation among ideas is "nothing but sophistry and illusion." A justification of the former would thus be the rationale that logical empiricists sought to supply for the latter.

Carnap does not actually offer a general scheme for translating pseudo-object sentences into syntactical sentences and for marking sentences in a natural language as genuine object sentences, pseudo-object sentences, or nonobject and nontranslatable sentences, i.e., as metaphysical sentences. Nowhere in his writings of this period, does he provide an explicit procedure for classifying an arbitrary sentence from a natural language into one or another of these philosophical categories. But this by itself is not a damning criticism. If the theory

[14] *Ibid.*

of logical syntax offers a sufficiently rich conception of the ideal, artificial language, it might be a rather simple matter to determine such translations and failures of translation in a more or less practical way. Again comparing Carnap's theory to Hilbert's metamathematics, a general scheme for such translations would be analogous to a scheme in Hilbert's theory of the syntax of the language of mathematics for translating the statements of classical mathematics into the strings of marks that comprise the formulas of some suitable formal axiomatization of classical mathematics.[15] The point is that in Hilbert's conception of metamathematics there is no explicit procedure for translation but the characterization of a suitable formal axiomatic system is sufficient in general for us to determine what are and what are not acceptable translations from classical mathematics. Accordingly, if Carnap's conception of logical syntax provides a sufficiently rich conception of the ideal, artificial language, it might be possible to determine translations from a natural language in a similar fashion, without the aid of an explicit procedure for carrying out the process of translation. Hence, the question of the adequacy of Carnap's program is just the question of how adequately he has been able to formulate his concept of an ideal language.

However, his formulation of an ideal language was not

---

[15] There is a certain disanalogy here, namely, that in Carnap's case the primary emphasis is on the formulation of an adequate translation scheme per se, whereas in Hilbert's it is on the proof of a theorem in metamathematics about the nonderivability of contradictory formulas in the axiomatization. But this can be disregarded.

adequate at all. Carnap's program of constructing a theory of logical syntax fared no better than Hilbert's metamathematical attempt to prove the consistency of classical mathematics, and partly for similar reasons. That is, the limitation of provable consistency to incomplete formal axiomatizations of classical mathematics is paralleled in the case of Carnap's program by a similar limitation of linguistic description dealing with purely syntactic matters. In Carnap's program for developing a theory of logical syntax, this limitation manifests itself in the form of inadequate and ultimately question begging translations of sentences.

A now classical example of the inadequacy of Carnap's translations of pseudo-object sentences is his rendering of "Babylon was treated of in yesterday's lecture" as the allegedly syntactical sentence "The word 'Babylon' occurred in yesterday's lecture." In the first place, the translation is not really a syntactical sentence as it is supposed to be, since the expression 'occurred in yesterday's lecture' is a predicate for events, not linguistic types whose tokens can be used to designate events. In the second place, not only is the latter sentence different in meaning from the former—of which it is the alleged translation—it is not even equivalent to the former in the sense of their both being true and false under the same conditions. Consider the following cases. On the one hand, although the word 'Babylon' occurred in yesterday's lecture, that lecture need not have treated of the city of Babylon. (The lecture concerned Baltimore, but the lecturer once uttered the word 'Babylon' by mistake or by way of comparing Baltimore to Babylon.) On the other hand, although the lecture treated Babylon, there need have been no actual occurrence of the word 'Babylon' in it. (Everyone at the lecture knew what it was to be about and so Babylon was not referred to by using the word 'Babylon'; or perhaps the lecturer used 'that city' or 'the ancient city notorious for its luxury and wickedness' when he wished to refer to Babylon.) Carnap offers other putative translations of "Babylon was treated of in yesterday's lecture," of which "In yesterday's lecture the word 'Babylon' or a synonymous designation occurred" is typical. Clearly, however, such alternative translations merely beg the question of whether syntactical concepts alone suffice to express the content of such "pseudo-object sentences," for these alleged translations use the semantical concept of a synonymous designation. And they do not avoid all the objections we have raised, since, as we observed above, the occurrence of 'Babylon' or a synonymous designation does not guarantee that the lecture was about Babylon. That is, they appear to avoid counterexamples in the form of possible cases in which, though the lecture treated of Babylon, no occurrence of the word 'Babylon' occurred in the lecture. But they do not avoid counterexamples of the other sort.

Such translations suggest a general method for avoiding other criticisms similar to some of those we have leveled against Carnap's translations. For example, it might be true not only that no occurrence of 'Babylon' is to be found in the lecture but also that no occurrence of a synonymous expression appeared either. Accordingly, the translation would have to contain a further clause to the effect that the utterances that comprise yesterday's lecture entail that the discourse was about the city of Babylon. The general method would be to add such further qualifications until we have successfully distinguished between lectures that treat of Babylon and those that do not. This method can be regarded as an explication of our intuitive ability to tell what a discourse is about. However, the appearance of successfully avoiding counterexamples, which this method gives, is gained at the expense of forfeiting the whole enterprise of constructing a theory of logical syntax. The question begging character of such translations becomes obvious when we notice that their incorporation of concepts like 'a synonymous designation,' 'entails,' or 'about' is by no means just stylistic polish. Without them the translations do not work. But with them these translations are no longer purely syntactical. Thus, the essential use of these concepts, which are, at the very least, prima facie semantic concepts, not syntactical concepts, raises the question as to whether the whole enterprise of such translation of sentences into syntactical sentences of the formal mode is capable of being carried out as planned. Carnap claimed that semantical concepts can be defined in syntactical terms within the theory of logical syntax, but there is nothing in the definitions, theorems, or even in the informal exposition of his theory that takes the slightest step toward showing that semantic concepts can be syntactically defined.

The point is that Carnap's theory of logical syntax does not provide a sufficiently rich conception of an ideal, artificial syntactic language to accomplish his program. Not only does Carnap's theory illicitly appeal to semantical concepts instead of restricting itself to syntactical concepts, nothing is said concerning what formal relations between a pair of expressions or sentences are necessary and sufficient for them to be properly taken as synonymous, what formal relations between a pair of sentences are necessary and sufficient for one to be properly taken as entailing the other (as, for example, in the case of "Roses are red" and "roses are colored"), and what formal relations are necessary and sufficient for a sequence of sentences to be about some subject. Furthermore, almost all of the concepts which we are led by logical syntax to suppose will play a crucial role in the statement of an ideal, artificial language are equally empty. Nothing is said about the formal properties a term or expression must have to be meaningful, what formal properties a sentence must have to be meaningful, what formal properties a sentence must have to be analytic, i.e., true by virtue of the meanings of its terms (as, for example, "Bachelors are male"), what formal properties a sentence must have to be contradictory, i.e., false by virtue of the meanings of its terms (as, for example, "Bachelors are female"), and so on. The concepts in the theory of logical syntax are left substantially unclarified, unanalyzed, and unexplained. They are used in the definition of other concepts and in the formulation of translations, even though no hint is given as to what criteria must be used in applying them. But, since such concepts can be no less in need of clarification, analysis, and explanation after they are made the basis for a theory of logical syntax than before such a theory is erected upon them, it is clear that the whole theory suffers from their vacuity. Therefore, they cannot legitimately serve as part of the apparatus for translations that are supposed to rely on purely syntactic considerations, since it is just the question of the possibility of such translations that is then begged. Accordingly, an ideal artificial language built out of such concepts cannot claim either to distinguish sense from metaphysical nonsense or to express philosophical problems in a form in which they can more easily be solved.

Two other difficulties contribute to the failure of Carnap's attempt to construct a theory of logical syntax which achieves the empiricist's aims. One is that Carnap's account of translation from the material to the formal mode depends on a wholly unclear and undeveloped prior distinction between genuine object sentences and those pseudo-object sentences that express metaphysical statements. We may grant that Carnap can distinguish syntactical sentences from other types just on the basis of grammatical form, i.e., syntactical sentences have to do with linguistic entities and their formal properties rather than things in the world, but beyond this nothing is at all clear. Carnap's examples of object sentences that appear to be acceptable from the viewpoint of grammar but which are logically nonsense, such as

"Caesar is a prime number," are cases that seem to involve a category mistake, such as the attribution of numerical status to something that is a human not a number. But there is nothing by way of appropriate syntactical apparatus in the theory of logical syntax to enable us to tell when such mistakes occur and when they do not. Furthermore, Carnap's other examples of logical nonsense, such as "The Absolute is perfect" and "Nothing nothings," are not cases of this sort; and, concerning them, nothing whatever is said to indicate what mistake is involved or how they are to be distinguished from genuine object sentences. Hence, the theoretical categories "genuine object sentence," "translatable pseudo-object sentence," and "untranslatable pseudo-object sentence," which are essential to Carnap's theory, lack any description. No means is given, by Carnap or others, for deciding when a sentence from a natural language should be assigned to one or another of these categories, or what it means to so classify sentences. Without a distinction between genuine object sentences and pseudo-object sentences, on the one hand, and a distinction between translatable and untranslatable pseudo-object sentences, on the other, the lack of a syntactical correlate for a given material mode sentence S cannot be taken to mean that S is metaphysical nonsense. It may mean only that S is a genuine object sentence or an untranslated but potentially translatable pseudo-object sentence. There being no criterion to decide whether a sentence is a metaphysical sentence like "The absolute is perfect," or a genuine object sentence like "Roses are red," or a syntactically translatable pseudo-object sentence like "Time is continuous," Carnap's formulations can at best distinguish the set of explicitly syntactical sentences. This means that his idea of using failure of translation into the formal mode as the test for whether a sentence is a piece of metaphysics could succeed only if we already have a criterion for whether something is a piece of metaphysics, i.e., whether an untranslated sentence makes cognitive sense. That Carnap's test should work if and when we possess such a criterion comes as no great surprise.

The second difficulty to which we now turn would doom Carnap's program even if there were no others. Let us suppose that the sentences of a natural language are divided into the categories "object sentence," "translatable pseudo-object sentence," "untranslatable pseudo-object sentence," and "syntactical sentence," and that we are given a translation scheme that correlates sentences in the second of these categories with sentences in the fourth. Now, the question arises whether a sentence in the material mode which received no correlate in the set of syntactical sentences under this translation scheme is to be correctly regarded as nonsense, as having no cognitive meaning. This, of course, depends entirely on the adequacy of the reasons given for accepting the theory of logical syntax in which the categories and the translation scheme are formulated. No one would deny the possibility of different theories of logical syntax in which the metaphysician's sentences receive syntactical correlates. For example, we might construct such a theory so that a sentence like "The absolute is perfect" receives some syntactic correlate. Carnap offers no arguments for his way of constructing the theory of logical syntax. In fact, he even goes so far as to say that how we choose to construct such a theory is arbitrary from the viewpoint of philosophical justification. "Everyone," wrote Carnap, "is at liberty to built up his own logic, i.e., his own form of language, as he wishes. All that is required of him is that, if he wished to discuss it, he must state his methods clearly, and give syntactical rules instead of philosophical arguments."[16] Thus, which theory of logical syntax one accepts as the framework within which to formulate an ideal language, Carnap's or that of some metaphysician who maliciously plays Carnap's game and states his methods clearly, is wholly a matter of individual choice. But this freedom from any governing constraints that might otherwise provide a basis for deciding between different theories of logical syntax which lead to different translations of the same sentences is, in effect, anarchy. For this freedom introduces an arbitrariness at the foundations of the theory of logical syntax that deprives us of a motivated way of condemning anything as devoid of cognitive meaning.

These latter two difficulties have, in different forms, plagued all of Carnap's and other logical empiricists'

---

[16] This is a version of Carnap's principle of tolerance from *The Logical Syntax of Language*. Each version of this principle suffers from the same basic mistake, that of failing to appreciate that a form of language in Carnap's sense, unlike such simple communication systems as Morse code, are not just arbitrary systems for transmitting messages but make truth claims, reformulate philosophical problems and theses, and decide between the sides of various philosophical controversies.

further efforts to construct an ideal, artificial language that serves as a means of distinguishing philosophical sense from metaphysical nonsense. And we shall thus have occasion to consider them again. But the first difficulty, the limitation of linguistic construction in purely syntactic terms, was one that Carnap, under the influence of Tarski's work on the concept of truth,[17] came to appreciate. He was, accordingly, led to reject the idea that a theory dealing exclusively with syntax suffices to construct an ideal language which handles meaning.

Thus, the first step beyond *The Logical Syntax of Language* came with Carnap's recognition that there are semantic and pragmatic aspects of language as well as syntactic ones. A full theory of language, Carnap now held, has three branches: *syntax,* which concerns itself with the formal properties of linguistic constructions; *semantics,* which concerns itself with the relation between linguistic entities and the things, events, states of affair, etc., in the world to which such entities refer and with the relation between sentences and the conditions in the world that must obtain for sentences to be true; and *pragmatics,* which concerns itself with features of language use, such as the psychological motives of speakers, the reactions on the part of hearers, the sociology of various speech patterns, and so forth.

Carnap now concentrated his attention on semantics in the above sense. Syntax had already received atten-

[17] A clear elementary statement of Tarski's ideas can be found in A. Tarski, "The Semantic Conception of Truth," *Philosophy and Phenomenological Research,* vol. 4, 1944; reprinted in L. Linsky (ed.), *Semantics and the Philosophy of Language.*

tion, and pragmatics, because it had the flavor of an empirical science, was de-emphasized almost to the point of complete neglect. Carnap's first attempt to develop a theory of semantics was based on the idea that the meaning of a linguistic construction is the object, property, event, state of affair, etc., to which it refers in case it is a constituent less than a full sentence and the conditions under which it is true in case it is a full declarative sentence. Accordingly, an account of the semantics of a language is given once the *syntactic rules* are supplemented by *designation rules* which specify the things to which terms and expressions of the language refer and *truth rules* which pair sentences and their truth conditions. The syntactic rules provide the vocabulary for the language, which consists of two types of symbols: *descriptive symbols* and *logical symbols*. The former are the symbols that most directly describe aspects of the world, e.g., 'is red,' 'New York,' 'is more nearly square than,' etc., while the latter are the symbols from elementary logic, i.e., propositional variables and truth functional connectives from propositional logic (e.g., '*P*,' '*Q*,' '*R*,' . . . , 'or,' 'if,' 'then,' 'not,' etc.), and the quantifiers and individual variables of quantification theory ('For all *x*, such that · · ,' 'There exists an *x*, such that . . . ,' '*x*,' '*y*,' '*z*,' · .) and the sign of identity '=.' The syntactic rules also provide the rules of sentence formation. They dictate what concatenations of logical and descriptive symbols form sentences of the language. First, these rules determine the minimal sentences of the language, the 'atomic sentences.' These result from ap-

46   THE PHILOSOPHY OF LANGUAGE

plying a predicate, such as 'is red,' to the name of something or to an individual variable (with appropriate use of quantification) to form a sentence, such as 'Roses are red' or 'There exists an x, such that x is red.' Second, these rules determine the compound sentences, such as 'Roses are red and violets are blue,' by connecting atomic sentences to one another with truth functional connectives. The designation rules provide an interpretation for the descriptive symbols in the form of specified designata, e.g., one such rule might say that 'New York' is the symbol that designates such and such a place, where the location may be given in terms of coordinates or in some other suitable manner. Finally, the rules of truth lay down truth conditions for atomic sentences and a means of finding the truth conditions for a compound sentence in terms of the truth conditions for its component atomic sentences. The rule for atomic sentences is, roughly, that an atomic sentence is true if and only if the thing designated by its subject has the property designated by its predicate. Thus, "Roses are red" is true if and only if the things designated by 'roses' have the property designated by 'red,' such designations being determined by the designation rules. The truth rules also include the principles of propositional logic, quantification theory, and identity theory. These, together with the truth rule for atomic sentences, provide a necessary and sufficient condition for the truth of each compound sentence. For example, "Roses are red or violets are blue" is true just in case one of its atomic sentences is true [18]

[18] Cf. R. Carnap, *Introduction to Semantics,* Harvard University Press, 1946, for the conception of semantics summarized above.

This treatment of semantics also proved inadequate. The basic criticism of it is due to Frege,[19] who pointed out that meaning and designation are different: nonsynonymous constructions can refer to the same thing(s), as, in Frege's example, 'Morning Star' and 'Evening Star.' Further counterexamples of this kind abound: 'nine' and 'the number of planets'; 'creature with a heart' and 'creature with a kidney'; 'the largest city in America' and 'New York.' If the meaning of a term or expression is taken to be its referent(s), then paradoxes result such as that the meaning of the term 'New York' or the meaning of the expression 'the largest city in America' must change if Los Angeles surpasses New York in size, for then these two constructions will designate different objects. There are other types of counterexamples, too. Some terms in a language that are clearly meaningful do not designate anything at all, e.g., 'witch,' 'Santa Claus,' 'the average consumer,' etc. Given the identification of meaning with designation, unless we are prepared to populate the world with various and sundry mysterious entities, all such constructions must be taken to designate the null class, in which case they must all be taken to have the same meaning. Finally, parallel to these criticisms are those which refute the identification of the meaning of a sentence with its truth conditions. For example, some sentences have the same truth conditions, but different meanings—'The number of

---

[19] Only a small portion of Frege's work is available in English. The interested reader is referred to two convenient volumes: *The Foundations of Arithmetic* (translated by J. L. Austin), Basil Blackwell, Oxford, 1953, and P. Geach and M. Black (eds.), *Translations from the Philosophical writings of Gottlob Frege,* Basil Blackwell, Oxford, 1952.

planets is not prime' and 'Nine is not prime' or 'Scott was nasty' and 'The author of Waverly was nasty.' Again, just as there are meaningful terms that designate nothing, so there are meaningful sentences that have no truth conditions, e.g., 'How are you feeling?,' 'Stop bothering me!' and 'Oh, were I but rich and handsome.'

Criticisms such as these convinced the logical empiricists that meaning cannot be assimilated to designation and truth conditions. The next phase in the treatment of semantics thus saw a sharp distinction made between theory of meaning and theory of reference.[20] However, no change was made in their general conception of language. Attention was now focused on the crucial question of how to formulate the semantic structure of a language of the kind they sought to construct. The important questions in theory of meaning were how to indicate which terms, expressions, and sentences are synonymous, which are meaningful, which are analytic, and so forth.

Carnap at this point proposed the device of *meaning postulates* and *semantical rules* as the way to handle the semantic structure of language.[21] Meaning postulates and semantical rules of a language *L* are simply statements, formulated in analogy to the axioms and the inference rules of an axiomatic system, which express stipulations concerning the meaning relations between the descriptive symbols in the vocabulary of *L* and between expressions

[20] Cf. "Notes on the Theory of Reference" and other essays in W. V. Quine, *From a Logical Point of View,* Harvard University Press, 1953.

[21] Cf. R. Carnap, *Meaning and Necessity,* University of Chicago Press (2nd edition), 1956, which includes the paper "Meaning Postulates" as a supplement.

constructed out of these descriptive symbols. They are intended to provide an interpretation for the descriptive symbols of the vocabulary of L in a fashion similar to the way in which postulates and inference rules of a formal axiomatic system provide an interpretation of the logical symbols of the vocabulary.

One way to show the need for such a further interpretation of the vocabulary of L is to observe that some inferences in L depend not only on the meanings of the logical symbols that occur in the premisses but also on the meanings of the descriptive symbols. For example, to state the fact that 'This apple is red' entails 'This apple is colored' requires us, on Carnap's new proposal, to lay down the statement 'Whatever is red is colored' as a meaning postulate. There has to be such a basis for sanctioning this inference, since, in addition to the interpretation of the logical symbols, i.e., the interpretation of 'For all x, such that . . . ,' 'If, then,' etc. (the sentence will be rendered as 'For all x, if x is red, then x is colored'), this inference depends on features of the meanings of the descriptive symbols 'is red' and 'is colored.' This meaning postulate expresses the inclusion relation between the meanings of these descriptive symbols upon which the inference is based. In a similar way, other semantic relations between descriptive symbols, such as synonymy, incompatibility, etc., might be given. The claim made by this new proposal of Carnap's is that any semantic relation upon which an inference rests, which is not given by the interpretation of the logical symbols, can be given in the form of a meaning postulate or semantical rule within the ideal language. Further, it is claimed that the meaning postulates and semantical rules are the only supplementation needed to specify the set of analytic sentences, since they are those sentences that follow from the meaning postulates and semantical rules alone, i.e., without the aid of other sentences of the language to serve as premisses for inferences to them.

Therefore, in this proposal of Carnap's, the synonymous terms, expressions, and sentences of the language, the incompatible constructions, the analytic sentences, etc., are given in terms of what amounts to a list of conventions. No one need have doubts about what constructions in the language are semantically related in one of these ways or have one of these semantic properties because, with respect to these conventions, there is an objective means of deciding the matter. All we need to do is to check through the items on the list headed 'meaning postulates' or that headed 'semantical rules.'

But here an old difficulty, one first encountered in connection with Carnap's theory of logical syntax, returns to plague him. Again, he fails to provide relevant constraints for his theoretical construction. Thus, the stipulations offered by meaning postulates and semantical rules are too arbitrary to serve as the basis for settling any philosophical controversy. Carnap himself is quite explicit about the absence of such constraints. He writes, "Suppose the author of a system wishes the predicates 'B' and 'M' to designate the properties Bachelor and Married, respectively. How does he know that these properties are incompatible and that therefore he has to lay down [the meaning postulate 'For any x, if x is B, then x is not M']? This is not a matter of knowledge but a decision. His knowledge or belief that the English words 'bachelor' and 'married' are always or usually understood in such a way that they are incompatible may influence his decision if he has the intention to reflect in his system some of the meaning relations of English words. . . . Suppose he wishes the predicates 'Bl' and 'R' to correspond to the words 'black' and 'raven.' While the meaning of 'black' is fairly clear, that of 'raven' is rather vague in the everyday language. There is no point for him to make an elaborate study, based either on introspection or on statistical investigation of common usage, in order to find out whether 'raven' always or mostly entails 'black.' It is rather his task to make up his mind whether he wishes the predicates 'R' and 'Bl' of his system to be used in such a way that the first logically entails the second. . . . those who construct systems . . . are free to choose their postulates, guided not by their beliefs concerning facts of the world but by their intentions with respect to the meanings, i.e., the ways of use of the descriptive constants."[22]

This may sound like the best of tolerant liberalism, but tolerance is not always a good thing. As Goodman observed, "Reluctant as I am to cast a shadow on all this sweetness and light, there are limits to my tolerance of tolerance. I admire the statesman tolerant of divergent political opinions, and the person tolerant of racial and

[22] Carnap, "Meaning Postulates."

educational differences, but I do not admire the accoun-
tant who is tolerant about his addition, the logician who
is tolerant about his proofs, or the musician who is
tolerant about his tone. In every activity, satisfactory
performance requires meticulous care in some matters;
and in philosophy, one of these matters is the choice of
systematic apparatus or "linguistic form.' "[23] Without
motivated constraints upon the way in which we
construct an artificial language, the language may have
anything whatever included among its meaning
postulates and semantical rules. Indeed, it may have
whatever features its author decides to give it. With
different authors we can have different languages that
differ with respect to just those features which will decide
philosophical controversies. Thus, there will be no basis
on which to choose one such language to serve as *the*
ideal language for the purpose of philosophical therapy
or philosophical analysis. We can well imagine that every
side in a controversy over the solution to a given philosophical problem will have its own 'ideal,' artificial language and that these languages will embody different
partisan solutions to this problem. Since there is no ra-
tional basis for justifying the claim that one of these artificial languages offers the correct solution, we are in no
better position after having constructed such languages
than we were before going to the trouble.

Note that this unconstrained freedom to choose whatever set of meaning postulates or semantical rules we

[23] N. Goodman, "A World of Individuals," in *The Problem of Uni-versals*, University of Notre Dame Press, 1956.

like, so that it is arbitrary what set we actually incorporate into the allegedly ideal language, is not simply a consequence of Carnap's personal liberal attitude toward philosophy. Rather, it is a consequence of the vacuity of the conception of meaning postulates and semantical rules. For example, these conventions single out a set of statements from among those produced by the formation rules and designate these as analytic in the language. But, as Quine has pointed out in his now famous article "Two Dogmas of Empiricism": ". . . the difficulty is simply that the rules contain the word 'analytic,' which we do not understand! We understand what expressions the rules attribute analyticity to, but we do not understand what the rules attribute to those expressions."[24] Alternatively, construing analyticity in terms of the notions 'semantic rule' and 'meaning postulate' so that a sentence is analytic if it is true according to the semantical rules and meaning postulates is equally empty. "Still," Quine goes on to stress, "there is really no progress. Instead of appealing to an unexplained word 'analytic,' we are now appealing to an unexplained phrase 'semantical rule,'" (or 'meaning postulate').[25] Analytic sentences, synonymous constructions, and so on are thus distinguishable only by the fact that these constructions appear on a list under the heading 'analytic sentences,' 'synonymous constructions' etc. or by the fact that their being analytic, synonymous, etc., follows from sentences appearing on a

---

[24] W. V. Quine, "Two Dogmas of Empiricism," *Philosophical Review*, vol. 60, 1951; reprinted in *From a Logical Point of View*.
[25] *Ibid.*

list under the heading 'semantical rules' or 'meaning postulates.' Such headings provide no indication of what properties a sentence of the language must have to qualify for membership on the list or of why it is reasonable to believe that having certain properties so qualifies a sentence. Consequently, such lists might just as well be labelled with nonsense syllables and contain randomly chosen sentences. At least in this way of doing things no one would be misled into thinking that meaning postulates and semantical rules have philosophical import.

This sort of criticism, especially on the part of Quine, forced Carnap to turn from semantics to pragmatics. In pragmatics, the third and final component of his theory of language, Carnap sought to find a means for giving some content to the, so far, vacuous concepts of 'analytic sentence,' 'synonymous constructions,' etc., and for justifying the meaning postulates and semantical rules in an artificial language. The means he proposed was that of introducing operational definitions of these concepts which would provide a behavioral test to determine their application. As Carnap put it, ". . . the objections raised against these semantical concepts concern, not so much any particular proposed explication, but the question of the very existence of the alleged explicanda (i.e., the concepts that are clarified and refined in the process of explication). Especially Quine's criticism does not concern the formal correctness of the definitions in pure semantics; rather, he doubts whether there are any clear and fruitful corresponding pragmatical concepts which could serve as explicanda. That is the reason why he demands that these pragmatical concepts be shown to be scientifically legitimate by stating empirical, behavioristic criteria for them. If I understand him correctly, he believes that, without this pragmatical substructure, the semantical intension concepts, even if formally correct, are arbitrary and without purpose. . . . If for a given semantical concept there is a familiar, though somewhat vague, corresponding pragmatical concept and if we are able to clarify the latter by describing an operational procedure for its application, then this may indeed be a simpler way of refuting the objections and furnish a practical justification at once for both concepts."[26]

According to Carnap, the linguist seeks to find dictionary entries for the descriptive terms of a language which express their meaning, or, as he sometimes says, their 'intension.' By the meaning or intension of a descriptive term t in a language L, Carnap means the general condition C that things or events must satisfy for speakers of L to be willing to ascribe t to them.[27] An explicit statement of C is, then, the dictionary entry for t. To obtain such a dictionary entry for a given descriptive term, a linguist asks speakers whether or not they are willing to apply the term to various things. The linguist is not restricted to asking about the application of the term to real objects and events. He may also ask about fictional ones. He may ask a speaker whether an animal similar

---

[26] R. Carnap, "Meaning and Synonymy in Natural Languages," also a supplement to the second edition of *Meaning and Necessity*.
[27] *Ibid.*

in essential respects to a horse but with a horn in the middle of its forehead is properly called a 'unicorn.' Semantic relations, such as 'is synonymous with,' are to be defined in terms of such behavioral tests in a manner for which the following is paradigmatic. The linguist asks speakers about the things and events to which they will each apply the terms t_1 and t_2 and accepts t_1 as synonymous with t_2 just in case the speakers are willing to apply them to the same objects and events, real or imaginary, refuse to apply them to the same objects and events, again real or imaginary, and the cases in which they are undecided about whether or not to apply them are the same.

This new proposal of Carnap's is intended to provide a basis for demonstrating that there exist phenomena to be described by the definitions of pure semantics—in Carnap's own formulation, that there are explicanda for the intension concepts of pure semantics. But this is a complete misunderstanding of Quine's criticism. In the case of analyticity, for example, Quine argued, "The notion of analyticity about which we are worrying is a purported relation between statements and languages: a statement S is said to be *analytic for* a language L, and the problem is to make sense of this relation generally, that is, for variable 'S' and 'L.' "[28] Quine's criticism of Carnap here is not that speakers cannot be shown to react differentially to sentences like "Spinsters are females," "Bachelors are unmarried," "Dogs are animals," etc., on the one hand, and sentences like

---

[28] W. V. Quine, "Two Dogmas of Empiricism."

"Spinsters are rich," "Bachelors are lonely," "Dogs are friendly," etc., on the other, as if behavioral tests might supply any information that the intuitive judgments of speakers on which those tests are based cannot supply. Rather, Quine's criticism is that the explication that Carnap offers of the pragmatical concept of analyticity does not provide any explanation of that concept. In general, Quine's criticisms show that the semantic rules and meaning postulates do not make sense of the semantic properties and relations they are intended to reconstruct: they tell us what sentences are called 'analytic,' 'contradictory,' 'synonymous,' etc., but they do not explain what is attributed to them by such labels. But even if we reinterpret Carnap's proposal so that what he is offering is thought of as behavioral tests and as operational definitions that give an empirical interpretation for the concepts of pure semantics, and even if we forget that to satisfy Quine, Carnap must provide tests and definitions that work for variable 'S' and 'L,' Carnap's new proposal fails to do the job for which it is put forth.

The question is whether behavioral tests and operational definitions such as those Carnap introduced actually characterize such concepts as 'analytic,' 'synonymous,' etc., that is, whether they provide us with any understanding of the abstract concepts of pure semantics. The answer is again in the negative because such behavioral tests rely on the linguist's and the speaker's intuitive grasp of the concepts that they are meant to explicate, and thus the operational definitions presuppose these concepts rather than define them. Let us consider

58   THE PHILOSOPHY OF LANGUAGE

an example. Quine once proposed that an utterance type be taken as grammatically well-formed just in case its token occurrences have been and could be uttered without eliciting a bizarreness-reaction from fluent speakers.[29] But this operational test fails in both directions. Anyone who attends to actual speech notices that many utterances are ungrammatical because of repetitions, arbitrary breaks, failures of agreement, interjections, improperly placed clauses, etc., and yet few are ever greeted with a bizarreness-reaction. Conversely, many grammatical utterances occur in situations where they are somehow inappropriate and thus occasion quite marked bizarreness-reactions (e.g., in an ordinary conversation about this and that, someone says, "I just swallowed my nose"). One might try to save Quine's test by quite correctly replying that it depends on the kind of bizarreness-reaction (the sort of bizarreness to which the reaction occurs). However, this reply could be sustained only by distinguishing a reaction to bizarreness in the relation between the utterance and the situation from reactions to bizarreness in the semantic, phonological, and syntactic structure of the utterance and by distinguishing each of these latter sorts from the others. But such an analysis is just what operational tests fail to do because they provide no understanding of concepts such as 'situational bizarreness,' 'semantic bizarreness,' 'phonological bizarreness,' and 'syntactic bizarreness.' A highly refined

[29] W. V. Quine, "The Problem of Meaning in Linguistics" in *From a Logical Point of View;* reprinted in J. A. Fodor and J. J. Katz (eds.), *The Structure of Language: Readings in the Philosophy of Language,* Prentice-Hall, 1964.

analysis of the possible types of bizarreness, distinguishing each from the others, and giving us an understanding of each type, might, of course, enable one to reformulate Quine's test for grammaticality so as to avoid difficulties such as those cited above, but such an analysis would be a theoretical account of grammaticality, i.e., a theory about the nature of grammatical well-formedness. The difficulties would be avoided because we now have theories of situational, semantic, syntactic, and phonological bizarreness, with respect to which we can legitimately dismiss what were formerly counterexamples on the grounds that they involve sorts of bizarreness other than grammatical ill-formedness.

The same points apply to Carnap's operational definitions, such as the one given for synonymy. Attempts to define operationally such abstract semantic concepts fail in both directions. Speakers apply synonymous expressions to different things and events and they apply nonsynonymous expressions to the same things and events. For example, Quine observed that the synonymous words 'rotten' and 'addled' are applied in such a fashion that only eggs are called 'addled,' although eggs and other things as well are called 'rotten.'[30] There is a variety of reasons why speakers do not apply synonymous expressions in the same referential cases. One is that some synonyms are too long and cumbersome, e.g., in normal situations speakers do not use 'drink of diluted spirits served in a tall glass with ice' but instead simply use the word 'highball.' On the other hand, nonsynonymous

[30] W. V. Quine, *Word and Object*, M. I. T. Press, 1960.

expressions such as 'creature with a heart' and 'creature with a kidney' or 'New York' and 'the largest city on the east coast of the U. S.' would certainly be applied to the same thing in the world by speakers. Again, we could distinguish cases of genuine synonymous expressions that happen to be used in different sets of circumstances from nonsynonymous expressions used in the same circumstances if we had a theoretical account of synonymy to appeal to in order to decide when different applications indicate a real difference in meaning. But there is no such account, and so everything depends on the operational test. A further difficulty of such dependence is that when an expression is ambiguous and another is synonymous with only one of its senses, as in 'bachelor' and 'unmarried adult male,' without such an account to indicate this, we will not be able to come anywhere close to showing that speakers apply them in the same cases, since, as with our example, the other senses of the ambiguous expression will be applied to cases that the other expression will never be applied to.

The upshot of all this is simply that, in the absence of theoretical accounts that explain abstract semantic concepts, behavioral tests and operational definitions fail to give any insight into these concepts. Carnap thus wrongly supposed that behavioral tests and operational definitions could do the work of such theoretical accounts. He thought that, by themselves, they could make a theoretical account of these concepts unnecessary. But, not only do behavioral tests and operational definitions not give an understanding of the concepts they are put forth to define, the situation is reversed: only the possession of a theoretical account that gives such understanding makes it possible to use behavioral tests properly. Without an antecedent understanding of such concepts provided by an independent theoretical analysis, we can neither formulate behavioral tests properly nor correctly evaluate the results they may yield, since we need such analyses in order to decide if a particular formulation of a test will test for the right linguistic property or relation, i.e., to make a nonarbitrary selection from among all of the possible tests for a specific linguistic property or relation. Consequently, behavioral tests do not explain the nature of abstract concepts, thereby replacing theories, but rather, properly used, they serve as part of the procedures for confirming or disconfirming the theories within which abstract concepts are defined.

Thus, the last of Carnap's attempts to offer an acceptable theory of an ideal language ends in failure too. Underlying the failure of the attempts of Carnap and other logical empiricists to construct an ideal, artificial language are two, not clearly differentiated, conceptions about the nature of such a linguistic system. One is that such a system is designed to supply the linguistic conventions that natural languages lack. On this conception, the first step in philosophical analysis may be to consider the facts from natural language about the term, expression, or sentence undergoing analysis. But all further steps must go beyond such facts and focus on the stipulation of principles to govern the philosophically acceptable use of the term, expression, or sentence within the ideal, artificial language. Moreover, such facts may or may not dictate features of these principles, at the discretion of the philosopher. Thus, the artificial language, and the principles incorporated in it, are designed, not to serve as a description of the natural language whose inadequacies made its construction necessary in the first place, but are intended to create the category distinctions and linguistic rules that are needed to prevent metaphysical statements from being confused with genuine statements about matters of fact and to make philosophical problems amenable to solution. Now, in terms of this conception, we have critically appraised the work of the logical empiricists and found that the constructions put forth to exclude metaphysical statements from ideal artificial language, and to make philosophical problems amenable to solution, cannot serve either of these purposes because these constructions are justified neither by the facts of natural language, nor in any other manner, and because they fail to explicate the semantic concepts for which they were intended.

On the other conception, none of these defects are avoided. The second conception is that an artificial language is a theory about the structure of a natural language in the form of an idealization. Carnap wrote that the structure of ". . . a particular word language, such as English, or of particular classes of word languages, or of a particular sublanguage of a word language, is best represented and investigated by comparison with a constructed language which serves as a system of reference.'[31] To make clear what he means by saying that "a constructed language . . . serves as a system of reference," he says, "The direct analysis of [natural languages], which has been prevalent hitherto, must inevitably fail [because of their incredible complexity], just as a physicist would be frustrated were he from the outset to attempt to relate his laws to natural things—trees, stones, and so on. In the first place, the physicist relates his laws to the simplest of constructed forms; to a thin straight lever, to a simple pendulum, to punctiform masses, etc. Then, with the help of the laws relating to these constructed forms, he is later in a position to analyze into suitable elements the complicated behavior of real bodies . . . ."[32] Thus, on this conception an artificial language is construed as an idealization of a natural language in just the sense in which ideal gases, perfectly rigid rods, complete vacuums, etc., are idealizations of physical phenomena. Its function is thus to reduce the complexity of such phenomena to manageable proportions so that regularities can be described in terms of simple laws. But although this analogy correctly represents the ideal character of a scientific theory of language, it is misleading as an interpretation of the status of the results actually produced by the logical empiricists in their attempts to construct artificial languages. For one thing, the artificial languages developed by Carnap and his followers are, unlike successful

[31] Carnap, *The Logical Syntax of Language.*
[32] *Ibid.*

idealizations in physics, under no strict empirical controls that determine their adequacy. A scientist who proposes an idealization must demonstrate that it predicts accurately within a reasonable margin of error and that the closer actual conditions approximate the ideal, the smaller this margin of error becomes. But, without effective empirical controls on the logical empiricist's artificial languages, we cannot determine which of two incompatible languages, i.e., two artificial languages which make inconsistent predictions about a natural language, deviates less from the linguistic facts. Logical empiricists failed to appreciate the fact that, without some means to determine how far an artificial language can deviate from the facts of a natural language, there is no way to evaluate its claims about the structure of that language and no validity whatever to the claim that an artificial language is an idealization of a natural language. Here, again, we find, in another form, the arbitrary character of the constructed languages proposed by logical empiricists.

But there is another point at which this analogy with physical theories breaks down. An idealization in physics is a theory of a highly systematic nature. The concepts which represent the ideal objects are the elements in terms of which the explanatory principles of the theory are formulated. These principles comprise a tightly integrated system upon which the coherence of the predictions and explanations afforded by the theory is based. The theory's predictions are determined by the kind of structure these explanatory principles attribute to the phenomena and thus correct predictions can confirm the belief that this, not some other, structure underlies the phenomena, while false predictions can serve to disconfirm this belief. However, the predictions made from an artificial language of the Carnapian variety are, from this viewpoint, quite empty. We can say that the linguistic constructions that are listed under the headings 'analytic,' 'synonymous,' etc., are the ones the Carnapian language 'predicts' are analytic, synonymous, etc. We can call such statements 'predictions.' But then, a successful prediction that a sentence has the property P establishes nothing more than that that sentence has the property P. There being no explanation of the concepts 'analytic,' 'synonymous,' etc., in terms of which to formulate a system of principles expressing an hypothesis about the semantic structure of the language concerned, there is no description of the systematic structure in the subject matter for successful predictions to confirm and unsuccessful ones to disconfirm. It is as if the Newtonian theory of mechanics were to specify examples of bodies, states of motion and rest, forces, actions and reactions, etc., but were to offer no laws of motion to explain the physical principles relating mechanical causes to mechanical effects. Hence, we know no more about a language after we find out that a Carnapian idealization 'predicts' that certain of its constructions have certain linguistic properties, and that others are linguistically related in certain ways, than we did before the idealization was formulated. The analogy with idealization in physics only conceals this fact behind a facade of scientism.

These two conceptions of the status of artificial languages conflict with each other. On the idealization-conception of an artificial language, such languages embody an hypothesis about the structure of a natural language and require empirical controls that constrain the idealization to account for the structure of the natural language. The adequacy of the artificial language thus depends upon how revealing it is as a description of the natural language. But, on the other conception, artificial languages are designed solely as a means of accomplishing philosophical therapy and analysis. They are not tied to any empirical controls just because it is assumed that natural languages are so vague, irregular, and amorphous that there are no philosophically significant facts for them to be faithful to. As Carnap first put it, there are no relevant semantic conventions to be found in a natural language. Hence, one conception assumes, as does any scientific investigation, that there exists regularity and structure to be described, while the other assumes it is lacking.

Thus logical empiricists equivocated on the issue of whether their artificial languages were idealized descriptions governed by empirical controls or ideal philosophical systems incorporating invented antimetaphysical stipulations. This equivocation made it wholly unclear what claims such artificial languages made and what constituted the justification for adopting one as the ideal language. Looked at as ideal philosophical systems, such languages are arbitrary because they have whatever features their authors decide they should have. But in order to embody convincing solutions to philosophical problems, they must do more than embody the solutions that their authors happen to believe correct. Some justification must be given. But if need for justification is filled by introducing empirical controls on artificial languages, then such languages are, at least in part, thought of as idealized descriptions, and it is admitted that there is something there for them to describe. Thus, to remove the arbitrariness by introducing empirical controls similar to those placed on idealization in other branches of science would be, to a significant extent, a denial of the assumption, central to logical empiricism, that semantic deficiencies of natural languages engender the conceptual confusions that create a need for the construction of artificial languages.

The basic problem is that neither Carnap nor any of his followers actually examined natural languages to determine whether it is true that the areas of a natural language that their artificial languages leave undescribed are sufficiently vague, irregular, and amorphous so that these areas may be legitimately left as the domain to be governed by stipulated conventions. Logical empiricists have assumed, but not established, that a description of these areas would not reveal them to exhibit a high order of systematicity underlying the superficial incoherence. Should this assumption prove false, a description of the semantics of natural languages might well produce results that accomplish their therapeutic and analytic aims, thus doing exactly what these philosophers thought only some constructed, ideal language could do. Therefore, the logical empiricists beg the fundamental question at issue. In the absence of any justification of their assumption, the failure of an artificial language to represent the semantic structure of a natural language can be construed *either* as a deficiency of the natural language *or* as a deficiency of the artificial language, in which case the supposed vagueness, irregularity, and amorphousness of the natural language is merely an artifact of the logical empiricist's own a priori assumption. Clearly, the only way to decide which is the case is to investigate natural languages, without a priori assumptions, to discover exactly what semantic structure they have. But this means we must try to construct descriptions of particular natural languages and a theory of language which are empirically motivated idealizations. Only such an investigation can offer substantive hypotheses about linguistic structure whose empirical validation or invalidation might settle the issue one way or the other. This, however, logical empiricists never attempted.

ORDINARY LANGUAGE PHILOSOPHY

The other major movement in twentieth-century philosophy, ordinary language philosophy, developed, in part, as a reaction to the logical empiricist's failure to come to terms with the facts of natural language. It took issue with their view that the conceptual confusions that generate metaphysical speculation are due to deficiencies of natural language which make it necessary to invent semantic conventions. What ordinary language philosophy urged instead was that natural languages are perfectly all right as they stand so long as they are used properly, i.e., in the ordinary way. Conceptual confusions are consequences of aberrations in usage. The restoration of normal, ordinary usage automatically clears them up, thus showing that the metaphysical speculations arising from these confusions are baseless, not because they are unable to arise in some artificial language, but because they do not arise in a properly used natural language. Thus, it is unnecessary to try to state linguistic conventions with full formal precision in an artificial language to correct aberrations in usage. Such corrections should be accomplished by a form of philosophical therapy and analysis which differs from that practiced by logical empiricists by concentrating on the description of linguistic facts.

The philosophical foundations of ordinary language philosophy were worked out by a number of philosophers, but one philosopher whose contribution was particularly significant was Wittgenstein. Wittgenstein began his philosophical career as a logical empiricist. His first book, *Tractatus Logico-Philosophicus*,[33] argued for the acceptance of an ideal, artificial language in which concepts are precisely defined and propositions unambiguously express the real form of facts. Indeed, on the basis of this book Wittgenstein himself became known as one

[33] L. Wittgenstein, *Tractatus Logico-Philosophicus*, Routledge & Kegan Paul, London, 1922.

of the founders of logical empiricism. But growing dissatisfaction with the concept of an ideal, artificial language eventually led him to take issue with logical empiricism in a way that laid the groundwork for an alternative conception of philosophical therapy and analysis.

Wittgenstein did *not* take the position that the artificial language approach failed because it was not scientific enough. Rather, he took the position that it failed because it was too scientifically oriented for its subject. The logical empiricists, Wittgenstein now argued, wish to imitate the activity of scientists and so model their artificial languages on scientific systems. Scientific systems, however, try to reveal the essence of objects, events, states, and processes in the form of precise, empirically motivated definitions that spell out the properties that are necessary and sufficient for something to be a phenomenon of a certain kind. Thus, in modelling their languages on scientific systems, logical empiricists try to reveal the essence of such linguistically given concepts as 'knowledge,' 'truth,' 'mind,' 'perception,' 'cause,' 'existence,' etc. They seek absolutely precise definitions that give their meaning as a condition which is necessary and sufficient for something to count as knowledge, truth, mind, perception, cause, existence, etc. But, Wittgenstein argued, such statements of meaning are simply not possible in philosophy. Unlike scientific terms, which have a single, technical function to perform, the terms of philosophical importance in ordinary language have a wide variety of uses, some of which depend upon features, such as vagueness and ambiguity, which would be eliminated in a logical empiricist's language. Wittgenstein stressed the need for philosophers to undertake a detailed descriptive examination of the ways in which speakers actually use words and expressions in their ordinary employment of a natural language. Such an examination, he contended, would show just how mistaken it is to suppose that the meaning of a word or expression can be given by a definition which states a necessary and sufficient condition for application. In this connection, Wittgenstein wrote, "Consider for example the proceedings that we call 'games.' I mean board-games, card-games, ball-games, Olympic games, and so on. What is common to them all?—Don't say: 'There *must* be something common, or they would not be called "games" '—but *look and see* whether there is anything common to all.—For if you look at them you will not see something that is common to *all*, but similarities, relationships, and a whole series of them at that. To repeat: don't think, but look!—Look for example at board-games, with their multifarious relationships. Now pass to card-games; here you find many correspondences with the first group, but many common features drop out, and others appear. When we pass next to ball-games, much that is common is retained, but much is lost.—Are they all 'amusing'? Compare chess with noughts and crosses. Or is there always winning and losing, or competition between players? Think of patience. In ballgames there is winning and losing; but when a child throws his ball at the wall and catches it again, this feature has disappeared. Look at the parts played by skill and luck; and at the difference between skill in chess and skill in tennis. Think now of games like ring-a-ring-a-roses; here is the element of amusement, but many other characteristic features have disappeared! And we can go through the many, many other groups of games in the same way; and can see how similarities crop up and disappear. And the result of this examination is: we see a complicated network of similarities overlapping and criss-crossing: sometimes overall similarities, sometimes similarities of detail."[34] Hence, the model which is to replace that of strict definition—the model which Wittgenstein believed gave a better picture of how the various uses of a word are connected with one another—is the notion of 'family resemblance.' As Wittgenstein put it: "I can think of no better expression to characterize these similarities than 'family resemblance'; for the various resemblances between the members of a family: build, features, color of eyes, gait, temperament, etc., overlap and criss-cross in the same way."[35]

It should be observed that Wittgenstein offers no specific arguments for his position that we cannot expect to find definitions which express a necessary and sufficient condition for applying a given word. What he does is to show that certain simple-minded conditions are not acceptable for certain words such as his example 'game.' But to show this is certainly not to establish that there is

[34] L. Wittgenstein, *Philosophical Investigations*, Basil Blackwell Oxford, 1953.
[35] *Ibid.*

no condition that is necessary and sufficient for a word such as 'game' to be applied correctly. Thus, he neither provides a reason why a statement of the family resemblance is the best we can do, nor does he try to analyze his cases to show that they amount to more than multiple senses of the same orthographic element, such that some of the simple-minded definitions he considers work for some senses and others work for other senses. The linguistic complexity he exhibits thus might shame a logical empiricist into becoming more careful about what he says concerning the way we use words, but it certainly cannot be grounds on which he would be reasonable to stop looking for definitions of the usual sort. Moreover, Wittgenstein totally ignores obvious cases that conflict with his position that there is nothing common to the instances, and only these instances, to which a word is correctly applied. Consider cases such as 'brother,' 'aunt,' and 'highball,' where it's quite clear that, for each, there is a unique defining condition: in the case of 'brother,' it is that the person be a male sibling of another; in the case of 'aunt,' it is that a person be someone's parent's sister; and in the case of 'highball' it is that something be a drink of diluted spirits served with ice in a tall glass. It might be replied that these cases are somehow different from cases like 'game,' but Wittgenstein gives no relevant distinction on which to support his position.

The logical empiricists' explanation of how speakers know when to apply a word to something is that speakers know a necessary and sufficient condition for its application and use this condition to decide whether to apply the word by determining if the particular case at hand has the features that satisfy the condition. But, according to Wittgenstein, speakers cannot decide whether to apply words in this way because such conditions do not exist. Thus, the logical empiricists' theory about how speakers know when to apply words leads them to mistakenly demand a sharp, formalizable boundary for concepts with blurred edges and indefinitely many divergent uses. Wittgenstein asks, "How should we explain to someone what a game is? I imagine that we should describe *games* to him, and we might add: 'This and *similar things* are called "games." ' " And do we know any more about it ourselves? Is it only other people whom we cannot tell exactly what a game is?—but this is not ignorance. We do not know boundaries because none have been drawn. To repeat, we draw a boundary—for a special purpose. Does it take that to make the concept usable? Not at all! (Except for that special purpose.) No more than it took the definition: 1 pace = 75 cm to make the measure of length 'one pace' usable."[36] Wittgenstein concluded this remark by saying, "And if you want to say 'But still, before that it wasn't an exact measure,' then I reply: very well, it was an inexact one—though you still owe me a definition of 'exactness.' "[37] The point is that the logical empiricist cannot actually pay this debt because he has no criterion for specifying the kind of precision on which his claims for the superiority of his linguistic constructions are

[36], [37] *Ibid.*

based. This debt cannot be paid with a definition of 'exactness' which requires that every distinction it is possible to make be made, nor can it be paid by saying that we must make every distinction necessary for some 'special purpose.' When do we stop making distinctions? When have we been precise enough? According to Wittgenstein, we need make only those distinctions that exist in the language, since to stop there is to stop at a natural point. But the logical empiricist's advice to make every distinction necessary to avoid imprecision affords us no criterion for stopping anywhere beyond the natural stopping point or short of the utopian goal of making every logically possible distinction.

The logical empiricist's approach regards a natural language as an imperfect approximation to some ideal language, which it is the logician's job to construct. "But," says Wittgenstein, "here the word 'ideal' is liable to mislead, for it sounds as if these languages were better, more perfect, than our everyday language," and he adds, "as if it took the logician to show people at last what a correct sentence looked like."[38]

According to Wittgenstein, philosophical problems arise when language is misused. Conceptual confusions and metaphysical speculations are the symptoms of such misuses. The treatment consists in a correct description of the actual use of the word or expression whose misuse caused the philosophical illness, together with an etiological account of how the departure from proper usage brought the illness about. Wittgenstein conceived of phi-

[38] *Ibid.*

losophy as a form of therapy which, by correcting misuses of language, removes the conceptual confusions and metaphysics arising from them. Philosophical analysis, for Wittgenstein, was a description of the ordinary uses of words and expressions aimed at dissolving the philosophical problems caused by their misuse. He wrote that in philosophy, "What we do is to bring words *back* from their metaphysical to their everyday usage."[39] ". . . when philosophers use a word—'knowledge,' 'being,' 'object,' 'I,' 'proposition,' 'name,'—and try to grasp the *essence* of the thing, we must always ask: is the word ever *actually* used in this way in the language which is its original home."[40] "For philosophical problems arise when language *goes on holiday*."[41]

Wittgenstein anticipated the criticism that his way of doing philosophy has only the negative objective of destroying our most cherished flights of philosophical imagination, for if he is successful, much of traditional philosophical speculation about knowledge and valuation is shown to rest merely on a style of language that departs radically from ordinary usage. In reply, he writes, "Where does our investigation get its importance from, since it seems only to destroy everything interesting, that is, all that is great and important? . . . What we are destroying is nothing but houses of cards and we are clearing up the ground of language on which they stand. The results of philosophy are the uncovering of one or another piece of nonsense and of bumps that the understanding has got by running its head up against the limits of

[39-41] *Ibid.*

language. These bumps make us see the value of the discovery."[42]

Part of Wittgenstein's therapy consists of making explicit the absurdities that derive from misusing language, "converting concealed nonsense into overt nonsense"[43] as he phrased it. Some philosophers have put forth the view that the meaning of a word is what it names, and this, in turn, has led to the metaphysical doctrine that there exist certain occult, supersensible entities named by such meaningful abstract nouns as 'truth,' 'virtue,' etc. But, Wittgenstein argues, if the meaning of a word like 'slab' were the actual physical bricks, blocks, etc., that a laborer fetches in carrying out the foreman's orders, rather than the ways in which 'slab' is used by the laborer and the foreman in giving, acknowledging, carrying out, etc., orders, then we could say such obviously absurd things as, "I broke part of the meaning of the word 'slab' " or "I laid a hundred parts of the meaning of the word 'slab' today."[44] Making such absurdities explicit enables us to see the absurdity in the view that a word's meaning is what it names. Thus, the metaphysics about supersensible entities based on this view of meaning is left without foundation.

Consider another example of Wittgenstein's kind of investigation. One might think of trying to define 'understanding' in terms of a condition which expresses the essence of the conscious mental process that occurs when someone understands something. But, according to Wittgenstein, such mental processes are neither necessary

[42-44] *Ibid.*

nor sufficient for understanding. " 'B understands the principle of the series' surely doesn't mean simply: the formula '$a_n = \ldots$' occurs to B. For it is perfectly imaginable that the formula should occur to him and that he should nevertheless not understand. 'He understands' must have more in it than: the formula occurs to him. And equally, more than any of those more or less characteristic accompaniments or manifestations of understanding"[45] (such as the 'Ah, ha' sensation). Conversely, inner conscious processes could be eliminated (say in favor of objective inscriptions) without eliminating the possibility of understanding. Thus, Wittgenstein cautions, "Try not to think of understanding as a 'mental process' at all.—For *that* is the expression which confuses you. But ask yourself: in what sort of case, in what kind of circumstances, do we say, 'Now I know how to go on,' when, that is, the formula *has* occurred to me?"[46] Here Wittgenstein changes the original question 'How do we formulate a definition that captures the essence of 'understanding'?' into one he considers it more reasonable to ask, namely, 'Under what conditions do we use the word 'understanding' correctly when we apply it to individuals on the basis of what they do?' To answer such questions involves describing the family resemblance between such locutions as 'understanding the rule,' 'understanding the problem,' 'understanding the directions to the road,' 'understanding poetry,' and so on. "Essence," says Wittgenstein, "is expressed by grammar: grammar tells us what kind of object anything is."[47] We need only

[45, 46] *Ibid.*

point out that, by 'grammar,' he does not mean such a thing as parsing sentences into nouns, verbs, adjectives, etc., but rather describing the complex pattern of overlapping and criss-crossing similarities that constitute the family resemblance which different instances of the use of 'understanding' bear to each other.

Ordinary language philosophy was put into practice not only on the Wittgensteinian model but also on what can be thought of as the Oxford model. Wittgenstein taught at Cambridge, and so Cambridge was the first home of ordinary language philosophy. But, subsequently, with intensive cultivation of ordinary language philosophy at Oxford, Oxford became the recognized center of this philosophical school. Under the leadership of philosophers such as Ryle, Austin, and others, Oxford evolved a version of ordinary language philosophy which, although strongly influenced by Wittgenstein, is somewhat different from Wittgenstein's. "At Oxford," Passmore comments, "Wittgenstein's ideas entered a very different philosophical atmosphere from that which prevailed at Cambridge. Oxford philosophers, for the most part, have learnt their philosophy as part of a course of study which is based upon classical scholarship. . . . At Oxford, then, Wittgenstein's ideas were grafted on to an Aristotelian-philological stock; the stock has influenced the resultant fruits which, amongst other things, are considerably drier and cooler than their Cambridge counterparts."[48]

[48] J. Passmore, *A Hundred Years of Philosophy*, Gerald Duckworth & Company, London, 1957.

At Oxford certain alterations in doctrine and changes in emphasis produced a somewhat modified and broadened conception of ordinary language philosophy. The anti-ideal, artificial language tendency of Wittgenstein's thought survived virtually intact, and so did his view that philosophical inquiry proceeds from and fundamentally concerns itself with the ordinary uses of words and expressions in a natural language. But the Wittgensteinian doctrine that philosophical problems are *merely* the result of failures to use locutions in their ordinary, everyday employment and that philosophical solutions are *just* forms of linguistic rehabilitation was markedly weakened. Ordinary language philosophers at Oxford were prepared to admit that many philosophical problems were due only to misuse and that, accordingly, many philosophical solutions were just therapy, but they also were willing to make a place for more constructive philosophizing. They held that in some cases entanglements with linguistic rules reflect genuine conceptual puzzles whose solutions offer genuine insights into the structure of the conceptual system underlying language. Philosophical solutions can thus provide a map of such entanglements which not only guides us out of present entanglements and enables us to avoid similar ones in the future—thereby accomplishing a piece of philosophical therapy or immunizing us against some possible future exposure to metaphysics—but which charts the conceptual terrain, thereby opening up the prospect of discovering some as yet unnoticed features of the boundaries of our concepts or even some new concepts and conceptual relations. Philosophical problems were thus capable of solution by an analysis which revealed the geography of the unexplored conceptual terrain where the problem arose. Wittgensteinian dissolution whereby a problem is shown to evaporate once we fully appreciate how the words concerned are ordinarily used is, consequently, one but not the only way of handling the problems that current philosophy inherits from past philosophy.

One example of an attempted linguistic solution to a classical philosophical problem is Strawson's treatment of the justification of induction.[49] Hume had raised the question of why we have confidence in inductive extrapolations from known cases to unknown ones. We usually infer that unknown cases of a certain type will have a certain property because we found that all known cases of that type have that property. Thus, we infer that the sun will rise in the future because it has always done so in the past. Hume argues that this is not a deductive inference, since the falsity of the conclusion is not logically inconsistent with the truth of the premisses. But, he continues, if it is not deductive, then the principle upon which the inference is based, viz., that observed regularities hold for unobserved cases, can only be based on experience. This, however, makes the whole thing circular because, then, any justification of this principle is an argument from observed cases, which, accordingly, appeals to the very principle it purports to justify. Strawson argued that the apparent insolubility of this

[49] P. F. Strawson, *Introduction to Logical Theory*, John Wiley & Sons, 1952.

problem derives from the fact that we are asking the
wrong question. We are asking whether inductive inference can be justified, which is as odd as asking whether
the law of the land is legal. Instead, we should be asking
whether it is reasonable to believe the conclusions of inductive inferences. If we put the question this way, it
is an easy matter to justify our belief. "Being reasonable"
(about such matters of fact) means "Having a degree of
belief in a statement which is proportional to the
strength of the evidence in its favor."[50] Hence, Strawson
concludes, it is necessarily the case as a consequence of
the meanings of words in our language that it is reasonable to believe conclusions that have been established by
proper applications of inductive inference.

Another example of an attempted linguistic treatment
of philosophical concepts is Ryle's discussion of the relation between voluntary action and normal
responsibility.[51] "The tangle of largely spurious problems,
known as the problem of the Freedom of the Will, partly
derives from . . . (an) . . . unconsciously stretched use
of 'voluntary.' " ". . . philosophers, in discussing what
constitutes acts voluntary or involuntary, tend to
describe as voluntary not only reprehensible but also
meritorious actions, not only things that are someone's

[50] The difficulty with Strawson's argument is that the notion of
'strength of the evidence in favor of a statement' begs the question,
since, as Goodman has pointed out, the whole question is just what
constitutes evidence in favor of a hypothesis that is not at the same
time evidence in favor of indefinitely many hypotheses inconsistent
with it. Cf. N. Goodman, *Fact, Fiction, and Forecast*, Harvard University Press, 1955 (the article, "The New Riddle of Induction").
[51] G. Ryle, *The Concept of Mind*, Hutchinson & Company, London,
1949.

fault but also things that are to his credit."[52] But, Ryle argues, "It should be noticed that while ordinary folk, magistrates, parents and teachers, generally apply the words 'voluntary' and 'involuntary' to actions in one way, philosophers often apply them in quite another way."[53] "In their most ordinary employment 'voluntary and 'involuntary' are used, with a few minor elasticities, as adjectives applying to actions which ought not to be done. We discuss whether someone's action was voluntary or not only when the action seems to have been his fault. . . . In the same way in ordinary life we raise questions of responsibility only when someone is charged, justly or unjustly, with an offense. It makes sense, in this use, to ask whether a boy was responsible for breaking a window, but not whether he was responsible for finishing his homework in good time."[54] "In the ordinary use, then, it is absurd to discuss whether satisfactory, correct or admirable performances are voluntary or involuntary . . ."[55]

Perhaps more significantly, the liberalization of the Wittgensteinian conception of ordinary language philosophy that took place at Oxford also allowed for the adoption of quite general philosophical theses and positions. The clarification and analysis of the concepts underlying language could concern concepts crucial to the formulation or defense of some philosophical thesis or position and could thus provide positive or negative evidence for that thesis or position. One of the best known attempts to use linguistic evidence to support one philosophical

[52-55] *Ibid.*

thesis and undermine another that is found in Oxford philosophy is Ryle's defense of behaviorism and criticism of Cartesian dualism.[56] Ryle contends that Descartes' concept of the soul as, according to Ryle, 'a ghost mysteriously ensconced in a machine' and the philosophical problem (created by a noncorporeal conception of mind) of how an immaterial entity can causally affect the workings of a material body are both the result of a category mistake resulting from a failure to follow the ordinary use of mentalistic words. On Ryle's account, Descartes' mistake is to regard the soul as some special sort of object, ontologically distinct from physical objects, belonging to a category of objects that are nonspatial, immaterial, and knowable only through introspection. To correct this mistake and clear up the problem of mind-body interaction, Ryle analyzes the ordinary use of mentalistic words to show that the facts about the proper use of these words reveal that they do not refer to an entity belonging to a special category distinct from the categories dealing with material objects and their behavior. Ryle tried to show, in particular, that predications about a person's mental qualities and states attribute dispositions, abilities, and propensities to his body, rather than attributing properties to a private, immaterial entity housed in the body. Ryle regards such dispositions, abilities, and propensities as similar to those we attribute to physical objects to which no mentalistic predicates apply. For example, they are similar to the disposition to break on impact which is attributed to a teacup when it is correctly

[56] *Ibid.*

described as fragile. Correspondingly, to describe someone as intelligent, generous, treacherous, etc., is to say something about how he will behave in a certain class of situations where he is appropriately stimulated. Ryle's evidence for this claim is derived from an analysis of the use of mentalistic words, in which a typical result is that describing someone as intelligent is a dispositional description meaning that he will exhibit a high degree of ability to solve conceptual problems under normal conditions. Since, on Ryle's account, the function of mentalistic words is to provide us with the means for describing regularities in the way persons carry on some of their publically observable behavior, and not to provide us with the means of referring to and chronicling private, introspectively observable events, Ryle concludes that using them as if they served this latter means is to misuse language by mistaking the category to which mentalistic words belong. Such linguistic evidence is taken as a refutation of Cartesian dualism and as support for the behaviorist position.[57]

We may mention two further points on which ordinary language philosophers at Oxford came to disagree with Wittgenstein's position. One disagreement arose over the question of supplying a theoretical foundation for the ordinary language brand of philosophical analysis. Wittgenstein wrote, "Philosophy may in no way interfere with the actual use of language; it can in the end

[57] For a discussion of Descartes' concept of the soul that casts serious doubts on Ryle's interpretation of Cartesian dualism, see N. Chomsky, *Cartesian Linguistics* (in preparation).

only describe it. For it cannot give it any foundation either. It leaves everything as it is . . . ."[58] Austin not only acknowledged the occasional necessity "to be brutal with, to torture, to fake, and to override, ordinary language"[59] but, on the issue of what it is about ordinary language that justifies the ordinary language philosopher in using his brand of philosophical analysis, he disregarded Wittgenstein's 'hands-off attitude' by trying to give some philosophical foundation for the appeal to ordinary language. He wrote, ". . . our common stock of words embodies all the distinctions men have found worth drawing, and the connections they have found worth making, in the lifetimes of many generations: these surely are likely to be more numerous, more sound, since they have stood up to the long test of the survival of the fittest, and more subtle, at least in all ordinary and reasonably practical matters, than any that you or I are likely to think up in our armchairs of an afternoon—the most favored alternative method."[60]

Finally, another divergence from Wittgensteinism can be found in the attempt, on the part of certain Oxford philosophers, to explicitly formulate certain of the technical concepts which were found useful as part of the methodology for their form of philosophical analysis. We may mention as examples Ryle's attempt to formulate a well-defined notion of 'category' which would incorpo-

---

[58] Wittgenstein, *Philosophical Investigations.*
[59] J. L. Austin, "A Plea for Excuses," *Proceedings of the Aristotelian Society*, vol. 57, 1956–1957; reprinted in *Philosophical Papers*, Clarendon Press, Oxford, 1961.
[60] *Ibid.*

rate a technique for deciding when two locutions belong to different categories in the language, and also Austin's attempt to develop apparatus for his theory of performatives.[61] Such clarification of methodology was quite uncharacteristic of Wittgenstein who was content to use his stock of special concepts, i.e., 'family resemblance,' 'use,' 'language,' 'language game,' etc., without subjecting them to explicit formulation.

Both versions of ordinary language philosophy were characterized by an intense, but narrowly restrictive, concern with the details of particular words and expressions in English. This was both their major virtue and their major vice. Because of this overriding concern with linguistic details, ordinary language philosophy made an important contribution to research in semantics, indeed far more of a contribution than was made by professional linguists in the first half of the twentieth century. For while professional linguists occupied themselves primarily with phonology, syntax, and various historical problems, ordinary language philosophers, with their attention focused on epistemological problems, occupied themselves primarily with semantics. In fact, their results, scattered and fragmentary though they are, provide some of the best examples of careful and insightful linguistic description. In this connection we may cite Austin's introduction of the concept of a performative verb and, in general, his classification of types of per-

<hr/>

[61] Cf. Ryle, "Categories," in A. G. N. Flew (ed.), *Logic and Language,* vol. 2, Basil Blackwell, Oxford, 1955, and J. L. Austin, *How to do Things with Words,* Harvard University Press, 1962.

formative verbs and his analysis of the performative uses of language.[62] We may also cite Ryle's discussion of what he calls 'achievement verbs' and Vendler's subsequent reanalysis of them.[63] Also worth mention is Urmson's work on grading adjectives and parenthetical verbs.[64]

But the concern with linguistic details that brought to light so many specific facts about natural language went hand in hand with a failure to take into account the complex structural organization in which such facts are systematized in actual languages. It is indeed somewhat strange that a movement that achieved such a quantity of competent description should have done almost nothing in the way of theorizing about linguistic structure. The comparison with Babylonian astronomy or Greek geometry before Euclid comes most readily to mind.

This failure was not accidental. There were reasons why ordinary language philosophy made no substantive contributions toward a theory of English or a theory of language. Perhaps the most significant of these reasons was that the whole orientation of ordinary language philosophy was antitheoretical. Ordinary language philosophy was, as explained earlier, reacting to the logical empiricist's excesses in theory construction, and, to the extent that they shared the antimetaphysical bent of logical empiricism, they were also reacting to the theoretical systems developed in some traditional meta-

[62] Austin, op. cit.
[63] Ryle, The Concept of Mind, and Z. Vendler, "Verbs and Times," Philosophical Review, vol. 67, no. 2, April, 1957.
[64] J. O. Urmson, "On Grading," in A. G. N. Flew (ed.), Logic and Language, vol. 2, and "Parenthetical Verbs," in A. G. N. Flew (ed.), Essays in Conceptual Analysis, Macmillan & Company, London, 1956.

physical enterprises. Therefore, the antitheoretical character of ordinary language philosophy was to a large extent dictated by the very philosophical motives that led it to investigate language in the first place. Thus, Wittgenstein once said that the work of a philosopher consists in "assembling reminders for a particular purpose." Hampshire, one of the more prominent of the ordinary language philosophers at Oxford, wrote: "But we do not in philosophy need to state what are the necessary and sufficient conditions for calling a signalling system a language; for we are not particularly concerned with defining the word 'language.' Nor are we concerned with a systematic classification of the different grammatical forms of language; the interest of contemporary philosophers in forms of speech neither is, nor should be, scientific or systematic."[65] Hampshire goes on to say that linguistic description as performed by ordinary language philosophers ought to confine itself to characterizing the use of particular locutions in a natural language so that the features of these locutions may be cited as counterexamples to certain "philosophical preconceptions about the necessary forms and functions of language."[66] Hampshire might be considered a somewhat extreme case, but, nevertheless, judged by the standard of practice his antitheoretical attitude toward the study of language was to a very large extent shared, implicitly if not explicitly, by those who worked within the framework of

[65] S. Hampshire, "The Interpretation of Language: Words and Concepts," in C. A. Mace (ed.), *British Philosophy in the Mid-Century*, Macmillan Company, 1957.
[66] *Ibid.*

ordinary language philosophy. In a similar vein, Wittgenstein once remarked that "it is, rather, of the essence of our investigation that we do not seek to learn anything *new* by it."[67]

Underlying the ordinary language philosopher's avoidance of any systematic or theoretical concern with language and his corresponding preoccupation with only the most minute details of English is a thoroughgoing distrust of generalizations. Ryle once went so far as to generalize, paradoxically, that "in philosophy, generalizations are unclarifications."[68] Contrary to the scientific view that explanation consists in the systematization of detailed facts in the form of generalizations that reveal their underlying organization, the ordinary language philosopher's view, implicit in the above quotes from Hampshire, Wittgenstein, and Ryle, seems to be that explanation in philosophy consists in overthrowing generalizations by showing that the facts they purport to cover do not fit nicely as instances. The doctrine seems to be that generalizations are unfaithful to facts and stand between the philosopher and the facts so that they prevent him from having a clear view of them. The only way to see the facts clearly is to remove the intruding, opaque generalization. This is accomplished by producing appropriate counterexamples. Not all ordinary language philosophers share this doctrine, but their general practice of concentrating on elaborate examinations of detailed linguistic examples and their refusal to try to construct

---

[67] Wittgenstein, *Philosophical Investigations*.
[68] Ryle, *The Concept of Mind*.

generalizations to systematize the examples shows that very few have escaped its influence.

The ordinary language philosopher whose approach is governed by this skeptical doctrine fails to look beyond the fact that most generalizations about linguistic structure have not been formulated in an exceptionless fashion. What he fails to understand is that a generalization can be valuable even if there are, at present, clear cut counterexamples to it. Counterexamples are indeed conclusive against the *formulation* of a generalization, but this does not mean that the generalization which we seek to formulate is wrong or that every feature of the formulation shares equally in the guilt. The ordinary language philosopher also fails to appreciate the role of counterexamples to indicate the direction in which the formulation of a generalization should be revised, not just to accomodate them, but to increase the degree to which the generalization reveals the underlying organization of the facts. If the ordinary language philosopher valued generalizations for the account they give of underlying systematicity, he would not treat new counterexamples as further evidence that our mistrust of generalization was well-founded all the time, but as new avenues toward more powerful and revealing formulations of underlying linguistic structure. His failure to appreciate this forces him to forfeit any possibility of going beyond an item by item description of particular linguistic constructions.

The ordinary language philosopher's emphasis was on acquiring insights concerning the use of particular words that could be applied in their practice of philosophical therapy, in defending or refuting one or another philosophical thesis or position, and in clarifying traditionally significant concepts having to do with knowledge and valuation. On the basis of what appeared to be a certain measure of success in achieving these aims, ordinary language philosophers believed that they could continue to be successful without trying to provide generalizations that show how particular facts about linguistic constructions are systematically related as part of the pattern of organization in the language. But such generalizations, as we shall argue more fully in the last part of the final chapter of this book, are often the only way to obtain an adequate treatment of cases of words and expressions about which there is little clear-cut agreement among speakers on the basis of their linguistic judgments. That is, it is often the case, and especially with philosophically significant words and expressions, that our judgments about the item we wish to analyze are too unclear and variable to permit us to make any definite statement about its meaning. In such cases, the only alternative is to formulate generalizations based on clear cases and try to obtain a statement of the meaning of the unclear cases from the organization these generalizations impose on them predictively. But, without generalizations describing the systematic semantic relations between clear and unclear cases, such theoretical triangulation is impossible, and the result is that unclear cases, and with them many of the most interesting issues in philosophy, are relegated to the limbo of endless quibbling.

Moreover, it is certainly an open question how successful ordinary language philosophy can be in its attempt to deal with traditional philosophical questions if it does not cultivate the study of language in general. Clearly, the issues about knowledge raised by Plato, the issues about explanation raised by Aristotle, the issues about thinking raised by Descartes, the issues about causality raised by Hume, the issues about perception raised by Berkeley, and other philosophical issues as about the concepts of knowledge, explanation, thought, cause, perception, etc., cannot be settled on a linguistic basis without drawing upon the facts about all natural languages. Hence, without a theory of language, the linguistic treatment of philosophical issues, theses, positions, and concepts is so highly restricted that even the best of analyses cannot claim to apply beyond the boundaries of the conceptual systems underlying a narrow class of languages, more often than not a class that contains just one's own native language. It is a serious question, and one that has already arisen in the literature,[39] why we should regard a distinction in the use of words in English (or another particular language) as having epistemological significance in philosophical therapy, in decisions about philosophical theses and positions, and in the clarification of concepts with which

[39] Cf. J. A. Fodor and J. J. Katz, "The Availability of What We Say," *Philosophical Review*, vol. 72, no. 1, January, 1963.

philosophers have traditionally dealt. Languages do differ from one another in various and sundry respects, and any distinction found in English but not supported by cross-linguistic evidence may very well turn out to be idiosyncratic. Only if the distinction can be shown to be rooted in the nature of language in general will it be possible to argue convincingly that the distinction can support the solution to a traditional philosophical problem since, as Quine pointed out, the general concepts which enter into the formulation of traditional philosophical problems are concepts such as 'analytic in L,' 'synonymous in L,' 'meaningful in L,' 'category in L,' 'entails in L,' etc., for variable L, and so no particularistic analyses of the use of English locutions can, in principle, provide solutions to them. Consequently, in forfeiting the possibility of going beyond item-by-item descriptions of English locutions, ordinary language philosophy also forfeits the possibility of inferring anything about the nature of conceptualization from linguistic facts.

CONCLUDING REMARKS

It is now clear, therefore, why neither ordinary language philosophy nor logical empiricism produced a theory of language on the basis of which philosophy might arrive at a better understanding of conceptual knowledge. Ordinary language philosophers assumed they did not need to know anything systematic about the nature of language. But without such a theory they had no notion of the sort of system within which to represent linguistic facts and no motivated way of philosophizing from such facts. Their presentations of facts about English were thus informal and unorganized, so that the body of facts which they brought to light consisted of an unmanageably large assortment of heterogeneous data of undetermined philosophical relevance. The technical constructs which occasionally figured in the ordinary language philosopher's analyses, such as 'rule of language,' 'proper use,' 'linguistic oddity,' 'category,' 'family resemblance,' etc., were left entirely unexplained or else were described in terms of some quite unilluminating analogy.[70] On the other hand, the logical empiricists were content to assume that they pretty much knew everything there is to know about language on the basis of traditional, school-book grammar. Beyond this, it was just a matter of inventing conventions or carrying out operationalistic investigations of speech behavior. Thus, although ordinary language philosophy unearthed numerous minute details of English usage, it made no effort to go beyond such particular facts in the direction of a theory of language that would reveal their systematic structure, and, although logical empiricism constructed general theories, it confined its efforts to highly arbitrary and conceptually impoverished theories about a class of artificial languages whose structure bears little similarity to the structure of natural languages.

---

[70] Cf. the further discussion of this point is Fodor and Katz, "What's Wrong with the Philosophy of Language?"

Neither one of these movements took the indispensable first step toward attaining the goal of the philosophy of language, the construction of a theory of the nature of language. But, since neither took the *first* step toward obtaining significant inferences about conceptual knowledge or convincing solutions to major problems in philosophy, it is not surprising that neither was able to take any further steps.

 4

THE THEORY
OF LANGUAGE

In this chapter we present a theory of language that combines the logical empiricist's conception of a formalized theory of linguistic structure in general with the ordinary language philosopher's demand that linguistic description be concerned with and governed by the facts of natural languages. Such a theory has the virtues that made each of these movements promising approaches to the philosophy of language while avoiding the vices that prevent both of them from achieving the goals of the philosophy of language.

BACKGROUNDS

Natural languages are vehicles for communication in which syntactically structured and acoustically realized objects transmit meaningful messages from one speaker to another. They are not the only vehicles for communication that humans have at their disposal, but they are, without a doubt, the most flexible and important ones. The basic question that can be asked about natural languages is: what are the principles for relating acoustic objects to meaningful messages that make a natural language so important and flexible a form of communication?

Roughly, linguistic communication consists in the production of some external, publicly observable, acoustic phenomenon whose phonetic and syntactic structure encodes a speaker's inner, private thoughts or ideas and the decoding of the phonetic and syntactic structure exhibited in such a physical phenomenon by other speakers in the form of an inner, private experience of the same thoughts or ideas. Behavioristically oriented investigations of linguistic communication focus exclusively on the publicly observable aspects of communication situations: speech sounds, nonverbal behavior of the participants in the situation, and physical properties of available stimuli. Thus, such investigations neglect the essential aspect of successful linguistic communication, the congruence of speaker's and hearer's thoughts and ideas that results from verbal exchanges.

Indeed, this is the only aspect that makes verbal exchanges genuine linguistic communication. We can perfectly well imagine two giant computers with no ability to formulate thoughts and ideas or understand them but with the ability to produce speech sounds alternately in such a fashion that verbal exchanges between the computers replicate the publicly observable phenomena that occur when human speakers communicate in a natural language. Since we have no inclination whatever to regard such computer exchanges as genuine linguistic communication—as no different in kind from what goes on between human beings—we ought to have no inclination either to accept the behaviorist's claim to be investigating actual linguistic communication.

But just as we must appreciate the cognitive dimension of linguistic communication, it is equally important to appreciate the physical dimension and its connection with the cognitive. We can also imagine a pre-established harmony that makes the occurrence of any mediating acoustic phenomena unnecessary. Suppose that whenever a speaker wants to impart one of his thoughts or ideas to an audience, the same thought or idea occurs almost simultaneously in the minds of the members of his audience, appropriately marked to indicate whose thought it is, when such an indication is relevant, and that, regardless of what thoughts or ideas occur to a speaker, when he has no desire to impart them to others, no congruent thoughts or ideas occurs to them (or if such thoughts or ideas do occur to them, they are not marked as the speaker's). Clearly, such a pre-established harmony of mental events, although it has certain decided advantages over linguistic communication, is no more genuine linguistic communication than the denatured process envisaged by behaviorists.

To understand the ability of natural languages to serve as instruments for the communication of thoughts and ideas we must understand what it is that permits those who speak them consistently to connect the right sounds with the right meanings.

It is quite clear that, in some sense, one who knows a natural language tacitly knows a system of rules. This is the only assumption by which we can account for a speaker's impressive ability to use language creatively. Fluent speakers both produce and understand sentences that they have never previously encountered, and they can do this for indefinitely many such novel sentences. In the normal use of language, the production and comprehension of new sentences, created on the spot, is the rule rather than the exception. The exceptions are such things as customary greetings, stereotyped exclamations, clichés, direct quotations, and so forth. Normally, what we say and what we hear others say is intelligible not because it is a repetition of some utterance with whose previous occurrences we are already familiar, but because we possess the means for creating new sentences and interpretations for new sentences. The creativity that exhibits itself in the production and comprehension of novel sentences is thus like the creativity exhibited when someone successfully multiplies two numbers that he has never multiplied or seen multiplied before. Both types of creativity are cases of rule-governed behavior in which rules that abstractly represent infinitely many possible constructions are used to produce one or another actual construction falling under them. We do not credit someone with mastery of arithmetic if he is only able to perform well with problems in whose solutions he has been well drilled. Rather, like the criterion for mastery of arithmetic, the criterion of a person's linguistic fluency is whether he can perform well in the production and understanding of sentences that he has not been previously taught, sentences that he encounters for the first time. Similarly, no test that contains only questions about sentences with which a subject is familiar from his lessons can inform us about his fluency; a high score might mean only that he had memorized the example sentences in his lessons. On the other hand, if we give him a test about sentences that are entirely new to him, he will be required to exhibit his mastery of the rules of the language, not the proficiency of his memory.

Thus, the basic feature of linguistic fluency is its creativity. By virtue of acquiring fluency, a speaker obtains the ability to produce and understand infinitely many sentences, even though he has had no previous exposure to them. This creative aspect of fluency is so commonplace in our daily use of language that it is seldom actually recognized or accorded its proper theoretical significance. But if we consider what is involved in learning a foreign language, we may avoid taking it for granted and accord it its proper significance. Suppose we are testing someone to determine whether or not he has gained

fluency in a foreign language. Obviously, we do not credit him with mastery of the foreign language if he is only able to understand or produce those sentences whose meaning he has been previously taught. Analogously, we do not credit animals with fluency in language if they merely respond appropriately to verbal commands in which they have been extensively drilled. Rather, the criterion to determine if someone has acquired fluency is whether or not he can understand any sentence of the foreign language that he has not before encountered (and that a speaker of that foreign language would be able to understand). The theoretical significance of the ability to produce and understand novel sentences is, then, that it is the real test of fluency.

Given that fluent speakers are fluent because of their knowledge of the rules of the language and that linguistic communication is a process in which the meaning that a speaker connects with the sounds he utters is the same meaning that the hearer connects with these same sounds, it seems necessary to conclude that speakers of a natural language communicate with each other in their language because each possesses essentially the same system of rules. Communication can take place because a speaker encodes a message using the same linguistic rules that his hearer uses to decode it. This becomes clearer when we think of how we learn a foreign language in the classroom. Our teacher and text present us with a more or less accurate approximation of the rules that any speaker of the foreign language tacitly knows. Our task is to learn them well enough for us to produce utterances that can be decoded by speakers of that foreign language and to understand utterances of those speakers themselves. This sort of example brings out the fact that our competence in a foreign language depends on whether, and to what extent, the rules we have been taught are equivalent to those that speakers of the foreign language acquired naturally. But it also shows that each speaker of the foreign language must use essentially the same system of rules, i.e., systems used by different speakers cannot differ significantly from each other, since this is a precondition for our being able to communicate with an arbitrary speaker of the foreign language on the basis of the rules we learned in the classroom.

Thus, contrary both to the behaviorist's conception of linguistic communication on which speakers are regarded as automatons and to the pre-established harmony conception on which there can be no causal explanation of linguistic communication, we offer a more realistic conception. Roughly, and somewhat metaphorically, we can say that something of the following sort goes on when successful linguistic communication takes place. The speaker, for reasons that are linguistically irrelevant, chooses some message he wants to convey to his listeners: some thought he wants them to receive or some command he wants to give them or some question he wants to ask. This message is encoded in the form of a phonetic representation of an utterance by means of the system of linguistic rules with which the speaker is equipped. This encoding then becomes a signal to the speaker's articulatory organs, and he vocalizes an utterance of the proper phonetic shape. This is, in turn, picked up by the hearer's auditory organs. The speech sounds that stimulate these organs are then converted into a neural signal from which a phonetic representation equivalent to the one into which the speaker encoded his message is obtained. This representation is decoded into a representation of the same message that the speaker originally chose to convey by the hearer's equivalent system of linguistic rules. Hence, because the hearer employs the same system of rules to decode that the speaker employs to encode, an instance of successful linguistic communication occurs.

This account of linguistic communication is far from anything more than a rough statement of our subject. We will try to distinguish various aspects of the investigation of linguistic communication and to formulate a theory about certain of these aspects. But until we have advanced quite far in the development of such a theory, it will not be possible to give a more precise statement of our subject than the one given above. After all, it is such a theory that provides a precise statement of the vaguer, more intuitively grasped conception of the subject. The attempt to explicate the concepts in which our initial rough statement of the subject is couched guides the development of the theory and also leads to new concepts that provide new demarcations of the subject, which could not be anticipated at the outset.

Linguistic communication takes as many forms as there are distant natural languages in which human beings communicate with one another. To describe linguistic communication in all its forms, linguists write *linguistic descriptions* for natural languages. A linguistic description is a scientific theory in a quite straightforward sense. Its subject matter is a particular one of the natural languages that have been or are spoken in the world, or, more precisely, the internalized rules common to speakers who communicate in that language. Thus, it describes the knowledge whose possession permits a fluent speaker to communicate with other speakers of his language *L* and whose absence prevents those who only speak another language from communicating with normal monolingual speakers of *L* in their language. The formulation of such internalized rules relates observable speech events to one another through complex deductive patterns formalized in the linguistic description. The rules of a linguistic description, which are analogous to the laws of a physical theory, relate such events because they are generalizations expressing invariant connections among classes of linguistic event-types. Thus, the entire linguistic description is a system from which the phonological, syntactic, and semantic facts about a language can be derived as consequences of its rules.

Linguistic descriptions in this sense treat the same phonological, syntactic, and semantic facts that we find discussed in traditional books on grammar. But their treatment is expressed in a formalized, deductive theory whose aim is to give an exhaustive, systematic account of the language, whereas traditional books on grammar express their observations informally, incompletely, and with little attempt to achieve systematization. The difference is much like the difference between mechanics after it was systematized on a Newtonian basis and before, at stages where mechanical phenomena were described independently of any unifying laws. Traditional books on grammar are catalogues of types of phenomena: at the phonological level, vowels, consonants, diphthongs, stress, syllables, etc.; at the syntactic level, parts of speech, word order, agreement, sentence types, tense, clauses, etc.; and at the semantic level, word meaning, synonymy, antonymy, reference, connotation, etc. They state their observations about such phenomena in the form of paradigms with informal commentary on the nature of the phenomena exhibited by the paradigm, leaving it to the reader's judgement to supply the extension to similar cases and the relation of such cases to others. Such treatment is nowhere near exhaustive, nor is any conception offered that might explain what an exhaustive treatment would be, because there is no notion of rule that could be used as a means of expressing general facts about the language. Traditional grammars also lack a notion of a system of linguistic rules. As a consequence, they must remain, regardless of how far they are expanded, mere catalogues of types of linguistic phenomena, with no systematization in terms of underlying structure that cuts across the types and with no generalizations that succeed in stating what is true about every case of a type.

What makes a linguistic description different from a traditional grammar is not its subject matter but its approach to its subject matter. In particular, the differentiating feature is that a linguistic description provides comprehensive formal organization of the subject matter in terms of a general conception of linguistic rule and system that it inherits from the theory of language, which is also a theory concerning the nature of linguistic descriptions.

The theory of language is a formulation of the universals of language, those principles of organization and interpretation that give particular natural languages the systematic form of a natural language. Linguists study the details of particular natural languages, formulating their facts in linguistic descriptions, in order to uncover the extent of diversity in forms of linguistic communication. Linguists study the features common to all natural languages, formulating such regularities in the theory of language, in order to uncover the limits of such diversity.

There are two ways to look at the theory of language. In one way, it is a specification of those features of natural languages that are invariant from language to language, and that form the basis on which speakers of natural languages pair sounds and meanings. In the other way, the theory of language is a model of which each empirically successful linguistic description in an instance, exemplifying every feature of the model. The model embodies a definite conception as to what kind of communication system a natural language is. Particular linguistic descriptions patterned on this model describe the diverse ways in which different languages realize this conception in the form of actual communication systems for human use. The former way of looking at the theory of language looks at it from the viewpoint of what it is a theory of, while the latter looks at it from the viewpoint of how the theory is formulated. That is, the statements in the theory of language are formulated as constraints on the form of any linguistic description, whereas these constraints are interpreted as expressing general principles embodied in the rules that any speaker of a natural language has internalized.

The construction of a theory of language and the construction of linguistic descriptions for particular languages are strongly interdependent. Given a set of empirically adequate linguistic descriptions, the linguist can abstract their common features and so generalize from them to a theory of linguistic structure in general. In this way, he asserts generalizations expressing linguistic universals that are inductively extrapolated from known regularities represented in the given set of already constructed linguistic descriptions. Alternatively, given a theory of language, a linguist can facilitate the construction of linguistic descriptions by using this model to provide a pattern on which to organize the facts about the language uncovered in field work. Similarly, the justification of the theory of language and particular linguistic descriptions are interdependent. The theory of language is empirically tested by determining whether its generalizations, which extrapolate an invariant property of all previously described languages, attribute properties to each subsequently investigated language that those languages actually have. A particular linguistic description, though it is primarily responsible to the facts about a language, is better confirmed if empirical support for it comes from general truths about language, themselves supported by a wealth of evidence from many natural languages, than if the evidence for the linguistic description is restricted to the language in question.

Thus, the evidence for the generalizations about language appearing in the theory of language comes from the same set of facts that confirms particular linguistic descriptions. Such generalizations are true just in case the features they ascribe to linguistic descriptions are actually those that must be attributed to linguistic descriptions for them to be empirically successful. This much is clear. But what is not yet clear is that the theory of language is, in a certain sense, a part of the statement of each particular linguistic description. That is, each linguistic description has a common part consisting of the set of linguistic universals and a variable part consisting of the generalizations that hold only for the given language. A rough, but only a rough, analogy is this: Just as in some poker games we lay a card face up on the table and have it serve as a wild card in every player's hand, so that each hand actually consists of the cards dealt plus this wild card, we consider the theory of language to be part of every linguistic description, so that each such description consists of an account of the idiosyncratic facts about a language plus an account of the general facts about language. Therefore, the properties of a natural language that are found in all other languages as well are not represented in the form of generalizations about that natural language. Rather, such facts are stated just once in the theory of language as facts about language, thereby making numerous particular statements of them unnecessary. In this way, linguistics achieves a high order of theoretical economy by avoiding the redundancy that would ensue if each truth about all languages were stated independently for each language, i.e., if each such truth were written down as many times as we write down linguistic descriptions in order to exhaust the range of natural languages. Moreover, from the viewpoint of the theory of language, where we are concerned not with the possible diversity among languages but with the necessary limits of such diversity, such increases in conceptual economy increase the strength of the theory. The more facts about particular languages that are found to be instances of general truths about language and are formulated as such, the tighter are the constraints imposed on systems that qualify as linguistic descriptions. The farther we thus empirically limit the logically possible diversity in natural languages, the richer the theory of universal structure given in the theory of language.

The theory of language consists of three subtheories, each of which corresponds to one of the three components of a linguistic description and provides a statement of the organization of that component in a linguistic description.[1] We use the terms *phonological theory, syn-*

[1] J. J. Katz and P. Postal, *An Integrated Theory of Linguistic Descriptions*, M.I.T. Press, 1964.

tactic theory (which together comprise *grammatical theory*), and *semantic theory* to refer to these sub-theories. We use the terms *phonological component, syntactic component,* and *semantic component* to refer, respectively, to the three corresponding parts of a linguistic description. The phonological component is a statement of the rules by which a speaker deals with the speech sounds of his language; the syntactic component is a statement of the rules by which he organizes such sounds into sentential structures; and the semantic component is a statement of the rules by which he interprets sentences as meaningful messages.

The syntactic component of a linguistic description is a set of rules that generates an infinite class of abstract formal structures, each of which describes the syntactic organization of a sentence. It is the source of the inputs to both the phonological and semantic components. The phonological component operates on such formal objects to determine their phonetic shape, while the semantic component operates on them to determine their meaning. Both the phonological and semantic components are, therefore, purely interpretive: they relate the abstract formal structures underlying sentences to a scheme for pronunciation, on the one hand, and to a representation of conceptualization, on the other. The absence of a connection between the phonological and the semantic components accounts for the generally acknowledged fact about natural languages that sounds and meanings are arbitrarily related. But the fact that the operation of each is performed on the same formal structure, or syntactically related formal structures, provides a basis on which a linguistic description can correctly pair semantic interpretations and phonetic representations, thus explaining what means speakers use to pair meanings and sounds.

It is thus the job of particular linguistic descriptions to say how semantic interpretations and phonetic representations are correlated in each of the languages spoken in the world. If this job is to be accomplished, it is obviously necessary to have some general means for representing sound sequences, meanings, and the mediating syntactic structures. Such a means must provide definitions of the concepts *semantic interpretation, phonetic representation,* and *syntactic description* which suffice to identify formally instances of semantic interpretations, phonetic representations, and syntactic descriptions that appear in particular linguistic descriptions. These definitions must specify what it is that certain formal objects in linguistic descriptions have in common by virtue of which they are all semantic interpretations, phonetic representations, or syntactic descriptions. Accordingly, such definitions must be linguistic universals, and the task of framing them becomes, respectively, the central concern of semantic, phonological, and syntactic theory.

Each of these theories is, therefore, concerned with three problems. First, a specification of the form of the rules that appear in the component of a linguistic description of which it is the general theory. Second, a specification of the system within which rules of the prescribed form will appear. Third, a specification of the universal constructs that provide a theoretical vocabulary for writing particular rules of the prescribed form.

As mentioned above, the theory of language contains a statement of the form of the connections between the phonological, syntactic, and semantic components of a linguistic description. This welds them into a coherent, integrated system, which is the linguistic description. We have given a rough version of this statement in saying that the semantic and phonological components operate to assign interpretations to the formal structures produced by the syntactic component, but this version will have to be spelled out in greater detail and with considerably more precision for it to stand as the theory of language's statement of these connections.

Beyond this statement and the theories of the components of a linguistic description, the theory of language must contain an explicit procedure for evaluating putative linguistic descriptions of a language to discern which one best fits the available data. Such a procedure will be a specification of principles of scientific methodology in a form that makes them directly applicable to the task of evaluating competing linguistic descriptions for a given language. The choice of a hypothesis in linguistics, as in any other science, is always underdetermined by the available data. Regardless of how much or what kind of data has been obtained, the data will be a very small proper subset of the indefinitely large set of possible observations about which the competing theories make, in many cases, conflicting predictions. Without some means of choosing that goes beyond successful prediction of the available observations, incompatible hypotheses will be equally well supported. Such underdetermination means that the slack must be taken up by considerations that have to do with the simplicity and generality of the hypotheses that predict the known facts equally well. Scientific methodology, relativized to the case of linguistics, tells us something about the simplicity of the form in which the data must be systematized, just as, in other cases, scientific methodology tells us that the form in which values expressing a relation between two variables must be the simplest curve that connects the observed values. But in order to use such general scientific considerations in linguistics, we must have a precise statement of what form they take in linguistics—how they are to be applied to decide choices in linguistic cases. It has been proposed that linguists explicate these general scientific considerations as a metric that determines which of two proposed systems is the simpler and more general account of the facts on the basis of the number of rules and symbols occurring in each. I will not comment on this proposal, beyond mentioning that it presupposes that we have adequate theories of the phonological, syntactic, and semantic components that fix the type of rules and the set of symbols with respect to which such a counting is to be used.

Finally, the theory of language must contain some general principle by which the derivations produced by the rules of the syntactic component can be mechanically converted into the syntactic description of the sentence generated in the derivation. We shall return to this later.

A linguistic description is an idealization in exactly the same sense in which any scientific theory, such as the dynamic theory of gases or the Newtonian theory of mechanics, is. Just as these physical theories do not state their laws for the behavior of actual physical objects but instead formulate them in terms of ideal objects under ideal conditions, so the rules of a linguistic description are not stated as a characterization of what any actual speakers tacitly know about their language but are formulated as a characterization of the tacit knowledge of an ideal speaker. Hence, it no more matters that the speech of some English speakers does not exhibit a distinction represented in the rules of a linguistic description of English than it matters in Newtonian mechanics that objects of certain shapes actually fall faster than do objects of other shapes.

But the idealization goes even further than this. It also abstracts away from the heterogeneity of natural speech, with its irregularities produced by memory lapses, shifts of attention, changes of interest, distractions, false starts, extraneous errors. To formulate this idealization we can say that a linguistic description is an explication of a fluent speaker's *linguistic competence*, i.e., what he tacitly knows about the structure of the sentences of his language that differentiates him from those who cannot speak his language, as opposed to his *linguistic performance*, i.e., what he does with this knowledge in actual speech situations. Linguistic descriptions seek to reconstruct the contribution of an ideal speaker's linguistic competence to his linguistic performance, independently of other psychological factors that influence the character of linguistic performance, ideal or not. Only under such idealization as this do the facts about actual speech constitute a true reflection of the competence of actual speakers.

This distinction between linguistic competence and linguistic performance is parallel to the distinction between language and speech, where by speech we understand an observable phenomenon with physiological, behavioral, and acoustic aspects and by language we understand a certain mental reality underlying observable speech phenomena. They may be regarded as indicating different ways of looking at the same difference. From the viewpoint of the empirical scientist, this dual distinction is between the subject of a scientific inquiry and the evidence for the theoretical constructions developed in the course of the inquiry. Facts about speech, appropriately sifted to remove the influence of linguistically irrelevant factors, are the data on which a linguist constructs and tests a theory of a natural language. From the viewpoint of the language user, it is a distinction between the speaker's inner representation of the rules of his language acquired in his transition from nonverbal infant to fluent speaker and his use of these rules to communicate in actual situations. Thus, again, we find that the construction of a linguistic description is concerned with the discovery of a mental reality underlying actual linguistic behavior.

Therefore, linguistic description can be no more concerned per se with the speech performance of members of a language community than a physicist is concerned per se with meter readings or a biologist is concerned with individual specimens of various sorts. Like other scientists, the linguist idealizes away from the heterogeneous phenomena that directly face him in nature. Thus, the linguist makes no effort to describe actual speech, the linguistic behavior resulting from the speaker's performance, but concentrates on language, the mental structure that constitutes the speaker's competence in the language.

Summarizing, linguistics studies the competence of ideally fluent speakers communicating with other similarly ideal speakers, where by 'ideal' is meant that their performance is regarded as totally unaffected by such linguistically irrelevant factors as those (1) that have to do with variations in performance from one speech situation to another, e.g., distractions, errors due to shifts of attention and interest, attempts to joke or deceive, false starts, nervousness, etc., (2) that have to do with variations from speaker to speaker, e.g., background, motives, intelligence, characteristic mannerisms, etc., and (3) that have to do with the general psychological limitations, e.g., the size of the number of items that can be stored in immediate memory, limitations on the scope of perception, and human mortality. This is just another way of saying that actual speech is a complex product of the interplay of a variety of factors, only one of which is the internalized system of linguistic rules that constitutes the speaker's tacit knowledge of his language. The linguist holds factors of the types (1), (2), and (3) constant and tries to assess the contribution of the speaker's competence to his performance. Thus he builds a theory of just what mental structure makes this contribution.

Accordingly, the linguist's idealization is under the empirical constraint that as actual conditions of speech approximate more closely to the ideal, predictions deriving solely and directly from a theory of competence must approximate more closely the structure of actual speech events. Further, it should be the case that, as we come to understand not only the contribution of the speaker's linguistic competence but also the contribution of factors such as (1), (2), and (3), we are better able to explain actual speech behavior in terms of the interplay of competence and linguistically extraneous psychological factors, each being accorded its proper function in the production of linguistic behavior. Hence, ultimately, although certainly not in the near future, the theory of linguistic competence must become a component in a broader psychological theory describing how verbal performance is causally produced.

Linguistic descriptions and the theory of language are, it seems to me, legitimately regarded as falling within the province of epistemology, rather than psychology proper. Admittedly, they are conceived of as descriptions of mental abilities and capacities, but this is in no sense psychologism or a psychological fallacy. Criticisms to the effect that some account of knowledge is just psychologism or commits the psychological fallacy are appropriate if the account criticized has offered a psychological analysis of the origin or development of a certain form of knowledge when instead it should have offered an analysis of its conceptual structure, the limits of its applicability, and the sort of grounds on which its validity rests. But theories of natural languages and of language do offer epistemological analyses of a certain kind of knowledge, that which speakers have of their language. Such theories seek to exhibit the structure of this knowledge, its limits, and foundations. For they are theories of competence, not theories of performance. On the other hand, a theory of performance, i.e., a theory dealing with how linguistic knowledge is put to use in the production and comprehension of actual speech, would be a straightforward psychological theory. But theories of language are different from psychological theories in just the respect relevant to the difference between epistemology and psychology. The former provide formal reconstructions of the concepts and principles within one of the cognitive spheres of interest to epistemology, whereas the latter assess the contribution of all factors influencing linguistic behavior, dealing with its origin, development, and consequences.

GRAMMATICAL THEORY

Grammatical theory is that branch of the theory of language that deals with the nature of the phonological and syntactic components of a linguistic description, or, alternatively, that branch in which the phonological and syntactic universals of language are stated. Phonological theory will come in for some treatment in this section, but, because of considerations of ultimate philosophical relevance, this section will concentrate on syntactic theory.

The rules of a linguistic description must pair phonetic representations with semantic interpretations as a reconstruction of the speaker's pairing of acoustic signals with meanings. The syntactic component will contain the rules for sentence generation and thus supply the input to the other two components. The phonological and semantic components operate on the formal objects generated by the syntactic component to assign them, in the former case, an interpretation in terms of pronunciation, and in the latter, an interpretation in terms of meaning. These phonetic and semantic interpretations are thus paired in a linguistic description by virtue of the fact that appropriate cases of each are assigned to the same syntactic object. The basic question that is faced in the construction of a model for syntactic components is what type of rules will be required in order that the inputs from the syntactic to the phonological and semantic components be sufficient to provide the information necessary to determine the proper pairing of phonological representations and semantic interpretations.

The primary consideration on which an answer to this question is based is that there is no longest sentence in a natural language. The set of novel sentences that a speaker can produce or understand would also be infinite were it not for the fact that his linguistic knowledge is stored within a psychological system that limits its use and accordingly limits the speaker's actual speech performance to a small finite set of sentences. Among the factors that prevent a speaker from using this knowledge of linguistic structure to produce or understand more than a finite subset of the set of sentences are the finite bound on memory storage, the finite restriction on the intake of sensory information, the finiteness of human life, and so on. Since all these psychological factors are irrelevant to the purely linguistic question about the formal character of the rules that comprise a speaker's linguistic knowledge, we may abstract away from them, and, thereby raise in a more revealing form the question of how a speaker can handle novel sentences.[2] Namely,

[2] We may ask why a speaker must be credited with possessing rules that ascribe to him the competence to derive the structure of any sentence from an infinite set, although the actual production and comprehension of all the relatively long members of this set are beyond his performance capabilities because of the nature of his memory, sensory apparatus, mortality, etc. If we do not, we commit ourselves to a syntactic theory that places a finite bound on the set of sentences. That is, the definition of 'sentence of L' given by this theory would say that any string of words having a certain syntactic property (shorter or equal in length to some number N) is grammatical whereas strings longer than N, regardless of their syntactic properties, are ungrammatical. Such a theory would be unacceptable for two reasons. Suppose S is a well-formed string of words in some natural language that is exactly N words long and we increase the length in some syntactically proper manner, e.g., by adding an adjectival modifier to one of its nouns. Now, ex hypothesi, the constituent of S whose length is increased to increase the length of S beyond N, e.g., the noun to which the adjectival modifier was added, is still a well-formed constituent of its type after its increase in length. Therefore, since the rest of the sentence S is well-formed and the new constituent is both well-formed and of the type that preserves sentential well-formedness when it occupies the position the old constituent had in S, we are in the embarrassing position of having to say both that the sentence obtained from S by this increase is well-formed and that it is not well-formed because

what types of rules enable an ideal speaker, one who is under no psychological limitation to finite performance, to produce or understand any one of the infinitely many sentences of his language?

The existence of a type of rule, technically called a "recursive rule,"[3] enables us to formulate the general character of the answer to this question. These rules are finitely statable, yet they specify an infinite output

---

it exceeds N in length. Second, a syntactic theory in which some fixed N determines whether or not a string of words is well-formed would be unmotivated. It would lack any justifiable means of choosing the N that divides the sentences from the nonsentences. Since the infinite set of strings that is considered too long is in no way structurally different from those that are granted the status of sentencehood, the length property that differentiates such strings from those that are accepted as sentences has nothing whatever to do with the structural property of syntactic well-formedness. If N is not fixed arbitrarily, the properties that fix an N are psychological properties that derive from the facts about a speaker's perceptual faculties, memory, mortality, etc. They are not like those properties that are disturbed when the words of a sentence are given in reverse order because any one of these properties can be found in strings of lengths greater than N.

It may be suggested that the mistake underlying such a syntactic theory is the failure to distinguish between the speaker's *linguistic competence* and his *linguistic performance*. Considerations that determine which strings are possible sentences and which do not so qualify have to do with his competence, while considerations that limit the speaker to an actual production and comprehension of only a finite number of the possible sentences have to do with his performance. Perhaps this point can be better appreciated if we notice that only by making this distinction and assuming that a speaker's competence provides him with information about the structure of the infinitely many sentences of his language, can we explain how it is that, as the finite limitation on performance is weakened, as with the change from speech to writing, his ability to handle longer sentences is correspondingly increased.

[3] The study of such rules in general, as opposed to the very special class of such rules that are used in the formal analysis of natural languages, is the subject of one of the most important branches of modern logic, that is, recursive function theory. Cf. S. C. Kleene, *Introduction to Metamathematics*, D. Van Nostrand Company, 1952.

because they are capable of being endlessly reapplied to their own output to yield an unbounded set of formal objects. The creative aspect of language thus provides us with good reason to hypothesize that some of the rules that compose a speaker's linguistic knowledge are recursive rules, since the ability of actual speakers to produce and understand novel sentences can be explained in terms of recursive rules which account for the structure of every sentence in the infinite set of sentences of a language. For example, given the initial axiom symbol S, the two rules $S \rightarrow X$, and $X \rightarrow X + X$, where '$\rightarrow$' is the instruction to rewrite the left-hand symbol as the right-hand symbols, yield the infinite output that consists of the formal objects X, $X + X, X + X + X$, ... Any one who learned these rules would have, ideally, acquired the ability to produce this infinite set of formal objects.

However, it is quite obvious that a linguistic description which contains only the rules $S \rightarrow X$ and $X \rightarrow X + X$ does not account for a speaker's knowledge of a natural language such as English, even though these rules specify an infinite output. The rules of a linguistic description must not only be capable of producing an infinite list of formal objects, but the formal objects on the list must be the sentences of the language under study and the list must exclude any string in the vocabulary of the language that is not a sentence in the language. Furthermore, these rules must somehow specify all the information about the sentences that a speaker utilizes to produce and understand them. If the rules of a linguistic description thus account for the infinitely many

124 THE PHILOSOPHY OF LANGUAGE

sentences of a language, a fortiori, they account for a
speaker's ability to produce and understand indefinitely
many sentences he has never before encountered. Hence,
in order to construct a model of the syntactic component
of a linguistic description, we must ask what further
characteristics such rules must have for them to represent
a speaker's linguistic competence.

The primary consideration in deciding what sort of
rules will appear in the syntactic component is the character of the sentence structure that these rules must describe. Sentences of a natural language are concatenations
of symbols in the vocabulary of the language. The

(1)   The cat likes the mouse

sentence (1) is a concatenation of the symbols 'the,' 'cat,'
'likes,' 'the,' and 'mouse.' We may think of these symbols
as belonging to the category of words, minimum units of
pronunciation, although, in fact, they are what linguists
call 'morphemes,' a category that includes nonwords such
as the prefixes 'mis,' 'de,' 'un,' etc., and such suffixes as 'ed,'
'able,' etc., and excludes such words as 'mismatch,' 'un-
usable,' 'determined,' etc. Obviously, one of the things that
a syntactic description of (1) must specify is the set of
words of which it is composed. Another is the order of
words, since two distinct sentences can contain the same
set of words. A third is the group of words that form
constituents of the sentence, such as, in (1), 'the cat' or
'likes the mouse.' Fourth, a syntactic description must
specify the syntactic categories to which each of the words
and constituents belongs, e.g., that 'the cat' is a noun

phrase. A description that specifies each of these four things about a sentence is what is called a *phrase marker*. For example,

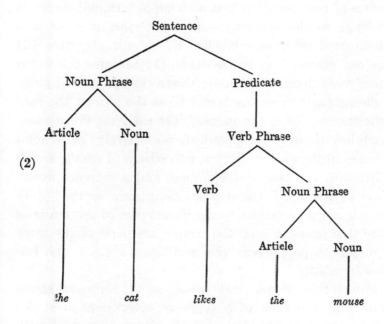

(2)

Such a diagram, or any equivalent of it such as a labelled parenthesization of the string of words, is a hierarchical bracketing which provides (i) the set of words of which the string is composed in terms of the condition that any element in the diagram is a member of this set just in case it is a terminal element of one of the branches, (ii) a segmentation of the string into syntactically significant parts in terms of the condition that any substring is a syntactically significant part of the whole string just in case it is the full string of terminal elements that is dominated by some node of the tree, and (iii) a classification of the words and syntactically significant sequences of words in terms of the condition that a string of terminal elements belongs to the syntactic category *C* just in case it is dominated by a node labelled *C*. Accordingly, from (2) we can predict that the sentence (1) contains the words 'the,' 'cat,' 'likes,' and 'mouse,' has as its syntactically significant parts these words as well as the strings 'the cat,' 'the mouse,' 'likes the mouse,' 'the cat likes the mouse,' and has these parts classified, respectively, as a noun phrase in the case of the first two strings of words, a verb phrase in the case of the second, and a sentence in the case of the third. Other predictions, such as that 'likes the' is not a syntactically significant part of the sentence and that 'the cat' and 'the mouse' are parts of the same syntactic type whereas 'the' and 'likes' are not, also follow from (2).

Given that phrase markers such as (2) represent structure that the rules of a syntactic component must describe, we can ask what sort of rules can produce such phrase markers. We can make our discussion more concrete by considering rules of the syntactic component of the linguistic description of English as examples.[4]

(3.1)   Sentence → Noun Phrase + Predicate,
(3.2)   Noun Phrase → Article + Noun,

---

[4] These rules are just for the purpose of illustration. For a more complete treatment with further explanation, cf. N. Chomsky, "A Transformational Approach to Syntax" in Fodor and Katz (eds.), *The Structure of Language: Readings in the Philosophy of Language*, Prentice-Hall, 1964.

(3.3) Predicate → $\begin{Bmatrix} \text{Verb Phrase} \\ be + \text{Adjective} \end{Bmatrix}$,

(3.4) Verb Phrase → $\begin{Bmatrix} \text{Verb Transitive} + \text{Noun Phrase} \\ \qquad\qquad\qquad + \text{(Adverb)} \\ \text{Verb Intransitive} + \text{(Adverb)} \end{Bmatrix}$,

(3.5) Adjective → *silly, fat, old, ugly, nice*, . . . ,

(3.6) Verb Transitive → *likes, eats, hits, astonishes*, . . . ,

(3.7) Verb Intransitive → *sweats, sleeps, barks, smells*, . . . ,

(3.8) Noun → *boy, man, cat, mouse, house*, . . . ,

(3.9) Article → *the, a, some*, . . . ,

(3.10) Adverb → *fast, loudly, on the truck, at nine*, . . . ,

where braces indicate obligatory choice and parentheses indicate optional elements. Technically, these rules are called 'phrase structure rules,' i.e., they are of the form $X \to Y$, where X and Y are strings of symbols of finite length, '→' is the instruction 'can be rewritten as,' and $X = NAM$ and $Y = NZM$, with Z nonnull and A a single symbol not identical to Z.[5] Thus, a phrase structure rule operates on a fixed string of symbols, rewriting a single, nonnull symbol in the string as a fixed nonnull string distinct from the replaced symbol.

These rules express empirical generalizations about the syntactic structure of English, rather than descriptions of the syntactic structure of specific English sentences, as do phrase markers. For example, (3.1) says that sentences in English are made up of two parts, the first of which is a noun phrase and the second a predicate, whereas the lower level generalization (3.8) says, among other things, that the words 'man,'

[5] For further discussion of the formal structure of such rules, cf. N. Chomsky, "On Certain Formal Properties of Grammars," *Information and Control*, vol. 2, 1959.

'cat,' and 'boy' are syntactically equivalent in that they are English nouns. Just as with empirical generalizations in other sciences, these linguistic rules make verifiable predictions about particular cases. That is, predictions concerning the syntactic properties of individual sentences can be made to follow from them. Such predictions, as mentioned above, are descriptions of the syntax of sentences that take the form of phrase markers. To obtain a phrase marker from rules such as (3.1)–(3.10), the rules must first be used to construct a derivation of the sentence. This is done by writing down the initial axiom symbol 'Sentence' and then applying the rules until a line of the derivation is reached none of whose symbols can be further rewritten by any of the rules. For example, one of the derivations that can be constructed from (3.1)–(3.10) is the following.

(4) Sentence
Noun Phrase + Predicate
Noun Phrase + Verb + Noun Phrase
Noun Phrase + Transitive Verb + Noun Phrase
Article + Noun + Transitive Verb + Noun Phrase
Article + Noun + Transitive Verb + Article + Noun
the + Noun + Transitive Verb + Article + Noun
the + *cat* + Transitive Verb + Article + Noun
the + *cat* + *likes* + Article + Noun
the + *cat* + *likes* + *the* + Noun
the + *cat* + *likes* + *the* + *mouse*

Derivation (4) is, of course, not the only derivation of (1) since the same rules used to construct (4) may be applied in different orders to obtain different derivations of the same sentence. Thus, it is desirable to have some means of representing the set of equivalent derivations of a sentence, i.e., the set of derivations that give the same syntactic description. Since the phrase marker is just such a representation, we require some procedure which associates a phrase marker with a derivation in such a fashion that equivalent derivations are mapped onto the same phrase marker and nonequivalent derivations are mapped onto different phrase markers. The procedure in question, called a *structure assignment algorithm*,[6] is a function F such that $F\ (i,j)$ is the set of phrase markers of the sentence S_i that are given by the syntactic rules R_j. This function makes it possible to determine what syntactic description is provided for a particular sentence by the syntactic component without relying on our intuitive judgments. Part of this function is a scheme for converting derivations such as (4) into phrase markers such as (2). Informally, the scheme is this: start with the second line of a derivation, the one immediately following the symbol 'Sentence'; proceed down and connect the symbols in each successive line with those in the immediately preceding line by linking a symbol either with the symbol it has helped to replace (as determined by the rule used to construct this line) or with its corresponding identity; all chains of identities (i.e., branches of the form 'x connected with x, connected with x, and so on') are reduced to a single member of

---

[6] Cf. N. Chomsky, "On the Notion 'Rule of Grammar,'" in Fodor and Katz (eds.), *The Structure of Language: Readings in the Philosophy of Language*.

the chain by eliminating all but the topmost symbol and connecting it to the symbol to which the bottommost member of the chain was connected. Using this scheme we can associate (4) with the phrase marker (2). The rules (3.1)–(3.10) are thus shown to yield the predictions contained in (2) for the sentence (1).

Some phrase markers describe only the observable syntactic form of a sentence. That sentences have a deeper underlying syntactic form, different from their observable form, and, accordingly, that a complete syntactic description cannot be given in terms of a single phrase marker has been demonstrated by overwhelming evidence. Indeed, it is this demonstration that constitutes the major achievement of the transformational approach to syntax.[7] Let us call phrase markers that describe the surface or observable structure of a sentence, 'final derived phrase markers.' A final derived phrase marker is, then, a labeled bracketing that segments a sentence's observable form into continuous constituents and that categorizes these constituents to provide whatever other information will be required for the phonological rules to determine the phonetic interpretation of the sentence. Thus, the final derived phrase markers for sentences will be the input to the phonological component.

Just as the final derived phrase markers describe the surface structure of sentences and are thus appropriate input to the phonological component, there is another

[7] For a convenient survey of this evidence, cf. P. Postal, *Constituent Structure*, Indiana University Press and Mouton & Company, The Hague, 1964.

type of phrase marker which describes the deeper underlying structure of sentences and is thus appropriate input
to the semantic component. Such phrase markers will be
called 'underlying phrase markers.'[8] The final derived
phrase marker for a sentence is connected with the underlying phrase marker for that sentence by another type
of syntactic rule, called a 'transformational rule.'[9] Transformational rules operate on underlying phrase markers
and convert them into derived phrase markers, and these
into other derived phrase markers, until the final derived
phrase marker is reached. Thus, a transformational rule is
a rule that operates on a phrase marker converting it into
another phrase marker. The structure assignment algorithm also has a scheme for determining the phrase
marker that results from a given pair of a phrase marker
and a transformational rule.

We may motivate the distinction between underlying
phrase markers and final derived phrase markers and also
explain the concept of a transformational rule, by showing why a linguist must theoretically infer the existence
of underlying phrase markers and why such phrase
markers must have syntactic features that their corre-

---

[8] Chomsky's latest work, *Aspects of the Theory of Syntax*, M.I.T.
Press, 1965, refers to such phrase markers as 'deep phrase markers'
and refers to those phrase markers we call 'final derived phrase markers'
as 'surface phrase markers.'

[9] The conception of transformational rule has undergone modification
in the course of recent work within the framework of generative grammar. The conception given in Chomsky's early book *Syntactic Structures*, Mouton & Company, The Hague, 1957, can no longer be accepted.
The reader is referred to Chomsky's *Aspects of the Theory of Syntax* and to Katz and Postal, *An Integrated Theory of Linguistic
Descriptions*. The above account is based on these two works.

sponding final derived phrase markers lack. Consider the case of the ordinary English imperative, such as

(5) Help the man.

which has the final derived phrase marker

(6)

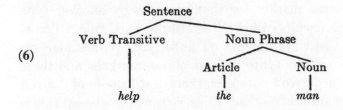

In (6) there is no indication of the presence of a noun phrase subject, as there is in the case of the phrase marker (2) where 'the cat' may be plausibly regarded as the subject of the sentence. In order to show that (5) actually has a subject, even though it does not appear in the observable form of the sentence, we may consider the way in which reflexive pronouns are handled by the syntactic component of a linguistic description for English. Consider the sentences:

(7) John likes himself.
(8) The woman admires herself.
(9) You underestimate yourself.

Sentences such as (7), (8), and (9) must be assigned phrase markers that provide a complete syntactic analysis of their reflexive forms. These phrase markers must be assigned on the basis of transformational rules that provide a means for handling the occurrence of any reflexive form in English. Among the evidence that determines the character of these reflexive transformations is the fact that sentences with the structure *Noun Phrase₁ + Verb + Reflexive Pronoun* occur just in case there are corresponding sentences having the structure *Noun Phrase₂ + Verb + Noun Phrase₁*. That is to say, verbs whose objects can be reflexive pronouns are also verbs which can occur elsewhere with objects identical to the subject of the sentences in which the reflexive pronoun object apears. Hence, for the verbs 'likes,' 'admires,' and 'underestimates,' we find other sentences in which the subjects of (7), (8), and (9) occur as objects of these verbs.

(10) She likes John.
(11) I admire the woman.
(12) People underestimate you.

However, for verbs which do not occur with reflexive pronoun objects, such as in:

(13) *You concede yourself,[10]
(14) *The woman completes herself,

there are no corresponding cases in which the subject can occupy the object position. For example,

(15) *They concede you.
(16) *Students complete the woman.

[10] An asterisk preceding a sentence indicates that the sentence is not grammatical. It does not mean that the sentence is unintelligible or that it is never used by speakers; only that it is to some degree a departure from full grammaticality. Thus it does not matter that many of the sentences so marked can be interpreted with reference to an appropriate situation. The point is that such a sentence must be distinguished from those that require no such special treatment.

Finally, notice that whereas (7), (8), and (9) are fully grammatical, (17), (18), and (19) are not.

(17)   *John likes themselves.
(18)   *The woman admires himself.
(19)   *You underestimate myself.

Here we see that such reflexive forms must agree with the subject of the verb in number, gender, and person. To explain these facts, the transformational rule for forming reflexive constructions derives these constructions, that is sentences like (7), (8), and (9) with their final derived phrase markers, from underlying phrase markers in which the object noun phrase is identical to the subject noun phrase. Hence the underlying phrase marker for (7) would be:

(20)

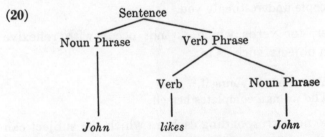

Phrase marker (20) is converted into the final derived phrase marker for (7) by a transformational rule which replaces the noun phrase within the verb phrase constituent by the appropriate reflexive pronoun on the condition that this noun phrase is identical with the first noun phrase. Consequently, there is no reflexive form for (10), (11), and (12). It must be noted that the phrase structure rules which give the underlying phrase markers for

(10), (11), (12), and similar cases also give the underlying phrase markers for cases like (7), (8), and (9).
In fact these rules are simpler if they are allowed to produce phrase markers such as (20), than if not, since with
free ocurrence of noun phrases there is no need for a
special *ad hoc* restriction preventing the case in which
the subject and object noun phrases are identical. There
are no sentences like

(21) *You overestimate you.

because the phrase marker of (21) is automatically converted into

(22)

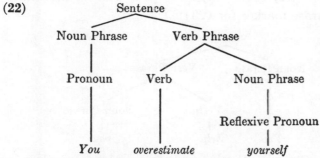

by the aforementioned rule. Note also that this transformational analysis of the syntactic structure of
sentences with reflexive pronouns explains why speakers
understand such sentences to involve identity of reference in the case of the subject and object.

Now let us return to the case of the imperative (5).
Imperatives can also contain reflexives in their object
position, as is illustrated by:

(23) Help yourself;

but no imperative can contain any reflexive pronoun except 'yourself.' Thus,

(24)   *Help myself (themselves, itself, herself, himself).

Referring to the above mentioned rule for the placement of reflexive pronouns, we observe that the occurrence of a reflexive pronoun in the object position of a sentence depends on the existence of an underlying phrase marker in which the object noun phrase corresponding to the reflexive form is identical to the subject noun phrase of the underlying phrase marker. From this it follows not only that imperatives have subjects but that, considering (23), and (24) their subject is 'you.' Hence, the underlying phrase marker for (23) is:

(25)

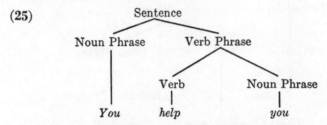

and, correspondingly, the underlying phrase marker for (5) is (26),

(26)

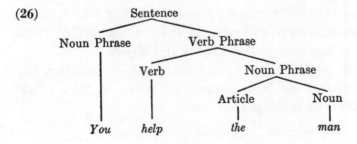

The transformational rule that produces the final derived phrase marker (6) from (26) simply deletes the noun phrase subject 'you' in (26). This underlying occurrence of 'you' as the subject of imperatives explains why such sentences are understood to refer to the person addressed. Further confirmation for this theoretically inferred feature of imperative sentences comes from tag questions such as:

(27)   The woman (John, I) will agree, won't she (he, I)?

Here the tag question is transformationally derived by a repetition of the auxiliary and subject of the main sentence, a change in their order, the addition of a negative, and a pronominalization of the subject. Thus, again, there is an identity condition between one part of the sentence and the subject. Since the tag questions that occur with imperatives permit only 'you,' i.e.,

(28)   Help the man, will you?

but not

(29)   *Help the man, will it (he, she, I, we, they)?

we can conclude again that imperatives have 'you' subjects. This conclusion is also reached by the need to explain the fact that some imperative forms contain an occurrence of a 'you' subject in their observable form, e.g.,

(30)   You help the man.

and that such forms are syntactically related to the normal imperative sentences. If the underlying phrase markers for all imperative sentences contain a 'you' subject which is optionally deleted in the derivation of the final derived phrase marker for the normal imperatives, then we have explained this fact. This convergence of evidence provides quite strong support for the claim that there is an underlying phrase marker with a 'you' subject even when 'you' is not present in the observable form of an imperative sentence and that the final derived phrase marker which represents the observable form of imperatives is derived from this underlying phrase marker.[11]

This example is, of course, only one case; but it is typical of the vast number of other cases where, for purposes of achieving a systematic explanation of a wide variety of linguistic data, we must introduce underlying phrase markers with syntactic properties different from those of the final derived phrase markers which they underlie. In other cases deletion also leads to sentences whose observable form does not contain features of their underlying syntactic structure. Consider the case of comparatives.

(31) John is better at complicated puzzles with tricky solutions than Bill.

[11] The discussion of the imperative and reflexive pronoun is adapted from P. Postal, "Underlying and Superficial Linguistic Structures," *Harvard Educational Review*, vol. 34, no. 2, 1964; Katz and Postal, *An Integrated Theory of Linguistic Descriptions;* and R. B. Lees, and E. Klima, "Rules for English Pronominalization," *Language*, vol. 39, 1963.

Comparative (31) is understood as if the whole verb phrase 'is good at complicated puzzles with tricky solutions' followed the occurrence of 'Bill,' since no one would interpret the comparison as between John's ability at complicated puzzles with tricky solutions and Bill's ability at driving racing cars, eating pies, or something else. This, as well as other linguistic considerations, leads to the formulation of rules that introduce an underlying phrase marker for cases like (31) which contains such duplicate verb phrases.

The transformational operation of permutation provides a still further set of cases in which certain features of the underlying syntactic structure of sentences do not appear in their observable form. Here the features do not include the loss of words but rather the loss of facts about segmentation and category membership of words and strings of words. Two very simple examples of this are the cases of particle permutation, as in sentences such as:

(32)   John looked the number of his friend up.

and object splitting, as in sentences such as:

(33)   Of the books you mentioned, I have read only one.

The final derived phrase marker of (32) does not represent the fact that 'look up' is a single constituent in the category Verb, but the underlying phrase marker, here given in much abbreviated form,

(34)

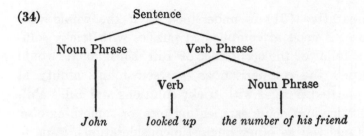

does provide this information. Similarly, the final derived phrase marker for (33) does not represent the fact that 'only one of the books you mentioned' is the object of the verb 'read,' but this fact is represented in the underlying phrase marker for (33).

(35)

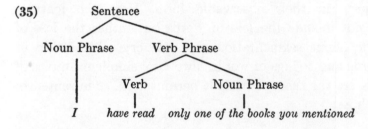

Further, deletion and permutation operations combine to produce final derived phrase markers in which there is no representation of such grammatical relations as 'subject of the verb' or 'object of the verb.' Consider the sentences:

(36)   John is easy to please,
(37)   John is eager to please.

The final derived phrase marker for these sentences is exactly the same except for the difference that one contains 'easy' where the other contains 'eager':

(38)

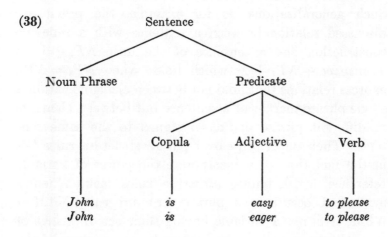

```
                        Sentence
            _____/        _____
           /                                \
     Noun Phrase                          Predicate
          |                        _____/   |   _____
          |                       /             |            \
          |                    Copula       Adjective        Verb
          |                       |             |             |
          |                       |             |             |
        John                     is            easy        to please
        John                     is           eager        to please
```

This means that, from the viewpoint of their final derived phrase markers, the only thing that can be predicted about one of these sentences that cannot also be predicted about the other is the presence of 'easy' or 'eager' in the set of words from which the sentence is composed. But it is entirely obvious that in (36) 'John' is the object of the verb 'please' while in (37) 'John' is the subject. Their respective underlying phrase markers make this distinction by, in the one case, representing 'John' as the anterior noun phrase of the verb 'please,' and, in the other, representing 'John' as the posterior noun phrase of the verb, which, it is to be noted, is the general basis on which these relations are determined.[12]

[12] Cf. Chomsky, "Current Issues in Linguistic Theory," in Fodor and

142 THE PHILOSOPHY OF LANGUAGE

The transformational rules of a syntactic component provide a means for expressing empirical generalizations that is not available with phrase structure rules alone. Such generalizations, as for example, the previously discussed relation between a sentence with a reflexive construction and a sentence of the form $NP_1 + Verb$ $Transitive + NP_2 + X$ which holds when $NP_1 = NP_2$, express relations that hold not between elements within a single phrase marker of a sentence but between elements in different phrase markers assigned to the same sentence. Their superiority over phrase structure rules lies in the fact that they incorporate the power of variable reference which phrase structure rules lack. When a symbol A occurs in a phrase structure rule, $NAM \rightarrow$ NZM, it is not a variable having some set of strings of symbols as its values, but refers to occurrences of the symbol A, i.e. tokens of this type, in lines of derivations. Thus, a phrase structure rule is an instruction to rewrite an occurrence of A by an occurrence of Z. On the other hand, the symbols that occur in a transformational rule are variables whose values can be any string of symbols dominated by any labeled node in a phrase marker.

Let us go into this more concretely. Among the transformational rules for the syntactic component of a linguistic description of English is the passive transformation:

Katz (eds.), *The Structure of Language: Readings in the Philosophy of Language,* and N. Chomsky, "Topics in the Theory of Generative Grammar," lecture 3 to appear in T. A. Sebeok (ed.), *Current Trends in Linguistics,* vol. 3, Indiana University Press, in press.

(39) [Noun Phrase – Auxiliary – Verb – (Particle) –
      1   2   3   4
Noun Phrase – by + Passive – X] →
   5   6   7   8
$$[5 - 2 - 3 - (4) - 6 - 1 - 8].$$

The left-hand side of this rule is a condition on the structure of phrase markers that determines whether or not (39) can be applied, whereas, the right-hand side expresses the structural change that is made in a phrase marker when it is operated on by (39). (It is not necessary to require that the verb constituent be transitive because there are the phrase structure rules,

(40) Adverb → Manner,
(41) Manner → by + Passive,

and these automatically restrict passivization to verbs that can freely co-occur with manner adverbials.) The structural condition of (39) incorporates the power of variable reference by stating the domain of this transformational rule in terms of the condition that a phrase marker falls in the domain of (39) if and only if its terminal elements are analyzed in the phrase marker as a sequence consisting of a Noun Phrase, followed by an auxiliary, followed by a verb, then optionally a particle; e.g., 'up' in "The phone number was looked up by John," another noun phrase, by + passive, and finally some other constituent or nothing. The power of variable reference enters by virtue of the fact that the symbols occur-

ring in the structural condition are variables ranging over
the members of classes of strings of words, the particular
variable determining the particular class of strings in each
case. With the power of variable reference, it is possible
to formulate rules that apply to a set of strings that share
only some abstract syntactic property, i.e., have a common configuration of symbols in their phrase markers,
such as the one described in the structural condition of
(39). Without this power, it would only be possible to
have rules that apply to a set of strings whose members
share a particular fixed subsequence of elements. In these
terms, it would be impossible to formulate the property
of necessary subject-object identity that reflexives share.
Transformational rules thus differ from phrase structure
rules in that, while a phrase structure rule can only make
use of information contained in the linear context of the
symbol to be rewritten, a transformational rule can use
any information in a phrase marker to which it applies.
The conclusion is simply that there is a wide range of empirical generalizations about syntactic structure that are
not expressible without transformational rules. Consequently, the model that the theory of language offers for
the construction of syntactic components of particular
linguistic descriptions requires that there be tranforma-
tional rules that connect underlying phrase markers with
final derived phrase markers.

We are now in a position to explain how a syntactic
component incorporates the recursive power that enables
it to generate an infinite set of sentences. The pattern
of sentence construction exhibited in (42)

(42)

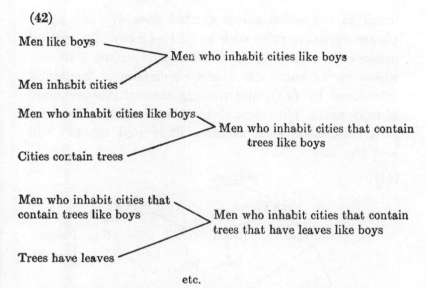

etc.

involves the recursive embedding of deformed versions of sentences into other sentences. Clearly, this sort of construction can theoretically be extended to produce sentences of ever increasing length, though, of course, there will be an upper bound on their utilization in speech performance. The most satisfactory way of formalizing this recursive construction is to add a phrase structure rule which is of the following sort:

(43)   Noun Phrase → (Article) + Sentence + Noun.

Whenever we develop a line of a derivation into another containing the symbol 'Noun phrase,' we can apply (43) to introduce the symbol 'Sentence' within the derivation. Such occurrence of 'Sentence' can then head subderivations within the over-all derivation, functioning very much as the initial axiom symbol does. We can apply phrase structure rules such as (3.1)–(3.10) in a cyclical manner by returning to the first rule in the sequence whenever we encounter a new occurrence of 'Sentence' introduced by (43), and running through the sequence of rules again. Thus, underlying phrase markers for compound sentences such as those illustrated in (42) will look like this:

(44)

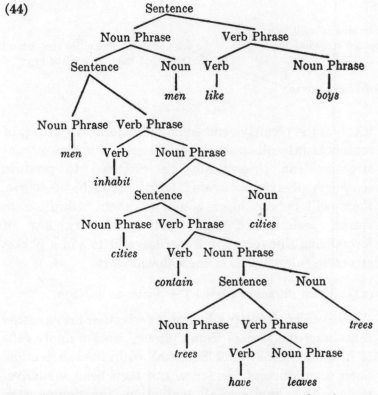

The transformations apply first to the most deeply embedded structure dominated by an occurrence of 'Sentence,' then to the next most deeply embedded one, and by such successive reapplication, proceed until the transformations are applied to the structure dominated by the topmost occurrence of 'Sentence,' the one which initiated the whole derivation. One transformation that will be applied to underlying phrase markers such as (44) is the relative clause transformation,

(45)   [X – Noun Phrase – Verb Phrase – Noun –
     1   2   3   4
     Verb Phrase – Y] →
         5   6
     [1 – 4 – Relative Pronoun – 3 – 5 – 6] just in case
                                     2 = 4.

Applying (45) and other transformations to (44) we obtain the final derived phrase marker (46),

(46)

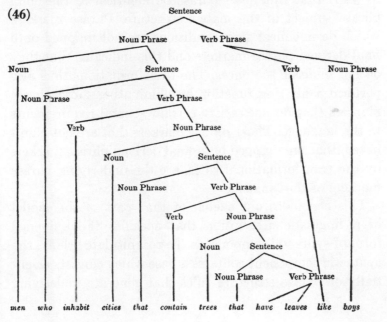

From this example we can see that the recursive power of the syntactic component comes from rules like (43) which can be applied to their own output any number of times within the same derivation.

Note, further, that the rules which generate underlying phrase markers such as (44) also generate infinitely many similar phrase markers that do not underlie any sentence. That is, these rules enable us to proceed from any occurrence of the symbol 'Sentence' to a subderivation for a structure whose subject noun can be whatever we like. For example, we might have introduced 'books' or 'tables' instead of 'trees' as the subject noun of the most deeply embedded structure of (44). But the resulting phrase marker would not meet the condition imposed by (45) that this noun phrase be identical to the noun phrase subject of the matrix structure. Phrase markers which do not meet such conditions are not mapped onto final derived phrase markers and this indicates that they do not underlie sentences. The transformations thus also perform a filtering function by eliminating those phrase markers that do not satisfy certain general requirements in the language. Those phrase markers that are not eliminated, that are mapped onto final derived phrase markers by the transformational rules, are the underlying phrase markers of the language.

This concludes our sketch of that part of the model of a linguistic description that specifies the universal form of syntactic components. To recapitulate briefly, the syntactic component contains a base which consists essentially of phrase structure rules that generate underlying phrase markers. Then, there is a set of transformational rules which convert underlying phrase markers into final derived phrase markers. The full syntactic description of a sentence consists of its final derived phrase marker and the set of its underlying phrase markers. There will be more than one underlying phrase marker for a sentence just in case that sentence is syntactically ambiguous. Syntactically ambiguous sentences such as (47)

(47) Vegetarians don't know how good meat tastes.

will have as many underlying phrase markers as there are different ways in which the sentence is syntactically ambiguous. Each distinct underlying phrase marker must correspond to a term of the ambiguity. For example, the two underlying phrase markers for (47) must differ in that in one case the relation of 'good' to 'meat' in (47) must derive from an embedded structure for 'meat tastes good' while in the other this relation must derive from an embedded structure for 'meat is good.' If they do so differ, the first case is one in which 'good' modifies the verb 'tastes' and the second is one in which 'good' modifies 'meat,' which corresponds directly to the two distinct ways in which (47) can be understood.

As mentioned above, the phonological and semantic components are purely interpretive systems which operate on the output of the syntactic component, viz., syntactic descriptions of sentences. These sets of abstract structures are formal objects which are uninterpreted in terms of sound and meaning until the phonological and semantic components have operated on them. These two components are thus functions whose arguments are, respectively, the final derived phrase marker of a sentence and the set of underlying phrase markers and whose values are appropriate interpretations of these abstract formal structures. We may picture the internal construction of a linguistic description as follows[13]:

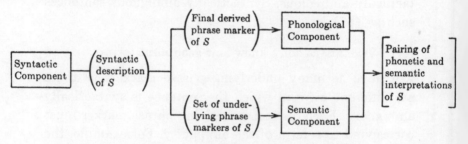

We need say very little about the phonological component because it has no significance for the discussion of conceptual knowledge in the next chapter.[14] This component interprets final derived phrase markers in terms of a representation in vocal sound. It assigns *phonetic interpretations* to these phrase markers which describe the pronunciation of sentences. The rules that perform

[13] As indicated in this schematic representation of a linguistic description, the semantic component and the phonological component operated independently of each other. This is the explanation that the theory of language gives for the quite generally recognized fact about natural languages that there is only an arbitrary connection between semantic structure and sound structure.

[14] For further discussion of the phonological component, cf. M. Halle, "On the Bases of Phonology" and "Phonology in Generative Grammar," in Fodor and Katz (eds.), *The Structure of Language: Readings in the Philosophy of Language,* and M. Halle and N. Chomsky, *The Sound Pattern of English,* to be published by Harper & Row.

this function are of both the rewriting and transformational variety. The output of these rules for a given sentence, the sentence's phonetic interpretation, is a matrix in which the rows represent physical acoustic properties and the columns represent successive segments of the sentence. A matrix entry (i,j) is a prediction as to whether or not the jth segment of the sentence has the ith property. The whole matrix is a complex set of predictions about the manner in which speakers of the language pronounce the sentence.

SEMANTIC THEORY

The semantic component interprets underlying phrase markers in terms of meaning. It assigns *semantic interpretations* to these phrase markers which describe messages that can be communicated in the language. That is, whereas the phonological component provides a phonetic shape for a sentence, the semantic component provides a representation of that message which actual utterances having this phonetic shape convey to speakers of the language in normal speech situations.[15] We may thus regard the development of a model of the semantic component

[15] This conception of the semantic component is elaborated in J. J. Katz and J. A. Fodor, "The Structure of a Semantic Theory," *Language*, vol. 39, pp. 170–210, 1963; reprinted in Fodor and Katz (eds.), *The Structure of Language: Readings in the Philosophy of Language*. It is also elaborated in J. J. Katz, "Analyticity and Contradiction in Natural Language" (same volume), and in Katz and Postal, *An Integrated Theory of Linguistic Descriptions*.

as taking up the explanation of a speaker's ability to produce and understand indefinitely many new sentences at the point where the models of the syntactic and phonological components leave off.

If the semantic component is to complete the statement of the principles that provide the speaker with the competence to perform this creative task, it must contain rules that provide a meaning for every sentence generated by the syntactic component. These rules thus explicate the ability a speaker would have were he free of the psychological limitations that restrict him to finite performance. These rules, therefore, explicate an ability to interpret infinitely many sentences. Accordingly, we again face the task of formulating an hypothesis about the nature of a finite mechanism with an infinite output. The hypothesis on which we will base our model of the semantic component is that the process by which a speaker interprets each of the infinitely many sentences is a compositional process in which the meaning of any syntactically compound constituent of a sentence is obtained as a function of the meanings of the parts of the constituent. Hence, for the semantic component to reconstruct the principles underlying the speaker's semantic competence, the rules of the semantic component must simulate the operation of these principles by projecting representations of the meaning of higher level constituents from representations of the meaning of the lower level constituents that comprise them. That is, these rules must first assign semantic representations to the syntactically elementary constituents of a sentence, then, apply to these representations and assign semantic representations to the constituents at the next higher level on the basis of them, and by applications of these rules to representations already derived, produce further derived semantic representations for all higher level constituents, until, at last, they produce ones for the whole sentence.

The syntactically elementary constituents in underlying phrase markers are the terminal symbols in these phrase markers. Actually, these are the morphemes of the language, but since we are simplifying our discussion, we will consider them to be words. Thus, we may say that the syntactic analysis of constituents into lower level constituents stops at the level of words and that these are therefore the atoms of the syntactic system. Accordingly, the semantic rules will have to start with the meanings of these constituents in order to derive the meanings of other constituents compositionally. This means that the semantic component will have two subcomponents: a *dictionary* that provides a representation of the meaning of each of the words in the language, and a system of *projection rules* that provide the combinatorial machinery for projecting the semantic representation for all supraword constituents in a sentence from the representations that are given in the dictionary for the meanings of the words in the sentence. We will call the result of applying the dictionary and projection rules to a sentence, i.e., the output of the semantic component for that sentence, a *semantic interpretation*. There are, therefore, three concepts to explain in order to formulate the model of the semantic component of a linguistic description: *dictionary, projection rule,* and *semantic interpretation.*[16]

Since the meanings of words are not indivisible entities but, rather, are composed of concepts in certain relations to one another, the job of the dictionary is to represent the conceptual structure in the meanings of words. Accordingly, we may regard the dictionary as a finite list of rules, called 'dictionary entries,' each of which pairs a word with a representation of its meaning in some normal form. This normal form must be such that it permits us to represent every piece of information about the meaning of a word required by the projection rules in order for them to operate properly. The information in dictionary entries must be full analyses of word meanings.

The normal form is as follows: first, the phonological (or orthographical) representation of the word, then an arrow, then a set of syntactic markers, and finally, *n* strings of symbols, which we call *lexical readings.* Each reading will consist of a set of symbols which we call *semantic markers,* and a complex symbol which we call a *selection restriction.* (Here and throughout we enclose semantic markers within parentheses to distinguish them from syntactic markers. Selection restrictions are enclosed with angles.) Thus, a dictionary entry, such as the one below, is a word paired with *n* readings (for it).

---

[16] The discussion to follow will explain these three concepts. Roughly, the dictionary stores basic semantic information about the language, the projection rules apply this information in the interpretation of syntactic objects, and semantic interpretations are full representations of the semantic structure of sentences given by the operation of the projection rules.

bachelor → N, N_1, . . . , N_k; (i) (Physical Object), (Living), (Human), (Male), (Adult), (Never Married); $<SR>$.

(ii) (Physical Object), (Living), (Human), (Young), (Knight), (Serving under the standard of another); $<SR>$.

(iii) (Physical Object), (Living), (Human), (Having the academic degree for the completion of the first four years of college); $<SR>$.

(iv) (Physical Object), (Living), (Animal), (Male), (Seal), (Without a mate at breeding time); $<SR>$.

Each distinct reading in a dictionary entry for a word represents one of the word's senses. Thus, a word with n distinct readings is represented as n-ways semantically ambiguous. For example, the word 'bachelor' is represented as four-ways semantically ambiguous by the above entry.

Just as the meaning of a word is not atomic, a sense of a word is not an undifferentiated whole, but, rather, has a complex conceptual structure. The reading which represents a sense provides an analysis of the structure of that sense which decomposes it into conceptual elements and their interrelations. Semantic markers represent the conceptual elements into which a reading decomposes a sense. They thus provide the theoretical constructs needed to reconstruct the interrelations holding between such conceptual elements in the structure of a sense. It is important to stress that, although the semantic markers are given in the orthography of a natural language, they cannot be identified with the words or expressions of the language used to provide them with suggestive labels. Rather, they are to be regarded as constructs of a linguistic theory, just as terms such as 'force' are regarded as labels for constructs in natural science. There is an analogy between the formula for a chemical compound and a reading (which may be thought of as a formula for a semantic compound). The formula for the chemical compound ethyl alcohol,

$$
\begin{array}{ccc}
\text{H} & & \text{H} \\
| & & | \\
\text{H} \!-\!\!-\!\!-\! \text{C} \!-\!\!-\!\!-\!\!-\!\!-\!\!-\!\!-\! \text{C} \!-\!\!-\! \text{O} \!-\!\!-\! \text{H} \\
| & & | \\
\text{H} & & \text{H}
\end{array}
$$

represents the structure of an alcohol molecule in a way analogous to that in which a reading for 'bachelor' represents the conceptual structure of one of its senses. Both representations exhibit the elements out of which the compound is formed and the relations that form it. In the former case, the formula employs the chemical constructs 'Hydrogen molecule,' 'Chemical bond,' 'Oxygen molecule,' etc., while in the latter, the formula employs the linguistic concepts '(Physical Object),' '(Male),' <Selection Restriction>,' etc.

The notion of a reading may be extended so as to designate not only representations of senses of words, but also representations of senses of any constituents up to and including whole sentences. We distinguish between 'lexical readings' and 'derived readings,' but the term 'reading' will be used to cover both. The philosopher's notion of a concept is here reconstructed in terms of the notion of a reading which is either a lexical reading or a derived reading for a constituent less than a whole sentence, while the philosopher's notion of a proposition (or statement) is reconstructed in terms of the notion of a derived reading for a whole declarative sentence.

Just as syntactic markers enable us to formulate empirical generalizations about the syntactic structure of linguistic constructions, so semantic markers enable us to construct empirical generalizations about the meaning of linguistic constructions. For example, the English words 'bachelor,' 'man,' 'priest,' 'bull,' 'uncle,' 'boy,' etc., have a semantic feature in common which is not part of the meaning of any of the words 'child,' 'mole,' 'mother,' 'classmate,' 'nuts,' 'bolts,' 'cow,' etc. The first set of words, but not the second, are similar in meaning in that the meaning of each member contains the concept of maleness. If we include the semantic marker (Male) in the lexical readings for each of the words in the first set and exclude it from the lexical entries for each of the words in the second, we thereby express this empirical generalization. Thus, semantic markers make it possible to formulate such generalizations by providing us with the elements in terms of which these generalizations can be stated. Moreover, such semantic generalizations are not restricted to words. Consider the expressions 'happy bachelor,' 'my cousin's hired man,' 'an orthodox priest I met yesterday,' 'the bull who is grazing in the pasture,' 'the most unpleasant uncle I have,' 'a boy,' etc., and contrast them with the expressions 'my favorite child,' 'the funny mole on his arm,' 'the whole truth,' 'your mother,' 'his brother's classmate last year,' 'those rusty nuts and bolts,' 'the cow standing at the corner of the barn,' etc. Like the case of the previous sets of words, the members of the first of these sets of expressions are semantically similar in that their meanings share the concept maleness, and the members of the second are not semantically similar in this respect either to each other or to the members of the first set. If the dictionary entries for the words 'bachelor,' 'man,' 'priest,' etc., are formulated so that the semantic marker (Male) appears in each, and if the projection rules assign derived readings to these expressions correctly on the basis of the entries for their words, then the semantic marker (Male) will appear in the derived readings for members of the first set but not in derived readings for members of the second. Again, we will have successfully expressed an empirical generalization about the semantics of a natural language. In general, then, the mode of expressing semantic generalizations is the assignment of readings containing the relevant semantic marker(s) to those linguistic constructions over which the generalizations hold and only those.

Semantic ambiguity, as distinct from syntactic ambiguity and phonological ambiguity, has its source in the homonymy of words. Syntactic ambiguity occurs when a sentence has more than one underlying structure. Phonological ambiguity occurs when surface structures of different sentences are given the same phonological interpretation. Semantic ambiguity, on the other hand, occurs when an underlying structure contains an ambiguous word or words that contribute its (their) multiple senses to the meaning of the whole sentence, thus enabling that sentence to be used to make more than one statement, request, query, etc. Thus, a necessary but not sufficient condition for a syntactically compound constituent or sentence to be semantically ambiguous is that it contain at least one word with two or more senses. For example, the source of the semantic ambiguity in the sentence 'There is no school now' is the lexical ambiguity of 'school' between the sense on which it means sessions of a teaching institution and the sense on which it means the building in which such sessions are held.

But the presence of an ambiguous word is not a sufficient condition for a linguistic construction to be semantically ambiguous. The meaning of other components of the construction can prevent the ambiguous word from contributing more than one of its senses to the meaning of the whole construction. As we have just seen, 'school' is ambiguous in at least two ways. But the sentence 'The school burned up' is not semantically ambiguous because the verb 'burn up' permits its subject noun to bear only senses that contain the concept of a physical object. This selection of senses and exclusion of others is reconstructed in the semantic component by the device referred to above as a selection restriction. Selection restrictions express necessary and sufficient conditions for the readings in which they occur to combine with other readings to form derived readings. Such a condition is a requirement on the content of these other readings. It is to be interpreted as permitting projection rules to combine readings just in case the reading to which the selection restriction applies contains the semantic markers necessary to satisfy it. For example, the reading for 'burn up' will have the selection restriction < (Physical Object) > which permits a reading for the nominal subject of an occurrence of 'burn up' to combine with it just in case that reading has the semantic marker (Physical Object). This, then, explains why "The school burned up" is unambiguously interpreted to mean that the building burned up. Selection restrictions may be formulated in terms of more complex conditions. We thus allow them to be formulated as Boolean functions of semantic markers. For instance, the selection restriction in the reading for the sense of 'honest' on which it means, roughly, 'characteristically unwilling to appropriate for himself what rightfully belongs to another, avoids lies, deception, etc.' will be the Boolean function < (Human) & $\overline{\text{(Infant)}}$ >, where the bar over a semantic marker requires that the marker not be present in the reading concerned.

We may note further that semantic anomaly is the limiting case of exclusion by the operation of selection restrictions. Semantically anomalous sentences such as 'It smells itchy' occur when the meanings of the component words of a sentence are such that they cannot combine to form a coherent, directly intelligible sentence. The semantic component of a linguistic description explicates such conceptual incongruence as a case where there are two constituents whose combined meanings are essential to the meaning of the whole sentence but where every possible amalgamation of a reading from one and a reading from the other is excluded by some selection restriction. Contituents below the sentence level can also be semantically anomalous, e.g., 'honest baby' or 'honest worm.' Thus, in general, a constituent $C_1 + C_2$ will be semantically anomalous if, and only if, no reading $R_i{}^1$ of C_1 can amalgamate with any reading $R_j{}^2$ of C_2, i.e., in each possible case, there is a selection restriction that excludes the derived reading $R_{i,j}$ from being a reading for the constituent $C_1 + C_2$. Consequently, the distinction between semantically anomalous and semantically nonanomalous constituents is made in terms of the existence or nonexistence of at least one reading for the contituent. We may observe that the occurrence of a constituent without readings is a necessary but *not* sufficient condition for a sentence to be semantically anomalous. For the sentence 'We would think it queer indeed if someone were to say that he smells itchy,' which contains a constituent without readings—which is semantically anomalous—is not itself semantically anomalous.

The projection rules of the semantic component for a language characterize the meaning of all syntactically well-formed constituents of two or more words on the basis of what the dictionary specifies about these words. Thus, these rules provide a reconstruction of the process by which a speaker utilizes his knowledge of the dictionary to obtain the meanings of any syntactically compound constituent, including sentences. But, before such rules can operate, it is necessary to extract the lexical readings for the words of a sentence from the dictionary and make them available to the projection rules. That is, it is first necessary to assign sets of lexical readings to the occurrence of words in the underlying phrase marker undergoing semantic interpretation so that the projection rules will have the necessary material on which to operate. We will simplify our account at this point in order to avoid technicalities with which we do not need to concern ourselves.[17]

It is at this point that the syntactic information in dictionary entries is utilized. The syntactic markers in the dictionary entry for a word serve to differentiate different words that have the same phonological (or orthographic) representation. For example, 'store' marked as a verb and 'store' marked as a noun are different words, even though phonologically (or orthographically) these lexical items are identical. Thus, lexical items are distinguished as different words by the fact that the dictionary marks them as belonging to different syntactic categories. Moreover, such pairs of lexical items have different senses so that, in the dictionary, they will be assigned different sets of lexical readings. Thus, it is important to know which of the n different words with the same phonological (or

---

[17] The assignment of lexical readings is actually accomplished by the same device that introduces the lexical items themselves, but, for the sake of avoiding complications, we shall not go into the formal structure of this device here. Cf. N. Chomsky, *Aspects of the Theory of Syntax*, and J. J. Katz, *Semantic Theory* (in preparation).

orthographic) representation is the one that occurs at a given point in an underlying phrase marker because only if we know this can we assign that occurrence of the element in the underlying phrase marker the right set of lexical readings. Since the underlying phrase marker will categorize its lowest level elements into their syntactic classes and subclasses, it provides the information needed to decide which of the lexical readings in the dictionary entries for these elements should be assigned to them. All that is required beyond this information is some means of associating each terminal element in an underlying phrase marker with all and only those lexical readings in its dictionary entry that are compatible with the syntactic categorization it receives in the underlying phrase marker.

In previous discussions of semantic theory, we suggested a rule of the following sort to fulfill this requirement:

(I) Assign the set of lexical readings R to the terminal symbol σ of an underlying phrase marker just in case there is an entry for σ in the dictionary that contains R and that syntactically categorizes the symbol σ in the same way as the labeled nodes dominating σ in the underlying phrase marker.

Iterated application of (I) provides a set of readings for each of the words in an underlying phrase marker. Thus, for example, given (I) and the fact that there will be two distinct entries for 'store' such that on one it is a noun while on the other it is a verb, 'store' would be assigned a different set of lexical readings in the underlying phrase marker for "The store burned up today" and in the underlying phrase marker for "The man stores apples in the closet." When (I) applies no more, the projection rules operate on the underlying phrase marker.

There is, however, another way of fulfilling this requirement which avoids the postulation of (I). Which way is chosen depends on how the rules in the syntactic component that introduce lexical items into underlying phrase markers work. If these rules are rewriting rules of the sort illustrated in (3.1)–(3.10), then a rule such as (I) is needed. But if lexical items are inserted into dummy positions in underlying phrase markers on the basis of a lexical substitution rule in the syntactic component, then we can do away with (I) by allowing the set of readings associated with the lexical item that is substituted to be carried along in the substitution. Since the restrictions on the substitution of a lexical item will be the same as those that are involved in the operation of (I), this procedure will have the same effect as (I). After all lexical substitutions, each lexical item in an underlying phrase marker will have been assigned its correct set of lexical readings. If it turns out that a lexical substitution rule proves to be better than a set of rewrite rules for introducing lexical items into underlying phrase markers, the postulation of (I) can be thought of as something that was, but is no longer, necessary to fill a gap that existed in the syntactic component.

Projection rules operate on underlying phrase markers that are partially interpreted in the sense of having sets of readings assigned only to the lowest level elements in them. They combine readings already assigned to constituents to form derived readings for constituents which, as yet, have had no readings assigned to them. The decision as to which of the readings assigned to nodes of an underlying phrase marker can be combined by the projection rules is settled by the bracketing in that phrase marker. That is to say, a pair of readings is potentially combinable if the two are assigned to elements that are bracketed together. Readings assigned to constituents that are not bracketed together cannot be amalgamated by a projection rule. The projection rules proceed from the bottom to the top of an underlying phrase marker, combining potentially combinable readings to produce derived readings that are then assigned to the node which immediately dominates the nodes with which the originally combined readings were associated. Derived readings provide a characterization of the meaning of the sequence of words dominated by the node to which they are assigned. Each constituent of an underlying phrase marker is thus assigned a set of readings, until the highest constituent, the whole sentence, is reached and assigned a set of readings, too.

There is a distinct projection rule for each distinct grammatical relation. Thus, there will be different projection rules in the semantic component of a linguistic description for each of the grammatical relations: subject-predicate, verb-object, modification, etc. The number of projection rules required is, consequently, dictated by the number of grammatical relations defined in the theory of the syntactic component. A given projection rule applies to readings assigned to constituents just in case the grammatical relation holding between these constituents is the one with which this projection rule deals. For example, the projection rule (R1) is the one designed to deal with modification, *viz.*, the grammatical relation that holds between a modifier and a head, i.e., such pairs as an adjective and a noun, an adverb and a verb, and adverb and an adjective, etc.

(R1)   *Given* two readings,

R_1: (a_1), (a_2), . . . , (a_n); $<SR_1>$
R_2: (b_1), (b_2), . . . , (b_m); $<SR_2>$

such that R_1 is assigned to a node X_1 and R_2 is assigned to a node X_2, X_1 dominates a string of words that is a head and X_2 dominates a string that is a modifier, and X_1 and X_2 branch from the same immediately dominating node X,

Then the derived reading,

R_3: (a_1), (a_2), . . . , (a_n), (b_1), (b_2), . . . , (b_m); $<SR_1>$

is assigned to the node X just in case the selection restriction $<SR_2>$ is satisfied by R_1.

This projection rule expresses the nature of attribution in language, the process whereby new semantically significant constituents are created out of the meanings of modifiers and heads. According to (R1), in an attributive construction, the semantic properties of the new constituent are those of the head except that the meaning of the new constituent is more determinate than that of the head by itself due to the information contributed by the meaning of the modifier. This rule enforces the selection restriction in the reading of the modifier, thus allowing the embedding of a reading for a modifier into a reading for a head only if the latter has the requisite semantic content.

It should not be supposed that other projection rules are essentially the same as (RI), in which the derived reading is formed by taking the union of the sets of semantic markers in the two readings on which it operates. If this were the case, there would be no semantically distinct operations to correspond to, and provide an interpretation of, each distinct grammatical relation. Moreover, the semantic interpretations of sentences such as 'Police chase criminals' and 'Criminals chase police' would assign each the same reading for their sentence-constituents, thus falsely marking them as synonymous. That is, since the same sets of semantic markers occur in the lexical readings that are assigned at the level of words in each case, their semantic interpretations would be the same. To indicate the sort of differences that are found among different projection rules, we may consider the projection rules that deal with the grammatical relations of subject-predicate and verb-object in terms of the two examples, 'Police chase criminals' and 'Criminals chase police.'

Neglecting the lexical readings for 'police' and 'criminals' and other senses of 'chase,' we may begin by considering the most familiar sense of 'chase':

chase → Verb, Verb Transitive, . . . ; (((Activity) (Nature: (Physical)) of X), ((Movement) (Rate: Fast)) (Character: Following)), (Intention of X: (Trying to catch ((Y) ((Movement) (Rate: (Fast)))); <SR>.

But, before considering the projection rules that combine senses of 'police' and 'criminal' with the sense reconstructed by this lexical reading, it is necessary to consider the motivation for this lexical reading.

The semantic marker (Activity) distinguishes 'chase' in the intended sense from *state verbs,* such as 'sleep,' 'wait,' 'suffer,' 'believe,' etc., and from *process verbs,* such as 'grow,' 'freeze,' 'dress,' 'dry,' etc., and classifies 'chase' together with other *activity verbs,* such as 'eat,' 'speak,' 'walk,' 'remember,' etc. The semantic marker (Activity) is qualified as to nature by the semantic marker (Physical). This indicates that chasing is a physical activity and distinguishes 'chase' from verbs like 'think' and 'remember' which are appropriately qualified in their lexical readings to indicate that thinking and remembering are mental activities. But (Activity) is not further qualified, so that, *inter alia,* 'chase' can apply to either a group or individual activity. In this respect, 'chase' contrasts with 'mob' which is marked (Type: (Group))—hence, we can predict the contradictoriness of 'Mary mobbed the movie star (all by herself),' i.e., both one person did something to the star alone and also more than one did that very thing to the star. Also, 'chase' contrasts, in this respect, with 'solo,' which is marked (Type: (Individual))—hence, we can predict that 'They solo in the plane on Friday' has the unique meaning that they each fly the plane by themselves on Friday. Moreover, the semantic marker (Movement) indicates that chasing involves movement of some kind that is left unspecified in the meaning of the verb 'chase,' in contrast with a verb

such as 'walk,' 'motor,' or 'swim.' This movement is necessarily fast, as indicated by the semantic marker (Rate:
(Fast)) which distinguishes 'chase' from 'creep,' 'walk,'
'move,' etc. Further, this movement has the character of
following, as indicated by (Character: (Following))
which distinguishes 'chase' from 'flee,' 'wander,' etc., and
classifies it together with 'pursue,' 'trail,' etc. Again, for
someone to be chasing someone or thing, it is not necessary that the person be moving in any specified direction.
This fact is marked by the absence of a qualification on
(Movement) of the form (Direction: ( )) which would
be needed in the lexical readings for 'descend,' 'advance,'
'retreat,' etc. But it is necessary that the person doing
the chasing be trying to catch the person or thing he is
chasing, so that 'chase' falls together with the verb 'pursue,' on the one hand, and contrast with 'follow,' 'trail,'
etc., on the other. This is indicated by (Intention of X:
(Trying to catch $((Y) ( )))$), where '( )' in the lexical
reading under consideration is the semantic marker
((Movement) (Rate: (Fast))) which indicates that the
person or thing chased is itself moving fast. It is sometimes held that the person chased must be fleeing from
someone or something, but this is mistaken, since a
sentence such as 'The police chased the speeding motorist'
does not imply that the motorist is fleeing at all. Finally,
note that 'chase' is not an achievement verb in the sense
of applying to cases where a definite goal is obtained.
It is not necessary for the person actually to catch the
one he is chasing for him to have actually chased him,
as is indicated by the nonanomalousness of sentences

such as 'He chased him but did not catch him.' Accordingly, 'chase' contrasts with 'intercept,' 'trap,' 'deceive,' etc.

Now, the slots indicated by the dummy markers 'X' and 'Y' determine, respectively, the positions at which readings of the subject and object of 'chase' can go when sentences containing this verb are semantically interpreted. The projection rule that handles the combination of readings for verbs with readings for their objects embeds the reading for the object of a verb into the Y-slot of the reading for the verb, and the projection rule that handles the combination of readings for predicates and their subjects embeds the reading for the subject into the X-slot of the reading for the predicate. Thus, there are appropriately distinct semantic operations corresponding to the distinct grammatical relations of verb-object and subject-predicate, and the sentence-readings for the two sentences 'Police chase criminals' and 'Criminals chase police' are appropriately different.

Preliminary to defining the concept 'semantic interpretation of the sentence S,' we must define the subsidiary notion 'semantically interpreted underlying phrase marker of S.' We define it as a complete set of pairs, one member of which is a labelled node of the underlying phrase marker, and the other member of which is a maximal set of readings, each reading in this set being a reading for the sequence of words dominated by the labeled node in question. The set of readings is maximal in the sense that it contains all and only those readings of the sequence of words that belong to it by virtue of the dictionary, the projection rules, and the labeled bracketing in the underlying phrase marker. The set is complete in the sense that every node of the underlying phrase marker is paired with a maximal set of readings. In terms of this definition for 'semantically interpreted underlying phrase markers or S,' we can define the notion 'semantic interpretation of an underlying phrase marker of S' to be (1) a semantically interpreted underlying phrase marker of S, and (2) the set of statements that follow from (1) by definitions (D1)–(D6) and any further such definitions that are specified in the theory of language,[18] where 'C' is any constituent of any underlying phrase marker of S,

(D1) C is *semantically anomalous* if and only if the set of readings assigned to C contains no members.

(D2) C is *semantically unambiguous* if and only if the set of readings assigned to C contains exactly one member.

(D3) C is *semantically ambiguous n-ways* if and only if the set of readings assigned to C contains n members, for n greater than 1.

(D4) C_1 and C_2 are *synonymous on a reading* if and only if the set of readings assigned to C_1 and the set of readings assigned to C_2 have at least one member in common.

(D5) C_1 and C_2 are *fully synonymous* if and only if the set of readings assigned to C_1 and the set of readings assigned to C_2 are identical.

(D6) C_1 and C_2 are *semantically distinct* if and only if each reading in the set assigned to C_1 differs by at least one semantic marker from each reading in the set assigned to C_2

We can now define the notion 'semantic interpretation of the sentence S' as (1) the set of semantic interpretations of S's underlying phrase markers, and (2) the set of statements about S that follows from (1) and definitions (D'1)–(D'3) and any further such definitions that are specified in the theory of language,[18] where 'sentence-constituent' refers to the entire string of terminal symbols in an underlying phrase marker,

(D'1) S is *semantically anomalous* if and only if the sentence-constituent of each semantically interpreted underlying phrase marker of S is semantically anomalous.

(D'2) S is *semantically unambiguous* if and only if each member of the set of readings which contains all the readings that are assigned to sentence-constituents of semantically interpreted underlying phrase marker of S is synonymous with each other member.

(D'3) S is *semantically ambiguous n-ways* if and only if the set of all readings assigned to the sentence-constituents of semantically interpreted underlying phrase markers of S contains n nonequivalent readings, for n greater than 1.

This way of defining semantic concepts, such as 'semantically anomalous sentence in L,' 'semantically ambiguous sentence in L,' 'synonymous constituents in L,'

---

[18] These further definitions include all those given in Katz, "Analyticity and Contradiction in Natural Language," those for concepts such as *presupposition of the question* (or *imperative*) S and *possible answer to the question S*, which are given in Katz and Postal, *An Integrated Theory of Linguistic Descriptions,* and any other definitions of semantic properties and relations that can be given in terms of configurations of symbols in semantically interpreted underlying phrase markers.

etc., removes any possibility of criticizing the theory of language in which these concepts are introduced on the grounds of circularity in definition of the sort for which Quine had criticized Carnap's attempts to define the same range of concepts. The crucial point about this way of defining these concepts is that their defining condition is stated solely in terms of formal features of semantically interpreted underlying phrase markers so that none of these concepts themselves need appear in the definition of any of the others. Moreover, these definitions also avoid the charge of empirical vacuity that was correctly made against Carnap's constructions. These definitions enable us to predict semantic properties of syntactically well-formed strings of words in terms of formal features of semantically interpreted underlying phrase markers. The adequacy of these definitions is thus an empirical question about the structure of language. Their empirical success depends on whether, in conjunction with the set of semantically interpreted underlying phrase markers for each natural language, they correctly predict the semantic properties and relations of the sentences in each natural language.

The semantic interpretations of sentences produced as the output of a semantic component constitute the component's full account of the semantic structure of the language in whose linguistic description the component appears. The correctness of the account that is given by the set of semantic interpretations of sentences is determined by the correctness of the individual predictions contained in each semantic interpretation. These are tested against the intuitive judgments of fluent speakers of the language. For example, speakers of English judge that the syntactically unique sentence 'I like seals' is semantically ambiguous. An empirically correct semantic component will have to predict this ambiguity on the basis of a semantically interpreted underlying phrase marker for this sentence in which its sentence-constituent is assigned at least two readings. Also, English speakers judge that 'I saw an honest stone' or 'I smell itchy' are semantically anomalous, as are 'honest stones' and 'itchy smells.' Hence, an adequate semantic component will have to predict these anomalies on the basis of semantically interpreted underlying phrase markers in which the relevant constituents are assigned no readings. Furthermore, English speakers judge that 'Eye doctors eye blonds,' 'Oculists eye blonds,' and 'Blonds are eyed by oculists' are synonymous sentences, i.e., paraphrases of each other, while 'Eye doctors eye what gentlemen prefer' is not a paraphrase of any of these sentences. Accordingly, a semantic component will have to predict these facts. In general, a semantic component for a given language is under the empirical constraint to predict the semantic properties of sentences in each case where speakers of the language have strong, clear-cut intuitions about the semantic properties and relations of those sentences. Where there are no strong, clear-cut intuitions, there will be no data one way or the other. But, nevertheless, the semantic component will still make predictions about such cases by interpolating from the clear cases on the basis of the generalizations abstracted from them.

Therefore, the empirical evaluation of the dictionary entries and projection rules of a semantic component is a matter of determining the adequacy of the readings that they assign to constituents, and this, in turn, is a matter of determining the adequacy of the predictions that follow from these readings and the definitions of semantic properties and relations in the theory of language. If the intuitive judgments of speakers are successfully predicted by a semantic component, the component gains proportionately in empirical confirmation. If, on the other hand, the semantic component makes false predictions then, as with any scientific theory, the system has to be revised in such a way that prevents these empirically inadequate predictions from being derivable from the dictionary and projection rules. However, deciding which part(s) of the component have been incorrectly formulated is not something that can always, or even very often, be done mechanically. Rather, it is a matter of further theory construction. We have to make changes which seem necessary to prevent the false predictions and then check out these changes to determine if they avoid the false predictions and do not cause special difficulties of their own. Thus, we are always concerned with the over-all adequacy of the semantic component, and it is on this global basis that we judge the adequacy of its subcomponents. The adequacy of a dictionary entry or a projection rule depends, then, on how well it plays its role within the over-all descriptive system.

Concluding Remarks

The model of a linguistic description that is provided by the theory of language seeks to explain the ability of speakers to communicate in a natural language on the assumption that, underlying their ability to communicate, there is a highly complex system of rules, which is essentially the same as that underlying the linguistic ability of others who speak the same language. On this model, the process of linguistic communication is conceived of as one in which the speaker, in his production of speech, encodes his inner, private thoughts and ideas in the form of some external, publicly observable, acoustic phenomena, and the hearer, in his comprehension of speech, decodes the structure of such objective phenomena in the form of an inner, private experience of the same thoughts and ideas. Language is thus viewed as an instrument of communication of thoughts and ideas which enables those who know the same language to associate the same meanings with each of the significant sound sequences in the language.

The explanation of linguistic communication afforded by the theory of language takes the form of a model that reveals the structure of the rules which constitute a speaker's linguistic competence and the organization of these rules into a system which relates meanings and sounds. The facts of linguistic communication are accounted for by showing them to be behavioral consequences of the use of rules with this structure and organized in the way that the model specifies. In particular, these rules explain the ability of a speaker of a natural language to produce and understand sentences that he never previously encountered in terms of a semantic process in which the meanings of new and unfamiliar sentences are obtained compositionally from the familiar meanings of their parts. If the facts of linguistic communication can be accounted for successfully on the assumption that they are consequences of a linguistic competence of the sort characterized in the model, then these facts provide strong empirical evidence for the model.

Before concluding this chapter, it will be worthwhile to anticipate a criticism of the theory of language which denies that languages are instruments for the communication of thoughts and ideas on the grounds that meanings cannot be identified with thoughts and ideas. One version of this criticism is found in Alston's book *The Philosophy of Language*,[19] and we can discuss the general criticism in terms of this typical version of it.

It will be recalled that semantic theory takes meanings to be representations of classes of equivalent thoughts or ideas, which thoughts and ideas are connected with linguistic constructions in the speaker's system of internalized rules. Thus, readings, which are the formal reconstructions of meanings, are composed of semantic markers, which represent the conceptual components of meanings. A semantic marker such as (Physical Object) represents the class of equivalent ideas that we as speakers of English have in mind when we distinguish

---

[19] W. Alston, *The Philosophy of Language*, Prentice-Hall, 1964.

the senses of 'stone,' 'man,' 'car,' 'book,' etc., from the senses of 'virtue,' 'tickle,' 'time,' 'shadow,' 'togetherness,' etc. Alston uses the label 'ideational theory' to refer to any theory of meaning that construes meanings in this way. Ideational theories are opposed, on the one hand, to referential theories, and, on the other, to behavioristic theories that treat meaning in stimulus-response terms. Thus, Alston's criticisms of ideational theories in general apply to the semantic theory presented in this chapter.

Alston says that three conditions must be met if ideational theories of meaning are to be adequate. First, whenever an expression or sentence is used in a certain sense the idea or thought of which it is the external, sensible sign must be present in the mind of the speaker. Second, the speaker must, except on those occasions where he uses words unthinkingly or automatically, utter sentences to make his hearers realize that certain thoughts or ideas are in his mind. Third, such sentences must evoke the same thoughts or ideas in the minds of the hearer if communication is successful. These conditions seem to me to be roughly correct, except for one thing. Alston understands the notion of 'present in the mind' (of a speaker or hearer) to mean 'consciously in his mind'[20] This is a natural interpretation if one is thinking of Locke, who is Alston's only example of an ideational theorist, but it does not fit the version of the ideational theory held by the major Cartesian linguists.[21]

[20] *Ibid.*
[21] Cf. N. Chomsky, *Cartesian Linguistics*, (in preparation).

And it is certainly not the interpretation of the notion 'present in the mind' that would be suitable to our discussion of the manner in which linguistic communication is explained within the theory of language. We used the term 'tacit' in order not to contradict the obvious fact of introspection that a speaker untutored in linguistics is not consciously aware of the complex of rules that enter into his uses of his language. We shall return to this matter shortly.

Given his interpretation of the notion 'present in the mind,' however, it is an easy matter for Alston to argue that the above mentioned three conditions are not satisfied. By way of showing that these conditions are not satisfied, Alston argues as follows: "Take a sentence at random, for example, 'When in the course of human events, it becomes necessary for one people to . . . ,' and utter it with your mind on what you are saying; then, ask yourself whether there was a distinguishable idea in your mind corresponding to each of the meaningful linguistic units of the sentence. Can you discern an idea of 'when,' 'in,' 'course,' 'becomes,' etc., swimming into your ken as each word is pronounced? In the unlikely event that you can, can you recognize the idea that accompanies 'when' as the same idea that puts in an appearance whenever you utter 'when' in that sense? Do you have a firm enough grip on the idea to call it up, or at least know what it would be like to call it up, without the word being present? In other words, is it something that is identifiable and producible apart from the word? Do you ever catch the idea of 'when' appearing when you utter other words—'until,' 'rheostat,' or 'epigraphy'?"[22] If someone talks about thoughts and ideas given in conscious experience, we know what it is that is being talked about, but if one talks about unconscious thoughts and ideas, it is no longer clear that one is talking about anything at all. Thus, Alston writes further, "What is disturbing about these questions is not that they have one answer rather than another, but that we do not know how to go about answering them. What are we supposed to look for by way of an idea of 'when'? How can we tell whether we have it in mind or not? Just what am I supposed to try for when I try to call it up out of context? The real difficulty is that we are unable to spot 'ideas' as we would have to in order to test the ideational theory."[23] If there are no conscious ideas in our minds antecedent to and expressed by our articulation of words such as 'when,' then a theory which says that such and such a word is connected with such and such an idea is not just false, as it would be if the word were connected with some other idea, but wholly untestable. Ideational theories are, on Alston's line of reasoning, without an empirical basis on which to rest their explanatory claims and so they cannot make a case for the thesis that meaning should be understood mentalistically.

This line of reasoning gains its plausibility from the fact that, except for introspective verification, which is ruled out by excluding the Lockean conception of

[22] Alston, *The Philosophy of Language*.
[23] *Ibid.*

thoughts and ideas as always and necessarily consciously experienced, there appears to be no way in which we can say what we mean by thoughts and ideas that is open to some empirical check on our ascription of them to the participants of a communication situation. But here is where critics of ideational theory have just overlooked a possibility; in fact, the one that we want to endorse as the proper basis for determining the empirical validity of an ideational theory of linguistic communication.

The alternative is this. When we say that thoughts and ideas need not be present in conscious experience and so need not be available to introspective observation, and further, as we would have to, that they are not publicly observable either, we are simply saying that they are un observable in much the same sense in which physical scientists say that certain microentities and microprocesses are unobservable. We are being, no more, or less, meta physical than they. What gives their claims about such entities and processes empirical content is that their theories connect the postulated existence of such things with certain observable phenomena through a complex chain of deductive relations. Hence, scientific method offers us a straightforward way of establishing the existence of un observable entities and processes, one which there is no legitimate reason to preclude from linguistics. The method is that of hypothetically postulating a theory within which some unobservable entity or process is de scribed and related to the observable behavior of public objects and of empirically verifying the theory by check ing to determine whether what it predicts on the basis of this relation between the observable and the unobservable accords with the data about the behavior of the relevant public objects.

Such theoretical systematization of observable linguistic phenomena in terms of some formulation of the underlying unobservable mental phenomena is no different from what is done in other branches of empirical science where we deal with causally effective yet observationally inaccessible phenomena. The linguist can no more look inside the speaker's head than a physicist can directly observe photons or a biologist directly inspect the evolutionary events that produced life. The linguist, like the physicist or biologist, achieves understanding of the phenomena with which he is concerned by constructing a theory of the unobservable system. If the consequences of the theory lead to correct predictions about the observable effects of the underlying system and would not do so if the theory were changed and if, moreoever, the theory is the simplest one that enables the scientist to derive the known facts and predict the unknown ones as consequences of the hypothesized system, then the scientist can say that the theory accounts for the observable behavior in terms of the functioning of an unobservable but causally efficient system and that the theory correctly represents the structure of this unobservable system. In this way, the linguist can empirically support the claim that his mentalistic theory of meaning describes a real, though unobservable, system that is the basis of the speaker's ability to communicate with other speakers and that causally underlies the observable speech events that occur in such communication.

The option of treating a theory of language and linguistic descriptions as hypothetically postulated theories, constructed on the basis of a step of positing an unobservable system and a step of confirming this posit in terms of its empirical consequences, permits us to formulate the connection between a linguistic construction and an idea in terms of rules which relate the phonetic representation of the linguistic construction with the semantic representation of the idea. Such rules, if they are systematically connected with one another in the hypothetically postulated theory, provide the basis for certain inferences to observable properties of speech phenomena. Therefore, an ideational theory has an empirical basis for claiming that a certain idea is in a speaker's mind, even though the speaker himself cannot find it in his consciousness, for the correctness of the inferences to observable properties of speech phenomena provides the empirical basis for such claims.

This option, then, blocks criticism of ideational theories such as Alston's. It does not, of course, show that we can construct an empirically successful theory of linguistic communication on a mentalistic basis or that thoughts and ideas which are not in the conscious experience of speakers play a role in linguistic communication. But it does show that *a priori* arguments such as Alston's do not eliminate the possibility of such theories in advance of their having an empirical run for their money.

One further point on this subject. The conception of the theory of language as a hypothetically postulated theory undercuts another of the assumptions implicit in criticisms such as Alston's. Alston assumes that an ideational theory must connect each of the meaningful words in an utterance with a specific idea (or set of ideas in case the word is ambiguous). Such as assumption is far too strong to impose on an ideational theory and any adequate linguistic description would violate it. Moreover, there is no need to impose it. The belief that an ideational theory has to go on this assumption lends plausibility to criticisms such as Alston's, but it is this assumption itself, not any feature of ideational theories, that makes it appear as if there is no idea corresponding to a word such as 'when.'

Consider a linguistic description of the sort given in the above account of the theory of language. This assumption of Alston's would mean that the semantic component must operate on final derived phrase markers, i.e., on the syntactic description of the utterance form of a sentence. Lexical readings would have to be associated with the terminal elements of final derived phrase markers. However, there are extremely strong reasons against this, which show that, rather, the semantic component must operate on underlying phrase markers.[24] Therefore, this assumption should be replaced by one that requires of an ideational theory only that it relate the representation of an idea or set of ideas to each of the constituents in the underlying phrase marker of a sentence. But replacing Alston's assumption with this one removes the plausibility of his criticism. Since

<hr />

[24] Cf. Katz and Postal, *An Integrated Theory of Linguistic Description,* for the reasons in this case.

underlying phrase markers are themselves highly abstracted, hypothetically postulated syntactic objects, direct introspective reports about the data of conscious experience cannot be thought of as the sole criterion for deciding what idea corresponds to a particular word in a sentence. Rather than asking what idea corresponds to the word 'when' in a sentence such as 'When in the course . . . ,' we should ask for the reading of the constituent in the underlying phrase marker for the sentence of which 'when' is the phonological or orthographic realization, namely, the reading of the constituent 'at whatever time.' And rather than asking if the idea can be identified introspectively on occasions when we utter such sentences, we should ask what reading for 'at whatever time' we should introduce in order that, when combined by projection rules with the readings for the other constituents of the sentence, we obtain the best set of predictions about the semantic properties and relations in the sentence. When the matter is reformulated in this way, all trace of Alston's criticism disappears, and we are left with a problem for further empirical research.[25]

[25] Cf. J. J. Katz, "The Semantics of Linguistically Expressed Time Relations" (in preparation).

IMPLICATIONS
FOR UNDERSTANDING
CONCEPTUAL KNOWLEDGE

We have claimed that the theory of language presented in the last chapter has significant implications for our understanding of conceptual knowledge. In this chapter, we will try to support this claim by taking four problems from philosophy that are widely acknowledged to be of importance for the investigation of conceptual knowledge and will show that fundamental progress toward their solution can be made on the basis of the theory of language.

The first falls under the topic of the logic of natural languages and concerns the extent to which deductive inferences are grounded in the structure of natural languages. To clarify this question we will show that the concepts of analyticity (contradiction, syntheticity, etc.) and entailment can be satisfactorily defined within the theory of language. That is, we will try to show that the problem of defining these concepts, with which Carnap and other logical empiricists struggled unsuccessfully, can be solved with appropriate definitions of the sort (D1)–(D6). Such definitions will reveal that deductive inferences that depend on the concepts 'analytic' and 'entailment' are, to the extent of their dependency, grounded in the structure of language. The second problem that we will consider is the nature of semantic categories. We will examine the general character a system of categories of the kind discussed by Aristotle has when it is embedded within a theory of language and will try to show that a theory of language answers questions about such a system that are left unanswered by the more informal treatments that semantic categories have received at the hands of traditional philosophers. In particular, we will deal with the problems of what such categories are, how to determine their number, what relations hold between them, and how to establish that something is a category. Third, we will consider the problem of innate ideas, or, alternatively, the issue of Rationalism versus Empiricism. Here we will try to show that the theory of language provides sound reasons for accepting the rationalist claim that there are innate ideas. Fourth, we will consider the nature of linguistic analysis in philosophy. In the case of each of these philosophical problems, we will seek a means of reformulating the problem as a problem within the theory of language itself and will try to solve the reformulated problem by further elaborating the theory of language.[1]

ANALYTICITY

In their study of conceptual knowledge philosophers have found it necessary to distinguish between truths of reason and truths of fact. According to Leibniz, truths of reason describe invariant features of all possible worlds while truths of fact describe actual features of some but not all possible words. Truths of reason are necessarily true while truths of fact are only contingently true, i.e., true contingent on the world about which they are asserted having the features they ascribe to it. Examples of the former truths include 'Bachelors are unmarried,' 'A child is younger than an adult.' Everything is identical with itself,' etc. Examples of the latter include 'Roses grow in the ground,' 'Lincoln freed the slaves,' 'Gases expand when heated,' etc. The truth of the former cases

---

[1] I am not claiming, and would certainly not want to claim, that every philosophical problem can be represented as a problem about the nature of language and dealt with as such in the theory of language. However, at the present early stage of development of the theory of language, it is not yet clear what class of philosophical problems is best treated within the framework of an empirical investigation of language. This monograph argues that part of the problem of the logic of language, the problem of categories of language, and the problem of innate ideas can be dealt with in this way. Perhaps with further development of the theory of language, this theory itself will make it clear which other philosophical problems should be approached in the way these three were and which must be left to other approaches.

can be ascertained by reason alone, but the truth of the latter cases requires investigation into the way the world is.

One trouble with this distinction is that it fails to explain what it is about a truth of reason which makes it ascertainable as such by reason alone. What process of reasoning permits us to recognize a truth of reason for what it is? One philosopher who proposed such an explanation for a significant class of truths of reason was Kant.[2] Kant's explanation went as follows. Sentences, or, rather, the judgments they express, are composed of a subject and a predicate. The judgment consists in connecting the subject and predicate. This constitutes an attribution of the predicate concept to the subject. The question of whether the judgment is true is, then, the question of whether the attribution is correct. It was one of Kant's major insights that in a certain class of truths of reason, the ones he called 'analytic,' the correctness of this attribution can be decided solely by examining the complex of concepts that make up the subject to determine if the predicate concept is already contained in them. Thus, the process of reasoning which permits us to recognize an analytic truth is a process of thinking through the subject concept to find out if the concept that the predicate attributes to it is already contained in it. If it is, then the attribution must be correct. Having established that the subject possesses this property, as it

[2] I. Kant, *The Critique of Pure Reason* (translated by N. K. Smith), Humanities Press, New York, 1929, and I. Kant, *A Prolegomena to Any Future Metaphysic* (translated by L. W. Beck), Bobbs-Merrill Company, 1950.

were, by definition, the predicate's attribution of it to the subject is necessarily valid. The denial of an analytic truth is accordingly contradictory because the subject is, by definition, asserted to have a certain property and yet, in connecting the predicate with the subject, the subject is asserted not to have this property. 'Bachelors are unmarried' is analytic because the concept of a bachelor contains the concept 'unmarried' which the predicate attributes to it, while 'Bachelors are not unmarried' is a contradiction because it asserts that some adult males are and are not unmarried.

The difficulties with Kant's explanation are that it is developed for constructions of subject-predicate form, which appears to severely limit its scope, and that it relies on such hard-to-pin-down notions as 'concept,' 'thinking,' 'containment,' etc., that are left without any analysis that might tell us how to understand them when we have to decide sophisticated or borderline cases. Partly for these reasons, the logical empiricists, again Carnap in particular, gave the term 'analytic' a different meaning. They took this term to mean 'truth by virtue of meaning alone' and sought to explicate it in terms of meaning postulates and semantical rules within a theory of artificial languages. Since, as we have seen, this attempt came to nought, it is plausible for us to go back to the Kantian notion of analyticity and try to remedy the deficiencies in Kant's explanation. Thus, we shall seek, within the theory of language, to find some way of extending the scope of Kant's explanation so that it covers cases which do not appear to be of subject-predicate form and to provide formal analyses of the informal notions in Kant's explanation that render them suitable to the job they were intended to do.

Casting this reconstruction of Kant's explanation in the terms of the theory of language, we can put our task as follows. The notions 'analytic,' 'synthetic,' and 'contradictory' have to be defined within the theory of language in the way that 'anomaly,' 'semantic ambiguity,' 'synonymy,' etc. were defined in Chapter 4. That is, we must present analyses of these notions in the form of definitions whose defining condition is framed exclusively in terms of formal features of semantically interpreted underlying phrase markers. Such definitions must enable us to predict which sentences of a natural language are analytic, which are synthetic, and which are contradictory.

The first step toward remedying the deficiencies of Kant's account of analyticity is to explicate his common sense ideas of subject and predicate in terms of the grammatical relations 'subject of the sentence S' and 'predicate of the sentence S.' (For simplicity, we use the term 'sentence' to mean a syntactically unambiguous sentence; thus, where a string of words is syntactically ambiguous, we use 'sentence' to refer to it under one and only one of its syntactic analyses.) The grammatical relation 'subject of the sentence S' is defined in the theory of language as follows:

The string of words σ is the subject of S just in case σ is the whole string of terminal elements in the underlying phrase marker for S that is dominated by a node labeled 'Noun

Phrase' and this node is immediately dominated by a node labeled 'Sentence' which is dominated by nothing.

The grammatical relation 'predicate of the sentence S' is defined as follows:

The string of words σ is the predicate of S just in case σ is the whole string of terminal elements in the underlying phrase marker for S that is dominated by a node labeled 'Predicate' and this node is immediately dominated by a node labeled 'Sentence' which is dominated by nothing.

Given these formal reconstructions, where Kant's account refers vaguely to subjects and predicates we will refer to strings of words in underlying phrase markers that satisfy defining conditions in these definitions. Thus, whereas on the basis of the informal notions of subject and predicate with which Kant worked it would be impossible to avoid saying that the subject of a sentence such as 'The policy was decided on by John' is 'the policy,' and that there is no subject of a normal English imperative such as 'Go home immediately,' on the basis of a syntactic theory such as the one developed in the previous chapter, it is possible to avoid these counter-intuitive conclusions. For the underlying phrase markers for these sentences contain as terminal elements, respectively, the strings 'John + Present + decide on + the + policy,' and 'You + Future + go + home + immediately,' and therefore, by the above definition for subject, the subjects of the above sentences are rather 'John,' and 'You,' respectively.

The next step is to observe that Kant's notion of a

concept is exactly the notion that semantic markers and readings formally reconstruct. This observation enables us to shift our attention from concepts to the formal elements in semantic theory that represent them. We can thus deal with such formal elements in the construction of the definitions we seek, instead of trying to work with the loose and rather elusive specifications of concepts that are characteristic of Kant's account. Thus, the notions of 'subject concept' and 'predicate concept' are replaced respectively, by the formal notions of the reading of the subject of a sentence and the reading of the predicate of a sentence, where these grammatical relations are determined according to the above definitions from syntactic theory and these readings are determined on the basis of semantically interpreted underlying phrase markers. Further, the Kantian notions of 'thinking through a concept' and 'the containment of a concept in another concept' are replaced by formally determined operations specified in terms of conditions on configurations of symbols in semantically interpreted underlying phrase markers. The obvious advantage of such replacement of concepts by formal elements, their configurations, and operations on them is that the application of semantic properties and relations, such as 'analytic,' 'contradictory,' etc., to sentences is now a matter that can be decided in a formal, mechanical way.

Let us now add the following definitions to the theory of language as an extension of the conception of a semantic interpretation of a sentence. We assume the following conventions: Let 'S' in the definitions below range over declarative copula sentences. Let the symbol 'R_1' stand for a reading of the subject of a S, the symbol 'R_2' stand for a reading of the predicate of S, and the symbol '$R_{1,2}$,' stand for the reading of the whole sentence S which results from the combination of R_1 and R_2. Then:

(D7) S *is analytic on the reading* $R_{1,2}$ if, and only if, every non-complex semantic marker in R_2 also occurs in R_1; for any complex semantic marker $((M_1) \cup (M_2) \cup \cdots \cup (M_n))$ in R_2, there is an (M_i), $1 \leq i \leq n$, in R_1; and the reading R_1 does not contain any antonymous semantic markers.[3]

(D8) S *is fully analytic* if, and only if, S is analytic on each reading assigned to its sentence-constituent, i.e., for each reading $R_{i,j}$ assigned to S, S is analytic on $R_{i,j}$.

These definitions formalize the Kantian idea that analyticity is the attributive vacuity that results from the failure of the meaning of a predicate to contribute any semantic content to the meaning of its subject. If we recall that the philosopher's notion of a statement or proposition is explicated within the theory of language as a reading of a declarative sentence, it will be clear that analytic statements (or propositions) are trivially true by virtue of the fact that in correctly determining the things to which their subjects refer we guarantee that these things have the properties their predicates attribute to them. Thus, (D7) in conjunction with the semantically interpreted underlying phrase marker for 'Bachelors are unmarried' enables us to predict that this sentence is analytic on a reading, but not fully analytic.

[3] The reader will find an explanation of this clause below.

On the basis of these definitions, it can be seen that analyticity is, on the sentence level, the counter-part of the semantic relation of meaning inclusion at the level of lower order constituents. We might bring this out more vividly by adding a definition which says that two expressions are such that the meaning of one is included in the meaning of the other just in case the reading of the former is related to the reading of the latter in the manner specified in (D7) for R_2 and R_1. We might then define two expressions as synonymous just in case the first meaning is included in the meaning of the second, and vice versa. In this way, we would explain the similarity and difference between analyticity and meaning inclusion.

Analogously, we want to be able to reconstruct contradictoriness as the counter-part, on the level of sentences, of the semantic relation of meaning incompatibility at the level of lower order constituents. We must thus seek definitions for 'S is contradictory on a reading' and 'S is fully contradictory' which are constructed in such a manner that the similarity and difference between contradictoriness and incompatibility is explained. Furthermore, these definitions must integrate with (D7), (D8), and the definitions for the concept 'syntheticity' to provide the desired logical relationships between these concepts.

Linguistically, the concept of incompatibility appears as antonymy, which is a relation between expressions. Under the general notion of antonymy are many specific types of antonymy relations. One example is the 'sex-antonymy' relation that holds between a pair of expressions just in case they have identical readings except that where the reading of one has the semantic marker (Male) the other has the semantic marker (Female). Some instances are: 'bride' and 'groom,' 'aunt' and 'uncle,' 'the cow in the barn' and 'the bull in the barn,' 'the foolish man who loaned me his car' and 'the foolish woman who loaned me her car,' etc. The majority of specific types of antonymy relations, however, hold for n-tuples of expressions, not pairs. For example, there are 'species-antonymous' cases, instances of which include: 'child,' 'cub,' 'puppy,' 'kitten,' 'cygnet,' etc. Another example is 'age-antonymy.' Age-antonymous n-tuples include: 'baby,' 'toddler,' 'child,' 'adolescent,' 'adult,' as well as the pairs 'puppy' and 'dog,' 'cub' and 'lion,' 'cygnet' and 'swan,' etc. There are, of course, many other types of antonymy.

The set of all and only the n-tuples of expressions that bear one of the types of antonymy relations to each other is *infinite* because it includes, besides the n-tuples of words, infinitely many n-tuples of syntactically compound expressions. Thus, the possibility of a longest expression in a set of X-antonymous expressions is precluded by the recursive character of the syntactic rules employed in the derivation of such expressions. Since each set contains infinitely many n-tuples of antonymous expressions, we will have to construct definitions both for each specific type of antonymy and for the general notion of 'antonymous n-tuple' which are adequate to specify such infinite sets. The most natural means of doing this within a theory of language is as follows. First, group semantic markers into antonymous n-tuples, i.e., n-tuples of incompatible semantic markers. This is accomplished by the notation which semantic theory will prescribe for the formulation of semantic markers. Semantic markers are so represented in this notation that the membership of any n-tuple of antonymous semantic markers can be uniquely determined on the basis of formal features of the symbols that comprise semantic markers. For example, we could represent the semantic markers (Male) and (Female) as respectively, '(S^m)' and '(S')'. Similarly, the other X-antonymous n-tuples of semantic markers could be represented using a common base symbol with variable superscripts, so that the general form of an antonymous n-tuple of semantic markers is: (M^{α_1}), (M^{α_2}), . . . ,(M^{α_n}). Second, we introduce the definitions:

(i)   Two semantic markers belong to the same antonymous n-tuple of semantic markers if, and only if, one has the form (M^{α_i}) and the other has the form (M^{α_j}), where $i \neq j$ and $1 \leq i \leq n$ and $1 \leq j \leq n$.

(ii) Two expressions are antonymous (on a reading) if, and only if, one has a reading R_1 and the other a reading R_2 and R_1 contains a semantic marker (M_1) that belongs to the same antonymous n-tuple of semantic markers to which a different semantic marker (M_2) in R_2 belongs.

(iii) The expressions e_1, e_2, . . . , e_n form an antonymous n-tuple of expressions if, and only if, each e_i has a reading containing a different semantic marker from the same n-tuple of semantic markers, i.e., $e_1, e_2, . . . , e_n$ are pairwise antonymous on a reading.

On the basis of these considerations, we may construct definitions for 'S is contradictory on a reading' and 'S

is fully contradictory' that reveal the way in which these concepts are a projection of antonymy relations between expressions.

(D9) S *is contradictory on a reading* $R_{1,2}$ if, and only if, the reading R_1 contains a semantic marker (M_i) and the reading R_2 contains a semantic marker (M_j) such that (M_i) and (M_j) are different semantic markers belonging the same antonymous n-tuple of semantic markers, and the reading R_1 does not itself contain any antonymous semantic markers.[3]

(D10) S *is fully contradictory* if, and only if, S is contradictory on every reading assigned to its sentence-constituent.

What is asserted about a sentence when its semantic interpretation marks it as a contradictory on a reading is that anything to which its subject refers possesses a property or properties incompatible with some of those attributed to it by the predicate. Thus, just as analytic sentences are true by virtue of meaning alone, contradictory sentences are false by virtue of meaning alone. The very condition that determines when something is correctly regarded as an instance of the subject concept guarantees the falsity of the predication. On the basis of these definitions, a semantic component of English would mark such cases as 'The bride is a groom,' 'My round table is square,' 'Spinsters are males,' etc., as contradictory on a reading.

In terms of the previous definitions, we can now define 'syntheticity':

(D11) S *is synthetic on a reading* $R_{1,2}$ if, and only if, there is a reading $R_{1,2}$ assigned to S's sentence-constituent such that S is neither analytic nor contradictory on $R_{1,2}$ and R_1 does not contain any antonymous semantic markers.[3]

(D12) S *is fully synthetic* if, and only if, S is synthetic on each of the readings assigned to sentence-constituents.

These definitions reconstruct the idea that a synthetic sentence is one whose truth or falsity cannot be decided solely on the basis of the meanings of its component words, but must be decided on the basis of consideration of certain facts about the world. That is, to decide the truth or falsity of synthetic sentences, we must go beyond meaning and consider whether or not what the sentence's subject refers to has the property that the predication says it has. Thus, 'Dogs are friendly,' 'My kitchen table is two feet high,' 'Bachelors are very tall men' are synthetic, and marked as such.

The interrelation of these definitions of analyticity, contradiction, and syntheticity is accomplished on the basis of a dictionary entry for 'not.' On this entry, we wish to show that, with these definitions, the negation of an analytic sentence is marked contradictory, the negation of a contradictory sentence is marked analytic, and the negation of a synthetic sentence is marked synthetic. Preliminary to formulating the dictionary entry for 'not,' let us define an operator which will be used in the formulation. Let $(M^{\alpha_1}), (M^{\alpha_2}), \ldots, (M^{\alpha_n})$ be an antonymous n-tuple of semantic markers, then

$$A/(M^{\alpha_i}), \text{ for } 1 \leq i \leq n = ((M^{\alpha_1}) \cup (M^{\alpha_2}) \cup \ldots \cup (M^{\alpha_{i-1}})$$
$$\cup (M^{\alpha_{i+1}}) \cup \ldots \cup (M^{\alpha_n})).$$

We call '$A/(-)$' the 'antonymy operator' and we

call the complex symbol inside the parentheses a 'complex semantic marker.' Complex semantic markers are treated exactly like ordinary semantic markers with respect to combination by the projection rules. Note that $A/A/(M^{\alpha_i}) = (M^{\alpha_i})$ is a consequence of this definition.

The 'not' for which we shall specify a dictionary entry is sentential negation. Superficially, sentential negation can be formed by a variety of different syntactic devices. For example, besides introducing an occurrence of 'not' in the proper position in a verb-phrase, we can prefix a sentence with 'It is not the case that' or 'It is false that,' we can embed a sentence in the frame 'That . . . is false' or 'That . . . is not true,' or we can put the sentence in quotes and suffix it with 'is false' or 'is not true.' Here we shall assume that all these forms are paraphrases of one another and that they all derive from an underlying form in which there is a syntactic symbol 'Neg' at a fixed position in the verb-phrase of the underlying phrase marker for the sentence.[4] Thus, the dictionary entry to be given may be regarded as an entry for the symbol 'Neg' which, in turn, may be regarded as realized phonologically and orthographically in a variety of ways.

The entry for 'Neg' will be a set of rules, each of which operates on readings for the predicate (except for the constituent 'Neg' itself). Since these rules operate before readings of constituents of a predicate combine to form readings for the whole predicate, the effect of their operation is incorporated into the readings for the whole

[4] Cf. E. Klima, "Negation," Fodor and Katz (eds.), *The Structure of Language: Readings in the Philosophy of Language*, and Katz and Postal, *An Integrated Theory of Linguistic Descriptions*.

predicate constituent. Thus, they will be able to impart formal features to the readings of a predicate that play a role in determining which of the definitions (D7)-(D12) is satisfied by the semantically interpreted underlying phrase marker of a sentence. We assume the following conventions: Let (X_1), (X_2), . . . , (X_n) be the semantic markers in a reading for the subject of a sentence and (Y_1), (Y_2), . . . , (Y_m) be the semantic markers in a reading for its predicate. Let '$(X) = (Y)$' express the identity of the semantic markers '(X)' and '(Y)' and let '$(X) \; \mathfrak{A} \; (Y)$' say that '$(X)$' and '$(Y)$' are different semantic markers drawn from the same antonymous n-tuple of semantic markers, i.e., that '(X)' and '(Y)' are antonymous semantic markers. The entry for 'Neg' is:

(i) If there is no (Y_i), $1 \leqslant i \leqslant m$, such that $(Y_i) \; \mathfrak{A} \; (X_j)$, $1 \leqslant j \leqslant n$, and there are (Y_i), (Y_{i+1}), . . . , (Y_{i+k}), $k \geqslant 0$, such that, for each (Y_{i_v}), $i \leqslant v \leqslant i + k$, $(Y_{i_v}) = (X_j)$, and there are (Y_1), (Y_2), . . . , (Y_{i-1}), (Y_{i+k+1}), . . . , (Y_m) such that no (Y_h), $1 \leqslant h \leqslant i - 1$ or $i + k + 1 \leqslant h \leqslant m$, $(Y_h) = (X_j)$ or $(Y_h) \; \mathfrak{A} \; (X_j)$, then (Y_1), (Y_2), . . . , (Y_{i-1}), (Y_{i+k+1}), . . . , (Y_m) is replaced by $A/(Y_1) \cup A/(Y_2) \cup \ldots \cup A/(Y_{i-1}) \cup A/(Y_{i+k+1}) \cup \ldots \cup (Y_m)$.

(ii) If there are (Y_i), (Y_{i+1}), . . . , (Y_{i+k}), $1 \leqslant i \leqslant m$ and $k \leqslant m$, such that, for each (Y_{i_v}), $i \leqslant v \leqslant i + k$, $(Y_{i_v}) \; \mathfrak{A} \; (X_j)$, then (Y_i), (Y_{i+1}), . . . , (Y_{i+k}) is replaced by $A/(Y_i) \cup A/(Y_{i+1}) \cup \ldots \cup A/(Y_{i+k})$. Any (Y_g) $1 \leqslant g \leqslant i - 1$ or $k + 2 \leqslant g \leqslant m$, is replaced by the null element if $(Y_g) \neq (X_j)$.

(iii) If, for each (Y_i), $1 \leqslant i \leqslant m$, $(Y_i) = (X_j)$, then (Y_1), (Y_2), . . . , (Y_m) is replaced by $A/(Y_1) \cup A/(Y_2) \cup \ldots \cup A/(Y_m)$.

First, let us show that, on the basis of this entry for 'Neg,' the negation of an analytic sentence is marked contradictory. The case of analytic on a reading is the basic case since marking full analyticity is a trivial consequence once it is shown that the former case can be handled. Let us assume we are given a sentence that is analytic on a reading by (D7), e.g., 'A spinster is a woman.' From this it follows that the semantic markers (Y_1), (Y_2), . . . , (Y_m) are such that, for each (Y_i), $1 \leqslant i \leqslant m$, there is an (X_j) such that $(Y_i) = (X_j)$. In our example, (Y_1) is (Physical Object), (Y_2) is (Living), (Y_3) is (Human), (Y_4) is (Adult), and (Y_5) is (Female), for $m = 5$. According to (iii), in the production of a semantically interpreted underlying phrase marker for the negation of an analytic sentence (Y_1), (Y_2), . . . , (Y_m) is replaced by $A/(Y_1) \cup A/(Y_2) \cup . . . \cup A/(Y_m)$. Thus, in our example, in the production of a semantically interpreted underlying phrase marker for 'A spinster is not a woman,' (Physical Object), (Living), (Human), (Adult), (Female) is replaced by $A/$(Physical Object) $\cup$ $A/$(Living) $\cup$ $A/$(Human) $\cup$ $A/$(Adult) $\cup$ $A/$(Female). Since *ex hypothesi* there are semantic markers (X_1), (X_2), . . . , (X_r), for $r = m$, such that each of the semantic markers (Y_1), (Y_2), . . . , (Y_m) is identical to some (X_j), $1 \leqslant j \leqslant r$, after this operation of (iii), there must be at least one semantic marker in the reading for the subject of the negation of an analytic sentence that is antonymous with a semantic marker in the reading of its predicate, e.g., (Female) and $A/$(Female), i.e., (Male). This makes these two expressions antonymous, and thus makes the sentence contradictory on a reading. Hence, the negation of an analytic sentence is marked contradictory.

Next, let us show that the negation of a contradictory sentence is marked analytic. We assume we are given a sentence that is contradictory on a reading by (D9), e.g. 'A spinster is a man.' From this it follows that there are semantic markers (Y_i), (Y_{i+1}), . . . , (Y_{i+k}), $1 \leqslant i \leqslant m$ and $k \leqslant m$, such that each (Y_{i_v}) $\mathfrak{A}$ (X_j), $i \leqslant v \leqslant i + k$. In our example, there is the single semantic marker (Male). According to (ii), in the production of a semantically interpreted underlying phrase marker for the negation of a contradictory sentence (Y_i), (Y_{i+1}), . . . , (Y_{i+k}) is replaced by $A/(Y_i) \cup A/(Y_{i+1}) \cup \ldots \cup A/(Y_{i+k})$. Thus, in our example, in the production of a semantically interpreted underlying phrase marker for 'A spinster is not a man,' (Male) is replaced by $A/$(Male), i.e., (Female). Since *ex hypothesi* there are semantic markers (X_1), (X_2), . . . , (X_r), for $r = i + k$, such that each of (Y_i), (Y_{i+1}), . . . , (Y_{i+k}) is antonymous with some (X_j), $1 \leqslant j \leqslant r$, after the operation of (ii), there must be only (Y_i), $1 \leqslant i \leqslant m$, such that $(Y_i) = (X_j)$. All the semantic markers in the reading for the predicate of the negation of a contradictory sentence must now also appear in the reading for its subject, since any that were not antonymous with one in the reading for the subject either is identical with a semantic marker in the reading for the subject or else is replaced by the null element as specified in (ii). For instance, if the sentence concerned were 'A woman is an uncle,' the semantic marker in the reading for 'an uncle' (Has a sibling who has a child, or has a spouse who has a sibling who has a child) would have been nullified, thus leaving only semantic markers that appear also in the reading for the subject. Hence, by (D7), the negation of a contradictory sentence is marked analytic.

Finally, let us show that the negation of a synthetic sentence is marked synthetic. Assume we are given a sentence that is synthetic on a reading by (D11), e.g. 'That adult is a woman.' Then, it follows that there are semantic markers $(Y_s), (Y_{s+1}), \ldots , (Y_{s+k}), 1 \leqslant s \leqslant m,$ $k \leqslant m,$ and $k \neq 0,$ such that no $(Y_{s_v}), s \leqslant v \leqslant s + k,$ is identical with or antonymous with any $(X_j),$ and that if there are $(Y_u), 1 \leqslant u \leqslant s - 1$ or $s + k + 1 \leqslant u \leqslant m,$ then $(Y_u) = (X_j).$ In our example, $s + k = 1, (Y_s)$ is (Female), and there are the semantic markers (Physical Object), (Living), (Human), and (Adult) which also occur in the reading for the subject. According to (i), in the production of a semantically interpreted underlying phrase marker for the negation of a synthetic sentence, $(Y_s), (Y_{s+1}), \ldots , (Y_{s+k})$ is replaced by $A/(Y_s) \cup A/(Y_{s+1}) \cup \ldots \cup A/(Y_{s+k}).$ With respect to the negation of our example, i.e., 'That adult is not a woman,' (Female) is replaced by $A/$(Female), i.e., (Male). Since *ex hypothesi* no (Y_{s_v}) is antonymous with or identical with any $(X_j),$ after the operation of (i), it must be the case that no $A/(Y_{s_v})$ is antonymous with or identical with any $(X_j).$ Also no (Y_u) is antonymous with any $(X_j).$ Hence, the negation of a synthetic sentence cannot be contradictory. Moreover, since *ex hypothesi* there is at least one such $A/(Y_{s_v}),$ it does not matter that there may be some (Y_u) which is identical with an $(X_j).$ The negation of a synthetic sentence cannot be analytic. Since the negation of a synthetic sentence is neither contradictory nor analytic, it is marked synthetic by (D11).

We may carry this formal treatment of logical features of natural language even further by showing how the notion of entailment may be defined within semantic theory. This relation holds between the antecedent and consequent of a conditional sentence when the latter follows from the former by virtue of their meanings alone. The philosophical problem here is to so construct the definition of this notion that the so-called paradoxes of material implication are not derivable and yet entailments that are acceptable can be predicted from the definition.

We can treat this problem as one whose solution requires an extension of the above theory of analyticity because we can define entailment using analyticity:

(D13) S_1 *entails* S_2 *on a reading* if, and only if, there is a conditional S_3 of which S_1 is the antecedent and S_2 is the consequent and S_3 is analytic on a reading or S_3 is metalinguistically true on a reading.[5]

(D14) S_1 *fully entails* S_2 if, and only if, there is a conditional S_3 of which S_1 is the antecedent and S_2 is the consequent and S_3 is analytic on every reading or S_3 is metalinguistically true on every reading.[5]

Due to technicalities, we shall not go into the syntactic

[5] A discussion of metalinguistically true sentences follows on pages 220–223. These clauses in (D13) and (D14) are included to handle entailments such as "Plato is dead" by either "Gregory knows Plato is dead" or "It is certain Plato is dead." Such cases are not treated as analytic conditionals because their truth depends not on vacuity of predication, but on the semantic structure of a constituent sentence (the subordinate sentence of the conditional) satisfying a condition imposed by the meaning of a particular word in the matrix sentence ("knows" and "certain" in the above examples).

considerations involved in identifying conditional sentences.[6] Rather, we shall assume that conditionals each have underlying phrase markers composed of two phrase markers conjoined by an element with the categorical status of a subordinating conjunction, subcategorized as a conditional. Let 'CS' stand for a conditional sentence and 'S_1' and 'S_2' stand, respectively, for its antecedent and consequent sentences. Let '$R_{1,2}$' be a reading for CS, where $R_{1,2}$ is formed from the readings R_1 for S_1 and R_2 for S_2, and where, in turn, R_1 is formed from the readings R_{Subj_1} and R_{Pred_1}, (respectively, the readings for the subject and the predicate of S_1) and R_2 is formed from the readings R_{Subj_2} and R_{Pred_2}, (respectively, the readings for the subject and predicate of S_2). Finally, let the relation $R_{Const_i} \varphi R_{Const_j}$ (where the symbol 'Const' stands for a constituent) hold just in case every noncomplex semantic marker in R_{Const_j} also occurs in R_{Const_i} and for any complex semantic marker $((M_1) \cup (M_2) \cup \ldots \cup (M_n))$ in R_{Const_j} there is an (M_k) in R_{Const_i} such that $1 \leq k \leq n$, and R_{Const_i} does not contain any antonymous semantic markers.

(D15)　CS *is analytic on the reading* $R_{1,2}$ if, and only if, it is both the case that $R_{Subj_1} \varphi R_{Subj_2}$ and that $R_{Pred_1} \varphi R_{Pred_2}$.

From the definition of $R_{Const_i} \varphi R_{Const_j}$ and the use of this concept in (D15), it is clear that (D15) is a direct extension of (D7). The following examples illustrate the types of conditional sentences whose analyticity by (D15) provides a basis for asserting that their consequents are

---

[6] The structure of an underlying phrase marker of a sentence will indicate whether or not that sentence is a conditional, and if so, what type of conditional it is.

entailed by their antecedents: 'If that person is a spinster, then that person is female,' 'If that spinster is foolish, then a woman is foolish,' and 'If that spinster is someone's aunt, then a woman is someone's relative.' The sentence 'If that person is a spinster, then that person is foolish' is not marked as analytic by (D15), as indeed it should not be, but, on a suitably formulated parallel of (D11), it will be marked as synthetic. Thus, the truth of such a sentence is not based on meaning but on the existence of an empirical regularity to the effect that any spinster is, as a matter of fact, foolish.

Although we have defined entailment in terms of the analyticity of the conditional, it was by no means necessary for us to have done so. We choose this approach because it brings out the relationship between entailment and analyticity and because a semantic theory must define analyticity for conditional sentences anyway. But by defining entailment as the analyticity of the conditional we thereby make the existence of entailment in a language depend on the existence of an appropriate class of conditional sentences in that language. If there were a language in which conditional sentences did not occur but there were pairs of sentences, one of which entailed the other, e.g., 'Mary is a spinster' and 'Mary is female', then, on our present definition of entailment, it would not be possible to mark such pairs as cases of entailment. It might also be objected that we are falsely claiming that a speaker can only determine entailments by first formulating the appropriate conditional sentences. However, neither of these possible objections need be taken seriously. Aside from the fact that there is good reason to believe that no genuine natural language lacks the means for constructing conditional sentences and no good reason to believe that the formulation of conditionals is not somehow the basis on which a speaker determines entailments, there is a simple extension of (D15) that does not depend on the notion of a conditional sentence. We can define S_1 *entails S_2 on the reading* $R_{1,2}$ by the condition that it is both the case that $R_{\text{Subj}_1} \varphi R_{\text{Subj}_2}$ and $R_{\text{Pred}_1} \varphi R_{\text{Pred}_2}$.

We cannot here carry the analysis of the concept of analyticity any further. We cannot, for example, give a full discussion of the analyticity of syntactically compound sentences such as 'The man who loaned the book to someone loaned someone a book,' 'The man who loaned the book to someone loaned someone something,' 'Dogs that bark bark,' 'People who are friendly and reasonable are friendly,' etc. But we can provide a sketch of the treatment of such cases. The underlying phrase marker for such sentences will have the general form:

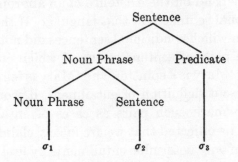

We can regard such underlying phrase markers as being composed of two phrase marker components, what we can refer to as the *matrix component*, the whole underlying phrase marker minus the branch under the highest node labelled 'Noun Phrase' which develops into an internal occurrence of 'Sentence' and minus whatever this occurrence of 'Sentence' dominates, and what we can refer to as the *maximal constituent component*, this first internal occurrence of 'Sentence' under the highest node labelled 'Noun Phrase' and whatever it dominates. Of course, the maximal constituent component can itself have recursive sentence-developments within it, just as the predicate of the matrix component can have such sentence developments in it. In terms, of this distinction, we introduce the symbols '$S_{\sigma_1\sigma_2}$' and 'S_{σ_2}' to refer, respectively, to the matrix sentence and the maximal constituent sentence. With respect to the examples above, we have, for the first, $S_{\sigma_1\sigma_2} = $ *The man loaned someone a book* and $S_{\sigma_2} = $ *The man loaned the book to someone*, for the second, $S_{\sigma_1\sigma_2} = $ *The man loaned someone something* and $S_{\sigma_2} = $ *The man loaned the book to someone*, for the third, $S_{\sigma_2\sigma_2} = $ *Dogs bark* and $S_{\sigma_2} = $ *Dogs bark*, and for the fourth, $S_{\sigma_1\sigma_2} = $ *People are friendly* and $S_{\sigma_2} = $ *People are friendly and reasonable*. Now, if we take the symbol 'S^*' to range over syntactically compound non-copula sentences:

(D16) S^* is analytic on a reading $R(S_{\sigma_1\sigma_2\sigma_2})$ if, and only if, $R(S_{\sigma_1\sigma_2})$ φ $R(S_{\sigma_2})$.

By (D16), our examples are each marked analytic, and, referring back to (D15), it is seen that they are so marked on the same basis as their corresponding conditional versions, i.e., 'If the man loaned a book to some-

one, then he loaned someone a book,' 'If the man loaned
the book to someone, then he loaned someone something,'
'If dogs bark, then they bark,' and 'If people are friendly
and reasonable, then they are friendly,' are marked analytic. Further, we can also introduce a definition for contradiction and a definition for syntheticity:

(D17) $S*$ *is contradictory on a reading* $R(S_{\sigma_1\sigma_2\sigma_3})$ if, and only
if, the reading for σ_3 and the reading for the predicate
of σ_2 contain different semantic markers from the same
antonymous n-tuple of semantic markers and σ_1 does
not itself contain any antonymous semantic markers.

(D18) $S*$ *is synthetic on a reading* $R(S_{\sigma_1\sigma_2\sigma_3})$ if, and only if,
there is a reading $R(S_{\sigma_1\sigma_2\sigma_3})$ assigned to $S*$'s sentence-
constituent such that $S*$ is neither analytic nor contra-
dictory on that reading and σ_1 does not itself contain
any antonymous semantic markers.

These definitions permit us to mark sentences such as
'Men who are old are young,' 'A woman who is married
is a spinster,' etc., as contradictory, and to mark a sentence such as 'Men who are old like girls who are young'
as synthetic, which if treated by definition (D9) would
be incorrectly marked as contradictory because the reading of its subject 'men who are old' contains semantic
markers that are antonymous with one in the reading of
its predicate 'like girls who are young.' This, then, is further motivation for this treatment of the concepts of
analyticity, contradiction, and syntheticity for syntactically compound non-copula sentences. Note, finally, that
definitions (D8), (D10), and (D12) do not need to be
supplemented in the manner in which we have supplemented definitions (D7), (D9), and (D11).

Next, we must fill out the semantic classification of types of sentences. This will explain the clause attached to the above definitions requiring that the reading of the subject of the sentence not contain a pair of antonymous semantic markers. Thus, we give the following two definitions:

(D19) *S is indeterminable on the reading $R_{1,2}$* if, and only if, *S* has a reading $R_{1,2}$ and the reading for its subject R_1 contains two different semantic markers from the same antonymous *n*-tuple of semantic markers.

(D20) *S is fully indeterminable* if, and only if, *S* is indeterminable on every reading assigned to its sentence-constituent.

With these two further definitions, we obtain the following classification of sentences:

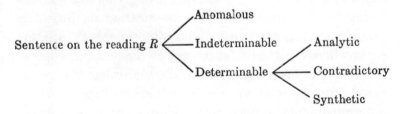

The rationale for (D19), which establishes the class of indeterminable sentences, involves a variety of considerations. Primarily, it involves a fundamental semantic distinction between the subject and the predicate of a sentence, with conditional sentences and the like being treated, as indicated above, in terms of the subjects and predicates of their component sentences. This distinction is based on the traditional idea that the subject is the term or expression that denotes that about which a declarative sentence states something, while the predicate is the expression that indicates the property, quality, etc., that the declarative sentence states is a property, quality, etc., of what is denoted by its subject. Thus, in general, whether or not a declarative sentence is true or false depends on whether or not that which its subject denotes has the property, quality, etc., ascribed to it in the predication. Analyticity is the case where truth is necessary because meaning of the subject includes the concepts expressed in the predicate, and the correctness of the predication is thereby guaranteed on linguistic grounds. Correspondingly, contradiction is the case where falsity is necessary because the meaning of the subject includes a concept that is incompatible with some component concepts in the meaning of the predicate, thereby guaranteeing the incorrectness of the predication on linguistic grounds. Synthetic truth and synthetic falsity are the cases where truth and falsity are contingent on whether or not what the subject denotes actually has the predicated property, quality, etc., as a matter of fact. But indeterminableness differs from each of these cases because of the inapplicability of questions of truth and falsity. Indeterminableness is the case where neither truth nor falsity, either of the linguistic or contingent variety, can obtain because there is necessarily nothing that the subject of an indeterminable sentence can denote, since its meaning contains incompatible concepts.

The class of indeterminable sentences must be disjoint from the class of synthetic sentences. These two classes must not have a member in common because such a sentence could not be synthetic in the intended sense. That is, its truth or falsity could not depend on a matter of fact, since, owing to the contradictoriness of its subject, there could not be anything about which to predicate a property, quality, etc. To put the matter another way, construing such a sentence as a genuine synthetic sentence would mean saying that there both is and is not something denoted by its subject. For a genuine synthetic sentence is either true or false. If true, there is something denoted by its subject, and that thing has the property, quality, etc., predicated of it. If false, there must be something denoted by its subject of which the predication fails. But, then, in either case, there is something denoted by its subject. However, the fact that its subject is, *ex hypothesi*, contradictory implies that there is nothing denoted by its subject. Therefore, because the internal inconsistency of the subject of an indeterminable sentence precludes it from being about anything, such sentences are not the sorts of sentences whose truth or falsity can be determined on the basis of factual considerations, and so indeterminable sentences must be distinguished from synthetic sentences.

Before considering why the class of indeterminable sentences must be disjoint also from both the class of analytic and the class of contradictory sentences, let us consider some points related to the foregoing matter. Sentences such as 'A female king is generous' and 'Living men who are dead prefer chocolate to vanilla,' which are straightforward cases of indeterminable sentences, are in

214 THE PHILOSOPHY OF LANGUAGE

a sense analogous to certain synthetic sentences, such
as 'A golden mountain has pine trees on it,' 'Witches have
a special dislike for New Yorkers,' 'The creatures that
now inhabit the moon prefer vanilla to chocolate,' and
so on, which are straightforward synthetic sentences. The
respect in which these synthetic sentences are like indeterminable ones is that their subjects do not denote anything and so they cannot be either true or false. But, note
that in the case of indeterminable sentences semantic
considerations alone suffice to decide that the subject of
the sentence cannot denote, whereas in the case of such
synthetic sentences this decision is a matter of fact. The
difference between indeterminable sentences and such
synthetic sentences is, then, that in the latter case there
are no semantic grounds on which to say that there is
nothing that their subjects denote, so that they fail to
be either true or false for quite different reasons. That
is, although their subjects do not denote, it is not necessary that they do not. For all we know about language,
there could be golden mountains, witches, and creatures
now inhabiting the moon. Of course, as a matter of empirical fact, we know that there are no such things, and
if we make the factual assumption that there are no such
things, then, on this assumption, such synthetic sentences
are like indeterminable sentences in the respect that they
cannot be true or false. Consequently, our analysis of indeterminable sentences suggests a way of accounting for
the situation where a synthetic sentence has a subject
which we know on factual grounds does not denote anything: such sentences are neither true nor false because

they fail to meet a condition on their making a genuine assertion. Indeterminable sentences fail the same condition, but their failure is a linguistic not a factual matter. We can think of this condition as built into the notion of a declarative synthetic sentence, but we cannot go into this suggestion here.

The next consideration in the rationale for distinguishing a class of indeterminable sentences has to do with why they are to be distinguished from analytic and contradictory sentences. Suppose we did not distinguish them from analytic and contradictory sentences, i.e., suppose the definitions (D7), (D9), and (D15) did not contain a necessary condition to the effect that the reading for the subject of a sentence must not contain two semantic markers from the same antonymous n-tuple of semantic markers. In this case a sentence like 'A female king is male' would be both analytic and contradictory.[7] That is, the theory of language would commit us to hold that such a sentence is both true and false, since, on the one hand, the concept of maleness is included in that of a male monarch, and, on the other, the concept of maleness is incompatible with the concept of femaleness. For this reason, then, we have made the class of indeterminable sentences disjoint from both the analytic and contradictory sentences by including in the definitions for these notions the condition that the subject's reading not contain distinct semantic markers drawn from the same antonymous n-tuple. Note that this condition must be

[7] I wish to thank Hans G. Herzberger for this example and also for discussing my treatment of it with me.

included in the definitions of *both* 'analytic sentence' and 'contradictory sentence,' since, as we have shown above, the denial of an analytic sentence is contradictory and the denial of a contradictory sentence is analytic. Thus, including this condition in the definition of one of these notions requires its inclusion in other in order to preserve our formal reconstruction of the principle that analyticity and contradiction are inversely related with respect to negation.

Consequently, the class of indeterminable sentences is mutually exclusive with the classes of anomalous sentences, analytic sentences, contradictory sentences, and synthetic sentences. Indeterminable sentences are cases where, by virtue of the meanings of their component words, it is necessary that they have no truth value because there can be nothing to which the attribution expressed in the predication can be made. The over-all systematization of indeterminable sentences within the framework of semantic theory provides a formal explanation of why sentences such as 'A female king is male,' 'A female king is generous,' etc., do not express truths or falsehoods and thus also provides a formal reconstruction of an essential condition on sentences which can express truths or falsehoods.

The logician will notice that my treatment of analytic, contradictory, synthetic, and indeterminable sentences is quite independent of truth functional logic and quantification theory. Sentences such as 'Any person who is female and not female is generous,' 'All female men are generous,' etc., are not, on my account, correctly trans-

lated into the propositional form '$(x)(P_x \cdot \sim P_x \supset Q_x)$';
thus they are not logical truths; and sentences such as
'Some persons who are female and not female are generous,' 'Some female man is generous,' etc., are not, on
my account, correctly translated into the propositional
form '$(\exists x)(P_x \cdot \sim P_x \cdot Q_x)$'; thus they are not logical
falsehoods. This does not mean to imply that a logician
would so translate such sentences, but only that criticism
of my account which is based on such translations and
which argues that my treatment of such sentences does
not square with truth functional logic and quantification
theory because some sentences we regard as indeterminable are truths while others are falsehoods is based on an
unacceptable assumption about translation from natural
language into logical notation. Also, the principle that a
logically false proposition implies any proposition has no
counterpart in my system because this principle rests on
the idea of material implication, while my system rests
on semantic relations such as entailment. Thus, we would
regard criticism to the effect that my system does not
reconstruct such principles of truth functional logic and
quantification theory missing the point both with respect
to the character of my system of semantics and to the
proper translation of sentences from natural language
into logical formulas.

Another question that arises in connection with the
concept of an indeterminable sentence is why we do not
also consider all sentences with contradictory predicates
to be indeterminable sentences. Sentences with contradictory predicates divide into two groups, those with contra-

dictory subjects and those without contradictory subjects. The former do not require special consideration
because they already fall in the category of indeterminable sentences. The latter, on the other hand, do not belong in that category. Consider a sentence of the latter
sort, such as 'The table is round and square' or 'Your
friend loves someone who is male and female' or 'He is
a living dead man'; these sentences are not indeterminable in the sense we have used but are rather contradictory
sentences in that they involve incompatible predications
made of the same unproblematic subject. Thus, instead
of expanding the definition of indeterminable sentence to
include such cases, we expand the definition of contradictory, syntactically compound sentences to include them.
We can add to (D17) the further condition that S^* is
contradictory on a reading in case there are two constituent sentences of the predicate of S^* such that their readings contain a different semantic marker from the
same antonymous n-tuple of semantic markers. The reason for handling this matter by so extending (D17) instead of expanding the definition of 'indeterminable sentence' to cover these cases is not only that they are indeed
cases of incompatible predication, and thus semantically
equivalent to those covered already by (D17), but also
that this method preserves the essential asymmetry between the subject and predicate of a sentence on which
our semantic interpretation of this grammatical relation
depends. That is, on this interpretation, the subject's
reading determines the thing about which the sentence
predicates something, while the predicate's determines

what is predicated, so that the operation of combining them reconstructs the assertion that is made by the sentence. Accordingly, this interpretation requires an asymmetry between that about which assertion is made and what is asserted of it, either consistently or inconsistently.

Furthermore, it should be made clear that, on this way of handling the matter, the sentence 'John hit a female man' and its passive, 'A female man was hit by John,' are both contradictory, whereas the sentence 'A female man hit John' and its passive, 'John was hit by a female man,' are both indeterminable. The reason is that in the former cases the subject is 'John' in both instances, which is certainly not internally inconsistent, while in the latter cases the subject is 'a female man' in both instances, which is internally inconsistent. For an active and its corresponding passive, on a transformational syntactic component, have the same subject and predicate. The point that must be kept in mind is that the subject of a passive sentence is determined by its underlying phrase marker, not by its final derived phrase marker in which the subject and object are in inverted order with respect to the corresponding active sentence and its underlying phrase marker. Also, one must bear in mind that the 'topic' of the sentence, the leftmost noun phrase in the final derived phrase marker of a sentence, does not coincide with the subject of the sentence in the case of passives.

One final point in this connection. Indeterminable sentences, unlike anomalous sentences, have readings and, therefore, they can bear semantic relations to one another. For example, the sentences 'A female man hit John' and 'John was hit by a female man' are genuine paraphrases, and will be marked as such on the basis of their semantic interpretations. This illustrates another facet of the distinction between paraphrase and logical equivalence in the usual sense of necessarily equivalent in conditions for truth and falsity. But it also illustrates the fact that a semantic relation, such as paraphrase, holds between sentences within the same general class of sentences, so that if one term of such a relation is indeterminable, so is the other, and if one term is not, neither is the other.

In concluding this discussion, we make one comment about the scope of analyticity as here defined. Analyticity in the above sense does not exhaust the range of truths that are such by virtue of the meanings of their component words without appeal to matters of fact. The failure of previous discussions to arrive at a precisely defined concept of analyticity and the tendency to apply this term to any sentence whose truth is guaranteed by meaning alone has either obscured the existence of other types of linguistic truths or led to their being misclassified as analytic truths. We want to consider one type of non-analytic linguistic truth in order to exhibit a limit on the scope of analyticity in natural language and we will leave open the question of whether this is the only such type.

Natural languages have various methods of commenting on their own sentences. In English, and other languages also, we find sentences specially designed to say something about other sentences, such as 'It is [   ] that S,'

'That S is [   ],' ' "S" is [   ],' 'The sentence S is [   ],' etc., where 'S' is a variable over sentences and '[   ]' represents some metalinguistic expression such as 'contradictory' (or in this sense 'impossible'), 'analytic,' 'synthetic,' 'anomalous' (or in this sense 'nonsense,' 'absurd,' etc.), 'ambiguous,' etc. Sentences such as 'The sentence spinsters are males is contradictory,' 'That trees are generous is absurd,' 'It is analytic that bachelors are unmarried,' ' "Old ladies like civil engineers" is ambiguous,' 'It is possible that the moon is made of green cheese' are true independent cf fact, while sentences such as 'The sentence spinsters are unpleasant is contradictory,' 'That trees are cut down for fire wood is absurd,' 'It is analytic that bachelors are intelligent,' ' "Old ladies like civil engineers" is not ambiguous,' 'It is possible that bachelors are female' are false independent of fact. The former cases are not analytic in the sense of my reconstruction of Kant's notion, i.e., they are not true by virtue of the fact that what is predicated is already a property of the subject definitionally. And the latter cases are not contradictory in the sense of my reconstruction of the concept of a contradictory sentence, i.e., they are not false by virtue of the fact that what is predicated of the subject is incompatible with one of its definitional properties. Rather, the former cases are true because the semantic structure of the constituent sentence is what it is claimed to be by the metalinguistic predicate, whereas the latter cases are false because their semantic structure is not what it is claimed to be. There is no analogue to synthetic sentences among the metalinguistic sentences.

We can handle these cases by introducing as a reading for the expressions 'contradictory,' 'impossible,' 'analytic,' 'synthetic,' 'nonsense,' 'ambiguous,' etc., conditions on the semantically interpreted underlying phrase marker for the constituent sentence which requires that it have the formal features that would satisfy the definition for the appropriate metalinguistic property. Thus, the lexical reading for 'contradictory' and one lexical reading for 'impossible' would be the condition that defines 'contradictory sentence' in the theory of language; the lexical reading for 'nonsense' or 'anomalous' would be the condition that defines 'anomalous sentence' in the theory of language; and so forth. We would also introduce the two further definitions:

(D21) *S is metalinguistically true* if, and only if, the semantically interpreted underlying phrase marker for its constituent sentence satisfies the condition in the reading for its metalinguistic predicate.

(D22) *S is metalinguistically false* if, and only if, the semantically interpreted underlying phrase marker for its constituent sentence does not satisfy the condition in the reading for its metalinguistic predicate.

Thus, by (D21), the sentence " 'the spinsters are males' is contradictory" is metalinguistically true because the constituent sentence 'spinsters are males' has the semantic structure which makes it contradictory by (D9) and this is what the metalinguistic predicate requires. Also, by (D22), the sentence " 'the sentence spinsters are unpleasant' is contradictory" is metalinguistically false because the constituent sentence 'spinsters are unpleasant' does not have the semantic structure which makes it contradictory, whereas the metalinguistic predicate requires that it have such semantic structure.

These additions to semantic theory enable us to distinguish and formally reconstruct another type of linguistic truth, one that involves a relation between two sentences, one of which talks about the semantic structure of the other. The fact that this relation is explicated in the same theory that describes the semantic structure of the sentence talked about is no more peculiar than that both sentences are expressed in the same natural language.

Given that it is possible to mark sentences *linguistically true* and *linguistically false,* either because they are analytic or metalinguistically true, on the one hand, or because they are contradictory or metalinguistically false, on the other, it is also possible to mark sentences that are conjunctions and disjunctions of such linguistic truths and falsehoods as either true or false. Suppose, following propositional logic, we construe the words 'and' and 'or' to have a reading that formulates the truth conditions for such compound sentences in terms of the truth values of their components. Thus, the truth condition for 'and' is that both components are true, and the truth condition for 'or' is that at least one is true. Consequently, on the basis of the semantically interpreted underlying phrase markers for such compound sentences and the definitions in semantic theory for 'analytic,' 'contradictory,' 'synthetic,' 'metalinguistically true,' and 'metalinguistically false,' it will be possible to mark each such compound sentence as linguistically true, linguistically

false, or linguistically undetermined (e.g., in the case
where we have a conjunction containing a synthetic sentence as a conjunct). But we cannot go into the details of
this interesting problem here.

SEMANTIC CATEGORIES

Early in the study of conceptual knowledge, philosophers sought to order concepts from all fields of knowledge in terms of their degree of abstractness. The major
systematic treatment of the most general classes into
which concepts divide was given by Aristotle. Aristotelian
categories claim to be the most general classificational di-
visions under which ideas of any sort can be subsumed.
They are the ultimate, unanalyzable, maximally abstract
set of natural kinds that are given in natural language.
Aristotle enumerated ten (perhaps eight) such
categories: substance, quantity, quality, relation, place,
time, posture, possession, action, and passivity (with the
last two of somewhat questionable status). But Aristotle
neither shows how he erected these categories nor how
to determine exactly the membership of this set. Moreover, he gives us only the roughest indication of the criterion by which these particular ten categories can be
picked out from other contenders. Namely, each is the
most general answer to a question of the form 'What is
X?' Thus, substance is a category because 'a substance'
or 'substances' is the most general answer to questions

such as 'What is Socrates?,' 'What is the earth?,' 'What are tables?,' etc. Likewise, quality is a category because 'a quality' is the most general answer to such questions as 'What is greenness?,' 'What is smoothness?,' 'What is roundness?,' and so forth for each of the others on Aristotle's list. But even if this rough test were an adequate criterion for categoryhood, it would tell us nothing about the nature of what it sorted out, since its application relies on intuitive judgments about what are and what are not the most general answers to the test questions. That is, even if those things that are proper answers to such questions are just those things that are the most general types or genera for classifying every possible idea, still we know no more about the concept of category than before we obtained its extension in this manner. The criterion itself presupposes our intuitive understanding of the notion of maximal generality as a condition of its application without providing any analysis of it. Yet this notion is central to the concept of category.

Philosophical concepts that are as loosely defined as this are sooner or later singled out for criticism by subsequent philosophers, and here we have no exception. We may mention two criticisms. Arnauld wrote, "To speak the truth, they are in themselves of very little use; they help but slightly in the formation of judgments, the true end of logic. Indeed, they often hinder this formation considerably . . . . These Categories are regarded as being established by reason and by truth, rather than as entirely arbitrary, and founded on the imagination of a man who had no authority to prescribe a law to others.

For others have just as much right to arrange the objects
of thought in another way, each according to his own
manner of philosophizing."[8] Kant criticized Aristotle's
theory in the following terms: He agreed with Aristotle's
linguistic approach, saying that "To search in our
common knowledge for the concepts which do not rest
upon particular experience and yet occur in all knowledge
from experience, of which they as it were constitute the
mere form of connection, presupposes neither greater reflection nor deeper insight than to detect in a language
the rules of the actual use of words generally and thus to
collect elements for a grammar"[9] (here 'grammar' is intended in the wide sense to include semantics). But he
pointed out that in Aristotle's theory ". . . we are not
able to give a reason why each language has just this
and no other formal constitution, and still less why any
precise number of such formal determinations in general,
neither more nor less, can be found in it."[10] "This
rhapsody," by which Kant means Aristotle's set of
categories, "must be considered (and commended) as a
mere hint for future inquirers, not as an ideal developed
according to rule; and hence it has, in the present more
advanced state of philosophy, been rejected as quite
useless."[11]

We may reformulate and supplement these criticisms
as follows. First, Aristotle's system of categories does not
itself, and is not embedded within a more general theory

---

[8] A. Arnauld, *The Art of Thinking*, Bobbs-Merrill Company, 1964.
[9] Kant, *A Prolegomena to Any Future Metaphysic*.
[10] *Ibid.*
[11] *Ibid*

that might, provide us with an explanation as to why all natural languages utilize just these categories; why, that is, the categories set forth in Aristotle's particular proposal ought to be regarded as linguistically universal in scope. Second, Aristotle's account is arbitrary because it does not answer the question of why these categories should be *the* categories of language and not others. His account provides no means for deciding empirically what are and what are not genuine semantic categories of language. As Arnauld points out, we are given no idea of how to empirically assess the claim that a certain concept is a genuine semantic category. Thus, we have no means to determine if a set of categories is correct and exhaustive. Third, there is no theoretically satisfactory statement that explains what a category is. Moreover, there is no explanation of the kind of structure that a system of categories exhibits, and no explanation of how one is to go about showing that a certain structural relation alleged to hold among a set of categories does, in fact, hold. Finally, neither Aristotle nor Kant considers the relation of a theory of categories to other theories having to do with the structure of language. In particular, no account is given as to how semantic categories are related to syntactic structure. However, since we are not here to criticize Aristotelian categories, but to resurrect them, we shall argue that these difficulties can be removed in principle if the theory of semantic categories is incorporated into the theory of language in the way to be suggested.

The task of the theory of language is to set forth the linguistic universals. 'Formal universals' prescribe the form of a linguistic description of a particular language, i.e., the way in which the syntactic, phonological, and semantic components are related, the form of the rules in each component, and their relations to one another. They are distinguished from 'substantive universals' which are generalizations, not about the form of linguistic descriptions, but about the constructs which are used in particular rules of the form specified by the formal universals. Such a generalization says that certain syntactic, phonological, or semantic constructs are used in the construction of certain rules of any linguistic description. Alternatively, such a generalization says that the property or relation represented by the construct is a feature of the syntactic, phonological, or semantic structure of natural languages.

We can embed the theory of semantic categories into the theory of language by regarding the semantic categories of language to be given by a subset of those semantic markers which semantic theory specifies as substantive universals. The semantic categories can thus be distinguished from the syntactic and phonological categories, and the claim that something is a semantic category can be interpreted in a straightforward way as the empirical claim that it is an essential feature of the theoretical vocabulary for the construction of particular linguistic descriptions. We must now provide some empirically motivated means for determining the semantic categories of language and the semantic categories of a particular language L which fits into the model of a linguistic description already presented.

As we have characterized the entries for lexical items in the dictionary, lexical readings contain a semantic marker for each independent conceptual component of the sense of the lexical item that they represent. Formulated in this way, almost every lexical reading will exhibit some amount of redundancy in the manner in which it specifies the semantic information in a sense. For example, the semantic markers (Physical Object) and (Human) that appear in the lexical readings for the words 'bachelor,' 'man,' 'spinster,' 'child,' 'uncle,' 'priest,' etc., are subject to a regularity governing their occurrence with respect to one another in the dictionary: whenever (Human) occurs in a lexical reading, so does (Physical Object), but the converse is, of course, not true (as examples such as the lexical readings for 'hammer,' 'bear,' 'potato,' etc., would show). Thus, the occurrence of (Physical Object) is actually redundant in the lexical readings for 'bachelor,' 'man,' 'spinster,' 'child,' etc., by virtue of the generalization that expresses this regularity. However, at present, we have no way to express this regularity in the formalism of the theory of language so that the redundancy of (Physical Object) for these cases is forced on us in order that we be able to fully represent the senses of these words. Without a means for expressing such regularities, linguistic descriptions that are written in accord with the theory of language, as so far formulated, can be correctly criticized for having missed an important generalization about their languages. With a means of representing such regularities, the actual occurrence of the semantic marker (Physical Object) is dispensible because its occurrence in the lexical readings for 'bachelor,' 'man,' 'spinster,' etc., is predictable from the occurrence of (Human) in these lexical readings and the generalization that says that (Human) never occurs in a lexical reading unless (Physical Object) occurs. Moreover, this case is not an isolated one. Not only is there a broader regularity covering the occurrence of (Physical Object), *viz.*, whenever (Human), (Animal), (Artifact), (Plant), etc., occurs in a lexical reading, so does (Physical Object), but other semantic markers besides (Physical Object) are redundant in the same way and are similarly predictable from generalizations expressing the appropriate regularities, *viz.*, (Animal) occurs whenever (Mammal) does. Hence, from the viewpoint of the whole dictionary with its thousands of entries, there will be an incredible amount of redundancy in the specification of the senses of lexical items unless we provide some way to eliminate such unnecessary occurrences of semantic markers by finding some formalism to express the appropriate lexical generalizations.

The obvious way to make dictionary entries more economical and to provide a means of expressing these regularities is to extend the conception of the dictionary presented in Chapter 4 so that the dictionary includes rules which state the appropriate generalizations and thereby enable us to exclude redundant semantic markers from lexical readings. In general, these rules will be of the form

$$[(M_1) \lor (M_2) \lor \ldots \lor (M_n)] \to (M_k)$$

where (M_k) is distinct from each (M_i), $1 \leq i \leq n$ and where $\lor$ is the symbol for disjunction. In the case discussed above, we have an example of a rule of this type:

$$[(M_1) \lor (M_2) \lor \ldots \lor (\text{Human}) \lor (\text{Animal}) \lor$$
$$(\text{Artifact}) \lor (\text{Plant}) \lor \ldots \lor (M_n)] \to (\text{Physical Object})$$

Adding this rule to the dictionary will enable us to capitalize on the regularity noted above and economize lexical readings that contain one of the semantic markers (M_1) (M_2), $\ldots$, (Human), (Animal), (Artifact), (Plant), $\ldots$, (M_n) by dropping the occurrence of the semantic marker (Physical Object). Such rules will comprise a new component of the dictionary, whose list of entries can now be regarded as containing only lexical readings in maximally reduced form. They thus function to enable us to compress the readings in dictionary entries. But they also operate as expansion rules by applying to lexical readings once those readings are assigned to the terminal nodes of an underlying phrase marker. That is, just after the operation of the rule (I) of Chapter 4 and just prior to the operation of the projection rules, these redundancy rules come into operation. They expand a lexical reading associated with a node in an underlying phrase marker by introducing into it the semantic markers on the right-hand side of those redundancy rules whose left-hand side is satisfied by the semantic markers already present in the reading. For example, since the lexical reading for 'child' has the sematic marker (Human), the redundancy rule presented above

expands this reading by introducing the semantic marker
(Physical Object), which it did not previously contain
because this reading was in maximally reduced form in
the dictionary. The reason why the redundancy rules
must operate at this point is that the projection rules
require the semantic markers that are introduced by
these rules in order to have the information they need
to determine whether or not selection restrictions are
satisfied. That is, the semantic markers introduced in this
way are required by the projection rules in order for them
to combine the right lexical readings in the formation of
the derived readings for the higher levels constituents of
sentences. For example, the semantic marker (Physical
Object) is required in the reading for 'child' in order that
this reading satisfy the selection restriction in the reading
for the verb 'hit' in the partially semantically interpreted
underlying phrase marker for the sentence 'The child hit
the ground with a thud.' Without this marker in this
reading, there would not be a combination of the subject's reading with the reading for the predicate and the
sentence would neither be marked as nonanomalous nor
be given its proper sentence-readings. Note also that it
would be mistaken to argue that the redundancy rules
need not be used to expand lexical readings on the
grounds that the semantic markers introduced by these
rules are not needed to obtain proper derived readings,
since, for example, the selection restriction for 'hit' might
be stated in terms of a disjunction of semantic markers
such as (Human), (Animal), (Artifact), etc., instead of
(Physical Object). But such a treatment would over-

whelmingly complicate the formulation of selection restrictions and would miss generalizations such as that it is only by virtue of being a physical object that something can hit something else.

So much for the formalism. The redundancy rules not only economize the formulation of the dictionary and state generalizations, they also represent inclusion relations among the concepts which semantic markers represent. For such rules can be interpreted as saying that the concepts represented by the semantic markers on the left-hand side are included under the concept represented by the semantic marker on the right-hand side. Here, then, is where the application of this formalism to the problem of semantic categories enters. With this interpretation of the redundancy rules, we can formally determine which of the semantic markers in a linguistic description of a language L are the *semantic categories of L*. Let

(RRL) $[(M_1^1) \lor (M_2^1) \lor \ldots \lor (M_g^1)] \to (M_p)$

$[(M_1^2) \lor (M_2^2) \lor \ldots \lor (M_h^2)] \to (M_q)$

$$\bullet$$
$$\bullet$$
$$\bullet$$

$[(M_1^n) \lor (M_2^n) \lor \ldots \lor (M_i^n)] \to (M_r)$

be the redundancy rules in the dictionary of the linguistic description for the language L. We can define *a semantic category of L* to be any concept represented by a semantic marker that occurs on the right-hand side of some rule in (RRL) but does not occur on the left-hand side of any rule in (RRL). Thus, to find the semantic categories of a particular natural language, we simply check over the list of redundancy rules in the linguistic description of L and pick out each semantic marker for which there is a rule saying that that marker subsumes other markers under it but for which none of the rules say that the marker is subsumed under other semantic markers. The significance of this definition is that it makes it possible empirically to justify claims to the effect that such and such concepts, and only these, are the semantic categories of a certain language and that it explicates the notion of a concept's being maximally general that enters into the notion of its being a genuine semantic category. Such justification for putative semantic categories is simply a matter of empirically establishing that no simpler statement of the lexical readings for the dictionary of the language is provided by redundancy rules other than those which, by the given definition of semantic categories of L, yield the semantic categories in question. This, it is to be noticed, is the same sort of empirical justification used in other branches of science when it is claimed that some theoretical account is best because it is based on the simplest set of laws for describing the phenomena.

In essentially the same way, we can use redundancy rules to obtain the *semantic categories of language*, i.e., the semantic categories for all natural languages as opposed to the semantic categories of a particular language. This is obviously the philosophically more significant notion, although philosophers have not clearly distinguished the two. Roughly, the semantic categories of language are those concepts represented by the semantic markers belonging to the intersection of the sets of semantic categories for particular languages, as obtained in the manner just described. That is, they are those concepts represented by the semantic markers found in each and every set of semantic categories for particular languages. Let us suppose, then, that there are semantic categories of language, and ask how we can represent them in the theory of language and show that some set of semantic markers correctly represents them.

There will be a set of redundancy rules that is the intersection of the sets of redundancy rules found in the dictionaries of linguistic descriptions of each particular language. These will be the universal redundancy rules, which may be referred to with '(URR).' If we were to explicitly include the rules (URR) among the redundancy rules for each linguistic description, we would make the same kind of mistake that was avoided by having redundancy rules in the first place. That is, we would have missed generalizations that hold across languages (that the regularities expressed in the rules in (URR) are universally valid) and we would have unnecessarily complicated the description of particular languages by writing down the same set of redundancy rules each time we construct a linguistic description of another language. This complication is quite considerable, since the description of natural languages is thus complicated by a factor that is a function of both the number of such redundancy rules and the number of languages to be de-

scribed. We can avoid both these undesirable
consequences if we take the natural recourse of stating
the rules in (URR) once within the theory of language
and not stating them as a component of the redundancy
rules for particular linguistic descriptions. Stated within
the theory of language, (URR) becomes part of that theory's characterization of the semantic component of a linguistic description. The theory of language will specify
that once the rule (I) has operated to associate lexical
readings with terminal symbols in underlying phrase
markers, the set of redundancy rules specific to and
found within the semantic component of the linguistic
description of a particular language operates to further
expand these lexical readings. Then the rules in (URR)
operate to still further expand those lexical readings.
Thus, by including (URR) within the theory of language,
rather than in each individual linguistic description, we
can both state that the generalizations expressing the
inclusion relations concerned are linguistic universals and
economize the formulation of linguistic descriptions.

Given the set (URR), we can formally determine the
set of semantic categories of language, i.e., determine
which of the semantic markers specified in the theory of
language as substantive universals represent the most
general classes of concepts. A semantic marker represents
a category of language just in case that marker occurs
on the right-hand side of one of the rules in (URR) and
does not occur on the left-hand side of any rule in
(URR). Thus, to pick out the categories of language, we
simply check over the list of rules (URR) and select each

semantic marker that represents a concept under which others are subsumed but which is not itself subsumed under other concepts. The justifications for the claim that a certain set of semantic markers represents the categories of language is now a straightforward empirical matter in precisely the same way that deciding the semantic categories of a particular language L is. However, the sets of redundancy rules for each linguistic description must afford the best simplification of the lexical readings in their respective dictionaries whereas the set of universal redundancy rules must afford the best simplification of the sets of redundancy rules in each of the particular linguistic descriptions. Given that both these empirical hypotheses are well supported by the available evidence, the claim that a set of semantic markers represents the categories becomes just a formal question of whether each of the members of the set meets the condition that there is a rule in (URR) saying that that marker is made redundant by others but no rule in (URR) that says that that marker makes other markers redundant.

On the above considerations, the theory of categories, in just the sense in which the notion of a category was employed by philosophers from Aristotle through Kant, becomes an integral part of the theory of language. The theory of language provides a definite answer to the question, left open by Aristotle and pressed by Arnauld, of how to determine in a nonarbitrary way that a proposed set of categories is both correct and exhaustive. The theory of language answers this question by framing such determinations in terms of the methodology of linguistics. As we have argued above, determinations can be made on the basis of empirical methods of justification that are merely linguistic variants of commonplace methods for evaluating the simplicity of theories in empirical science. Further, the status of categories is clarified by giving them a well-defined role in the theory of language i.e., by construing semantic categories as elements in the vocabulary from which semantic components of particular linguistic descriptions draw theoretical constructs for the formulation of dictionary entries. Moreover, the theory of language brings out the relations between categories, especially the inclusion relations of concepts within each category. By providing a characterization of the way in which semantic categories function in the process of providing semantic interpretations for sentences, the theory of language also defines the manner in which semantic categories integrate with syntactic structure and their role in the process of semantic description.

Note, however, that the notion of category used by philosophers such as Ryle in discussions of topics such as 'category mistakes' is quite different from the one we have just been analyzing and for which we have proposed definitions. That notion of category is far less abstract than ours and includes the whole domain of concepts represented by semantic markers and readings for subsentential constituents. It is a notion that we have explicated by the formalism of semantic markers in general. Thus, the semantic markers that represent categories of language or categories of a particular language are a very small proper subset of the set of semantic markers. Category mistakes, such as those exhibited by sentences like 'The stone is thinking of its immobility' or 'My sister married a generous insecticide,' are due to a conceptual incongruity between the meanings whose combination is directed by the syntactic structure of these sentences. The semantic markers in the selection restrictions whose failure to be satisfied explicates this conceptual incongruity need not be ones that represent categories of either of the general senses defined above. Thus, within the theory of language such 'category mistakes' are represented as instances of semantic anomaly. This, then, provides a far richer set of semantic markers to use to predict semantic anomalies than would be possible if we limited ourselves to defining selection restrictions solely over the domain of the categories of language or those of a particular linguistic description.

Finally, there is the question that Kant sought an answer to, namely, why natural languages utilize just the set of categories they do. We cannot give a complete answer by saying that the theory of language is a definition of 'natural language,' so that utilization of these categories is one of the features a linguistic system must possess to be a natural language, although this is surely part of the answer. For we can still ask why humans cannot acquire some system of rules that is not a natural language in just this sense. The complete answer is thus some rationale for establishing that only systems of rules that have the properties of natural language can be acquired by humans. This, however, brings us to the philosophical problem we wish to discuss next.

INNATE IDEAS

The third philosophical problem is one of the most extensively debated problems in the history of philosophy —the issue of innate ideas. Rationalists such as Plato, Descartes, Leibniz, and Kant argued that men are born with a stock of ideas which determine to a very large extent both the form and content of their mature knowledge, while empiricists like Hobbes, Locke, Berkeley, and Hume argued that at birth men are a virtual *tabula rasa* on which experience writes its lessons according to the principles of associative learning. The rationalists claimed that our concepts originate in principles that form the inborn constitution of the mind, and the empiricists claimed that all our ideas come originally from experience. The controversy is fundamentally a conflict between two opposed hypotheses to account for how conceptual knowledge is built up from experience by the operation of innate principles of mental functioning. The basis for the controversy is not, as it is often conceived in popular discussions, that empiricists fail to credit the mind with any innate principles, but rather that the principles which are accorded innate status by empiricists do not place any substantive restrictions on the ideas that can qualify as components of complex ideas or any formal restrictions on the structure of associations which bond component ideas together to form a complex idea. On the empiricist's hypothesis, the innate principles are purely combinatorial devices for putting together items from experience. So these principles provide only the machinery for instituting associative bonds. Experience plays the selective role in determining which ideas may be connected by association, and principles of association are, accordingly, unable to exclude any ideas as, in principle, beyond the range of possible intellectual acquisition.

Thus, the empiricist's account of how conceptual knowledge develops is essentially this. Experience provides examples of things of a certain kind which are somehow copied by the mind to form a simple idea of such things. Empiricists differ among themselves about the sort of things that are represented as simple ideas, but this has no bearing on the present discussion. Simple ideas are combined to form complex ideas, and these are combined to form still more complex ideas, without any limit on the level of complexity that may be reached. Such combinations are dictated by the regularities exhibited in experience. The network of associative bonds instituted to form a complex idea from simpler ones is itself a copy of the pattern of regularities which connect items in experience, where these regularities are represented as associative bonds. Since the associative machinery does not place restrictions either on the intrinsic characteristics of the items from experience to determine which of them can be represented as simple ideas or on the structure of the complex ideas resulting from the process of combining ideas, any logically possible concepts can, given the appropriate experience, be realized in the mind in the form of some simple or complex idea. Since any simple ideas whatever are possible, since any simple ideas can become the elements associated in the formation of a complex idea, and since any complex idea is just a network of associative bonds whose ultimate elements can be nothing other than simple ideas derived from experience, it follows that the empiricist's principles of mental operation are, as it were, neutral with respect to which ideas from the totality of all logically possible ones are chosen for use in making sense of our actual experience. In this regard, these principles defer to experience to provide a basis for choice among the totality. To explain how this choice is made, empiricists introduce the doctrine that the causally effective factor in learning is the frequency of presentations of spatially and temporally contiguous items together with perhaps other precipitating factors such as drive reduction.[12] The components of every complex idea are bonded together by links forged by the operation of enumerative techniques of inductive generalization from frequently repeated instances of contiguously occurring items in experience.

Contrary to this, rationalists claim that the principles of mental operation with which man is innately equipped place quite severe restrictions on what a simple idea can be and on what ways simple ideas can combine with one another and with complex ideas in the production of complex ideas. To account for the attainment of conceptual knowledge, such restrictions are incorporated in the rationalist hypothesis in the form of a system of innately

[12] E.g., the law of effect or pattern of presentations, as in C. B. Ferster and B. F. Skinner, *Schedules of Reinforcement*, Appleton-Century-Crofts, 1957.

fixed conceptual forms which sharply limit the set of those ideas which the mind is capable of acquiring to a very small subset of the set of all logically possible ideas. These innate conceptual forms, or innate ideas, contribute directly to our stock of abstract concepts and indirectly organize the content of experience by serving as models for the construction of particular concepts, which, accordingly, have the structure of the abstract concepts on which they are modeled. For example, an abstract concept such as our concept of an object with spatially and temporally contiguous parts is not learned by copying experienced objects but is manifested as a functional component of our conceptual knowledge under precipitating sensory conditions. Similarly, experience does not present instances of a particular concept such as that of a stone or animal which the mind copies without the benefit of a template. Experience sets off a process in which such particular concepts are manufactured from the same innately fixed conceptual form which gives rise to the abstract concept that determines the category to which those particular concepts belong.

Hence, the rationalist is no more claiming that all our ideas arise from innate forms in a way that is wholly independent of a selective effect of experience than the empiricist is claiming that there are no innate principles of mental operation. "Necessary truths," wrote Leibniz, ". . . must have principles whose proof does not depend on examples, nor consequently upon the testimony of the senses, although without the senses it would never have occurred to us to think of them."[13] According to the rationalists, conceptual knowledge is a joint product of the mind and the senses, in which sense experience serves to realize the innately fixed form of mature conceptual knowledge. Leibniz phrased this point in terms of a particularly revealing analogy. He wrote, ". . . I have taken as illustration a block of veined marble, rather than a block of perfectly uniform marble or than empty tablets, that is to say, what is called by philosophers *tabula rasa.* For if the soul were like these empty tablets, truths would be in us as the figure of Hercules is in a block of marble, when the block of marble is indifferently capable of receiving this figure or any other. But if there were in the stone veins, which should mark out the figure of Hercules rather than other figures, the stone would be more determined towards this figure, and Hercules would somehow be, as it were, innate in it, although labor would be needed to uncover the veins and to clear them by polishing and thus removing what prevents them from being fully seen. It is thus that ideas and truths are innate in us, as natural inclinations, dispositions, habits or powers, and not as activities . . . ."[13] The rationalist thus denies the empiricist contention that all of our ideas come from sense experience, arguing instead that sense experience serves to activate such natural inclinations, dispositions, habits or powers, i.e., to transform the latent unperceived ideas with which men are innately equipped into clearly perceived, actual ideas. The senses, to return to Leibniz's

[13] G. W. Leibniz, *New Essays Concerning Human Understanding,* A. C. Langley (trans. and ed.), Open Court Publishing Company, La Salle. Ill., 1949.

analogy, play the role of the sculptor who by polishing and clearing away extraneous marble reveals the form of Hercules.

Rationalists claim that the set of possible ideas from which experience selects those that are actually acquired by us is a far narrower set than those which it is possible to imagine or formulate. Consequently, in denying the empiricist's contention that all our ideas come from experience, the rationalist is putting forth a stronger hypothesis about the innate contribution to conceptual knowledge. The controversy is, then, whether some version of this stronger hypothesis or the empiricist's weaker one best explains how a conceptual system of the sort that mature humans possess is acquired on the experience they have accumulated.

We make no effort here to review the traditional arguments of empiricists and rationalists. Instead we shall consider the form that the issue over innate ideas takes in the case of language acquisition. The reason for thus narrowing the issue is that in so doing we deal with the crux of the issue in terms of a case about which enough is now known in the theory of language to afford a substantial basis for deciding between the empiricist and rationalist hypotheses.

The major fact to be explained by the contending hypotheses is that a child who undergoes the transition from nonverbal infant to fluent speaker of a natural language on the basis of an exposure to a sample of speech has acquired an internal representation of the rules that determine how sentences are constructed, used, and understood. These internally represented rules constitute his competence in his native language. Thus, at the final stage of the nonverbal infant's transformation into fluent speaker, the product of the process of language acquisition is an internal representation of a linguistic description. This internal representation is, then, the object whose acquisition has to be explained by the contending empiricist and rationalist hypotheses. Accordingly, we may conceive of the nonverbal infant as initially equipped with a language acquisition device of undetermined constitution,

(D)

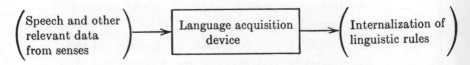

and we may think of the empiricist and rationalist hypotheses as hypotheses about its constitution. Since the input to (D) is a sample of utterances over a certain maturational period, and perhaps other linguistically relevant sensory information as well, and its output is an internalization of the rules of the language from which the sample was drawn, the best hypothesis about (D) is that hypothesis which accounts in the most revealing way for how such an output is produced on the basis of such an input. Therefore, our approach to deciding whether the empiricist or rationalist hypothesis is best will be to study the properties of the input and output of (D) to determine the kind of mechanism that can convert an input with the properties that the input to (D) is found to have into an output with the properties that the output of (D) is found to have. Whichever hypothesis thus provides the most fruitful model of the internal structure of the language acquisition device will be accepted as the best hypothesis.

The empiricist hypothesis claims that the language acquisition device operates essentially by principles of inductive generalization which associate observable features of utterances with one another and with other relevant sensory information to obtain an internalization of the rules of a linguistic description. These principles have been given a precise statement in various, from our point of view, equivalent forms in the work of taxonomic linguistics in the Bloomfieldian tradition and learning theorists in the tradition of American behaviorist psychology.[14] Such statements are attempts to work out a simulation model of the device (D). On the other hand, the rationalist hypothesis, which attributes a far richer structure to the device (D), has never been expressed in a precise enough form for it to receive serious consideration as a competing explanation. The rationalist hypothesis claims that the language acquisition device contains a stock of innate ideas that jointly specify the necessary form of language (realized in any actual natural lan-

[14] Cf. N. Chomsky, "Current Issues in Linguistic Theory" and "A Transformational Approach to Syntax," in Fodor and Katz (eds.), *The Structure of Language: Readings in the Philosophy of Language;* also Postal, *Constituent Structure,* provides a discussion of taxonomic linguistics; for behaviorist learning theory, a convenient survey is provided by W. K. Estes et al., *Modern Learning Theory,* Appleton-Century-Crofts, 1954.

guage) and thus the necessary form of a speaker's internal representation of the rules of his language. But no rationalist has given a precise formulation of these innate ideas, or an exact account of the process by which abstract and particular concepts are created from the interaction of innate conceptual forms and sensory stimulation. Thus, one might even say that there is no definite rationalist hypothesis, but just a general notion about the character of such a hypothesis. These difficulties with the formulation of the rationalist hypothesis have been one major factor which has discouraged cultivation of such an alternative to the empiricist conception of intellectual acquisitions. Another difficulty is the somewhat greater initial plausibility that the empiricist hypothesis has by virtue of its apparent greater simplicity. Consequently, we consider the empiricist hypothesis first, and ask whether there are fundamental inadequacies in it that force us to resort to the rationalist's apparently more complicated account of language acquisition and to take on the burden of trying to give their account a more precise formulation. This means that we shall examine the output and input to (D) to find out if an empiricist model of associative learning can provide an account of how the input is transformed into the output which squares with what is known about them.

For a predetermined output from an input-output device, there is a functional relationship between the input and the richness of the internal structure of the device. Namely, the weaker the input in structural organization, the richer the internal structure of the device must be in order to give the fixed output from the input, i.e., in order to make up for the poverty of the input. Let us take a rather mundane example. A very intelligent person can obtain the solutions to certain mathematical problems (the output) given just the barest formulation of the problems (the input) whereas a very unintelligent person might have to be virtually told the solutions before he gets them. Thus, we often infer the poverty of someone's intellect from how much has to be given him at the outset for him to arrive at the solution to a problem. Similarly, here we will try to show that the input to the language acquisition device would be too impoverished for it to be able to produce an internalization of the rules of a linguistic description were it to be constructed in accord with the empiricist hypothesis. That is, we shall try to establish that operations of inductive generalization and association cannot produce an internalization of a linguistic description from the kind of speech and other data that is available to the child.

One fundamental assumption of any associative theory of learning is that what is learned can be broken down into elements which have been each associated with observable and distinguishable constituents of the input in the following sense. The elements of the input which can have something associated with them must be distinguishable in terms of the discriminative and analytic capacities of the perceptual mechanism that codes the input into discrete parts and analyzes those parts as units within one or another category. Thus, limitations on the perceptual mechanism based on the discriminative and analytic distinctions it can make are also limitations on the richness of the information which the input provides for the associative machinery. Similarly, insufficiencies in the input itself are also limitations on the richness of the information with which the associative machinery can work. Therefore, if the associationist theory is to successfully explain the case of language learning, the physical speech sounds, or utterances, from which the child acquires his knowledge of the rules of the linguistic description must contain, or be analyzable into, observable and distinguishable elements such that for each constituent of the meaning of an utterance whose meaning has been acquired there is an observable and distinguishable component of its phonetic shape with which that semantic constituent can be associated. Since learning the meanings of the sentences of a language is conceived of as a process of associating semantic elements of some kind with observable features of the phonetic shape of the sentences to which the child is exposed, these observable features must provide a rich enough basis of distinct elements for each semantic component of the meaning of such sentences to have a distinct phonetic element(s) with which it can be correlated by association. If, therefore, we can show that this fundamental assumption is false—that there are, in the case of certain essential semantic elements, literally no observable features of the phonetic shape of sentences with which these semantical elements can be associated—then we will have established that the input to (D) is structurally too impoverished for the rules of a linguistic description to be derived from it by principles of inductive generalization and association. That is what we shall now attempt to establish.

To show this, we first define two notions, that of the *observable grammatical features of a sentence* and that of the *unobservable grammatical features of a sentence*. To define the first of these notions, we refer back to our earlier discussion of final derived phrase markers. It will be recalled that these phrase markers are the objects on which the phonological rules, the rules that determine the pronunciation of sentences, operate. These rules map phonetic interpretations onto final derived phrase markers. Since it is only the speech sounds represented by such phonetic interpretations which the child encounters in acquiring his fluency in the language—since, that is, this is the only data about the language that he can observe, it is natural to define the notion of observable grammatical features in terms of properties of final derived phrase markers, along with properties of their phonological interpretations where these are relevant. *Thus, we define the observable grammatical features of the sentence S to be any features of S which can be predicted directly from its final derived phrase marker or any feature that can be predicted directly from its phonological representation, and nothing else.* Anything that requires information from other sources, such as the rules of the linguistic description or other phrase markers of the sentence, in order to be predicted is *ipso facto* not an observable grammatical feature. Thus, in the case of example (1) in Chapter 4, the observable grammatical features of this sentence are those that can be predicted from (2), e.g., the set of words that make up (1), the segmentation of these words into continuous constituents, and the classification of these constituents into syntactic categories, and from (1)'s phonological representation.

Note that this definition of a sentence's observable grammatical features, although it seems natural in the sense that it permits us to count anything that we would intuitively regard as an observable grammatical feature as such, is nonetheless, overly generous to the empiricist. That is, it is overly liberal in the sense that it counts much more information about the grammar of a sentence as observable than a nonverbal child could be expected to be able to inductively extract from the sounds he actually encounters. For one thing, it is quite obvious that the child is in no sense given a classification of the constituents of a sentence into their syntactic categories. Furthermore, the essentially inductive techniques of data cataloguing devised by taxonomic linguists in order to provide a mechanical discovery procedure for final derived phrase markers on the basis of their phonological representation have always proved a dismal failure, not because there was little skill employed in their development, but because, without the general definitions of the grammatical properties they were to identify in particular cases, they lacked the conceptual apparatus to do their job.[15] For another thing, and perhaps more significantly, it has been found in recent work in acoustic phonetics that the physical sounds of speech do not them-

[15] Cf. Chomsky, *Syntactic Structures*, footnotes 3 and 7 of chapter 6.

selves provide a complete basis for identifying the significant phonological units of sentences. These two points are by themselves a strong argument against the empiricist hypothesis about language acquisition, but we shall not develop them here. If on the basis of this overly liberal definition of an observable grammatical feature we can show that the observable features of sentences are insufficient to enable a child to acquire the rules of his language by operations of inductive generalization and association, then we have an adequate refutation of the empiricist conception of language learning.

As we saw in Chapter 4, final derived markers do not, and could not, adequately specify all the information about the syntactic structure of sentences. This means that the syntactic structure of a sentence is not given by a single phrase marker which segments it into continuous constituents and labels these segments but must be given by other phrase markers also. These other phrase markers are connected with the final derived phrase marker by a system of transformational rules which convert underlying phrase markers into derived phrase markers, and these into still further derived phrase markers, until the final one is reached. The underlying phrase markers may be thought of, in contrast to the final derived phrase markers, as reconstructing the unobservable, theoretically inferred, features of sentences.

Now, in terms of the underlying phrase markers, we can define the notion unobservable grammatical feature of a sentence. *An unobservable grammatical feature of*

S is any syntactic feature of S which can be predicted directly from its underlying phrase marker but cannot be predicted from its final derived phrase marker. In general, if we compare final derived phrase markers with their corresponding underlying phrase markers, we find that the unobservable grammatical features of sentences form quite an impressive collection. The occurrence of a 'you' subject in normal English imperative sentences is one example of an unobservable grammatical feature. Another is the occurrence of a second verb phrase in comparative sentences, as illustrated in the discussion of examples (31) and (32) in Chapter 4. Still another is constituents whose existence cannot be revealed by bracketing in a final derived phrase marker, as described in the discussion of examples (32) and (33) in Chapter 4. And we may mention also grammatical relations such as the subject and object relations in examples (36) and (37) in Chapter 4. These are only a few of the very many cases of unobservable grammatical features. Such features cannot be detected in the perceptible or physically definable properties of the data in the sample of the language which a language learner encounters, but, nevertheless, they must, as we have already shown, be theoretically posited by the linguist as part of the structure of sentences in order that his linguistic description successfully explain observable grammatical features. Thus, the unobservable features of a sentence as well as its observable features must be considered as information that a speaker utilizes to produce it on the appropriate occasion and to understand it when it is produced by other speakers.

That unobservable grammatical features of sentences bear semantic content which makes an essential contribution to the meaning of sentences, i.e., that the meaning of sentences having such features is not complete without the semantic contribution made by them, is obvious from the examples we have already given. Thus, it follows that any hypothesis to explain how the rules of a language are acquired must explain how the semantic content contributed by unobservable grammatical features becomes part of the full meaning of sentences. Otherwise, the hypothesis fails to explain how a speaker knows what sentences with unobservable grammatical features mean. Now, the empiricist hypothesis claims that the meanings of sentences are learned by a conditioning process in which inductive generalization and association provide the steps of language acquisition. Since such steps must proceed exclusively from observable features of the utterances to which the child is exposed, the empiricist hypothesis is claiming that the meaning of sentences can be learned solely on the basis of operations of associating semantic elements with observable grammatical features of sentences. But this is simply false. First, the observable grammatical features account for only a small fraction of the semantic content of sentences; and, second, on the empiricist hypothesis, there is no means of associating the semantic content of unobservable grammatical features with the sentences whose meaning contains that semantic content. We conclude, then, that the empiricist hypothesis is, in principle, incapable of accounting for the acquisition of a natural language, whereby acquisition is meant mastery of rules that provide the full meaning of any sentence in the language.

To put the matter another way, since the observable structure of sentences is often quite severely impoverished from the point of view of semantic interpretation and since principles of inductive generalization and association add nothing structural or substantive to these structures on which they operate, it follows that such principles cannot account for the full range of semantic, as well as syntactic, properties on which the interpretation of sentences, essential to communication with them, depends.

We may anticipate a reply to part of the above argument. The empiricist might argue that he can account for the semantic effect of an absent feature such as the 'you' subject of imperatives on the basis of inductive generalization because some imperatives, such as (30) in Chapter 4, explicitly contain the word. The empiricist's counter-argument would then be that the language learner can make an inductive extrapolation of a second person pronoun subject from cases of sentences interpreted as requesting (commanding, etc.) something of the person addressed in which there is an explicit occurrence of 'you' to cases also interpreted in this manner but in which there is no explicit occurrence of 'you.' Similarly, the empiricist would have to argue that information about syntactic categorization and grammatical relations that are not observable features of sentences can be inductively inferred from sentences with the same meaning in which that information is observably represented. For example, the language learner would inductively infer that 'look' and 'up' constitute a single verb in (32) in Chapter 4, from the fact that 'look up' is such an observable constituent in 'John looked up the number of his friend.' This is the type of argument to which the empiricist must appeal because he must show that there are grammatical elements of the appropriate sort with which the relevant semantic information can be associated. If this argument breaks down, our previous conclusion about the absence of such elements and the consequent inadequacy of the empiricist's attempt to explain the meanings of sentences on associationist principles follows.

This counterargument of the empiricist's does break down because, on the empiricist hypothesis about the innate equipment of the language learner, the sort of inductive inference that the counter-argument claims the language learner can make is not, in fact, one he can make with this equipment and nothing more. The inadmissable assumption of the empiricist's counter-argument is the supposition that the sentences about which the inductive inference is made can, without begging the question, be correlated with just those sentences from which the desired conclusion can be drawn. Take the case of the 'you' subject in imperatives. Not only do sentences such as (30) in Chapter 4 occur, but sentences such as,

(a) John Jones help the man,
(b) Everyone help the man,
(c) No-one help the man,
(d) Everyone with a serviceable boat help the man,

and indeed any of infinitely many similar sentences with different noun phrase subjects also occur. If the desired conclusion about the critical cases is to be reached, the inductive inference can proceed only from cases like (30) of Chapter 4, yet, on the empiricist's account, there is nothing in the language learner's inferential equipment that prevents cases like (a)–(d) from leading to incorrect inductive conclusions about normal imperatives. There is indeed a transformational relation between cases like (30) and (5) of Chapter 4 which does not hold between (a), (b), (c), or (d) and (5). But this relation is as unobservable as the 'you' subject of (5) and hence cannot, without begging the question, be used as a basis for correlating (30) but nothing else with (5). The same point applies in the other cases discussed. In the case where the subject-verb and object-verb relations are unobservable features of sentences, the empiricist might argue in the same vein that (36) and (37) of Chapter 4 are correlated respectively with sentences like

(e)   It is easy for one to please John.
(f)   John is eager for John to please.

But if the reasons for this pair of correlations as opposed to some other is that (36) and (e) have the same meaning and (37) and (f) have the same meaning, he still has to show that John is the object of 'to please' in (e) and the subject of 'to please' in (f). It is clearly not sufficient to observe that in (e) 'John' follows 'to please' whereas in (f) it precedes it, since with respect to the observable form of indefinitely many sentences the situation can be the other way around. Thus, in

(g)   The boat was chosen by John

we have the subject 'John' following the verb and the object preceding it.[16] What the empiricist requires here is the general definitions of *subject of* and *object of* which are formulated in terms of configurations of syntactic symbols in underlying phrase markers and the transformations which connect the underlying phrase markers with their appropriate final derived phrase markers. Neither of these can be appealed to by him without begging just the question at issue. Finally, take the case of permutations in which syntactic categorization is lost. Basing such inductive inferences on information given in the final derived phrase marker resulting from permutations will lead to inadequate conclusions in a large number of cases. For instance, the inductive inferences which enable the language learner to obtain a complete object constituent for (33) in Chapter 4 are to proceed from the facts that (33) and (h)

(h)   I have read only one of the books you mentioned

have the same meaning and that (h) has the structure represented in (35) in Chapter 4. These inductive inferences are supposed to reach the conclusion that 'only one of the books you mentioned' is the object of (33), so that the semantic information specifying what (33) says its speaker read can be associated with the full object of (33). But then, (i), which has the same meaning

---

[16] That (g) must have an underlying phrase marker in which 'John' is the subject of 'choose' and 'the boat' is its object follows from facts such as that 'choose' requires an animate subject.

as (h),

(i) you mentioned some books of which I have read only one

would analogously be regarded as correlated with (j)

(j) *Of which I have read only one, you mentioned some books

which is clearly an unacceptable conclusion. Again, the relevant distinction, in this case between the structure of (h) and (i), is not something that the empiricist can take into consideration.

The empiricist's counter-arguments have a common feature. In each case, it is presupposed that the language learner understands a sentence S (whose final derived phrase marker is itself too impoverished to account on associationist principles for how he understands S) because he can correlate S with another sentence S' whose final derived phrase marker is not too impoverished (it being the same as the underlying phrase marker for S) This presupposition of the empiricist's can easily be seen to be very highly implausible, for it means that the language learner has *actually* encountered and learned the meaning of each S'. I do not have in mind here that this presupposition imposes an order in which sentences must be encountered for them to be learned, although this is by itself implausible enough given that different individuals who acquire the same linguistic fluency, as a matter of fact, have quite different linguistic histories with respect to the order in which they heard sentences and to what sentences were heard. What I am thinking of is the fallacy that, on this presupposition, being able to understand the meaning of any one of an enormously large class of sentences—which *ex hypothesi* a fluent speaker's mastery of a language makes him capable of—implies his having already encountered an occurrence of each and every sentence S' correlated to an S in that enormous class of sentences. However, the number of distinct sentences of the type S that a fluent speaker can understand—even limiting ourselves to those of the length found in books in a college library—is so astronomically high that in order for him to have had the time to have actually heard all such S' he would have had to have been living for centuries. On one calculation, the total number even of sentences of twenty-words or less (well below the upper limit for books in a college library) is 10^{30} while the number of seconds in a century is only 3.15 times 10^9.[17]

The above argument against the empiricist hypothesis shows that the set of observable features with which associations to semantic content can be made is too impoverished a set. We can also give an argument to show that the set of semantic elements which is allegedly associated with observable features is too impoverished itself. This argument is a psychologization of an argument of Goodman's in some recent work of his on the concept of confirmation in science.[18] In discussing the nature of lawlike statements, Goodman exhibited a paradox in a current version of confirmation theory

---

[17] G. A. Miller, K. Pribram, and E. Galenter, *Plans and the Structure of Behavior*. Holt, Rinehart, and Winston, 1960.

[18] N. Goodman, *Fact, Fiction, and Forecast*, Harvard University Press, 1955.

THE PHILOSOPHY OF LANGUAGE

which shows that on this theory any prediction about unknown cases is confirmed by any evidence whatever about the known cases. Goodman argued as follows: "Suppose that all emeralds examined before a certain time *t* are green. At time *t*, then, our observations support the hypothesis that all emeralds are green; and this is in accord with our definition of confirmation. Our evidence statements assert that emerald *a* is green, that emerald *b* is green, and so on; and each confirms the general hypothesis that all emeralds are green. So far, so good. Now let me introduce another predicate less familiar than 'green.' It is the predicate 'grue' and it applies to all things examined before *t* just in case they are green but to other things just in case they are blue. Then at times *t* we have, for each evidence statement asserting that a given emerald is green, a parallel evidence statement asserting that that emerald is grue. And the statements that emerald *a* is grue, that emerald *b* is grue, and so on, will each confirm the general hypothesis that all emeralds are grue. Thus, according to our definition, the prediction that all emeralds subsequently examined will be green and the prediction that all will be grue are alike confirmed by the evidence statements describing the same observations. But if an emerald subsequently examined is grue, it is blue and hence not green. Thus although we are well aware which of the two incompatible predictions is genuinely confirmed, they are equally well confirmed according to our present definition. Moreover, it is clear that if we simply choose an appropriate predicate, then on the basis

of these same observations we shall have equal confirmation, by our definition, for any prediction whatever
about other emeralds—or indeed about anything else."[19]
We will adapt this argument so that, instead of dealing with a definition of confirmation intended as a
reconstruction of the techniques for confirming laws in
science, it deals with the empiricist's hypothesis about
language acquisition. Goodman's argument then becomes a refutation of a psychological hypothesis rather
than an epistemological theory. The adaptation is possible because the empiricist's psychological hypothesis
about how languages are acquired employs the same
principles of inductive generalization as those on which the
conception of confirmation, which Goodman criticizes by
this argument, rest.

According to the empiricist, (D) operates by inductive
principles which associate contiguously occurring elements in the sensory input when their contiguous occurrence is repeated frequently enough. Thus, if a is always
accompanied contiguously by b, we form the association
ab, expecting b when a occurs again. Now, suppose that
a child learning a language has encountered a sufficiently
large number of instances, say N, in which two linguistic
events a and b have occurred together, where a is a word
in its phonetic form and b is a meaning. For example, a
might be the word /bɔyz/ and b the meaning of the
English word 'boys.' In analogy to Goodman's construction of the predicate 'grue,' we can construct other 'Goodman-type' meanings, representing other logically possible

[19] *Ibid.*

concepts, among which will be the case c. c is the concept which is the meaning of 'boys' during the period when the N instances of a and b were observed to occur together and the meanings of 'girls' at any time after that period. Now, by parity of argument, the empiricist must infer not only that the child associates b with a, thus giving /bɔyz/ the meaning of 'boys,' but also that the child associates c with a, thus giving it a different meaning. Moreover, he must also predict that the child associates d, e, f, etc., with a, where these are also 'Goodman-like' meanings and are each, like c, incompatible with b and one another. For parallel to the N contiguous occurrences of b with a, there are N contiguous occurrences of c with a, of d with a, of e with a, and so on. This implies that the empiricist must predict that, for any occurrence of /bɔyz/ which takes place after the period when the N cases were observed, it is understood not only to mean what the English word 'boys' means but also what the word 'girls' means, what the word 'stones' means, what the word 'monkeys' means, and so forth. Thus, with respect to the set of specifiable concepts, it will be taken to mean anything at all. Since this sort of adaptation of Goodman's argument can be made for grammatical features as well as for any meanings of any word in the language, what is shown is that the empiricist hypothesis completely underdetermines the output of (D), which means that the empiricist hypothesis completely fails to account for language acquisition.

Two further points. First, it is clear that counter arguments based on contentions such as that the meanings

c, d, e, etc., are defined using the meanings of the words
'boys,' 'girls,' 'stones,' etc., and are therefore less simple
or that there is some other asymmetry between the standard meanings and the various sets of 'Goodman-type'
meanings are to be met with exactly parallel arguments
to those Goodman himself uses to refute parallel criticisms of his argument.[20] Second, it is clear that Goodman's own appeal to the notion of entrenchment[21] as a
way out of the paradox for confirmation theory is of no
avail here. This notion is that of a scheme for ranking
predicates which must, by definition, be applied on
the basis of some antecedently given set of statements
that must be presumed to have been inductively established from past experience. Hypothetically, there are indefinitely many other possible sets of statements, each
differing from the others by having been established by
a different counter-inductive procedure. Goodman's con-
finement of his task to one of sheer explication enables
him to escape the criticism that there is no way to decide
which of the sets should be taken as the basis for
measuring the degree of entrenchment of a predicate.[22]
Here, however, we are dealing with the child's first intellectual acquisition in the realm of language, and hence
we are dealing with a case with respect to which no
extrapolations from past experience can be presupposed

[20] *Ibid;* also N. Goodman, "On Infirmities of Confirmation Theory,"
Philosophy and Phenomenological Research, vol. 8, no. 1, 1947. Also,
more recently, N. Goodman, "Positionality and Pictures," *Philosophical
Review*, vol. 69, no. 4, 1960.
[21] Goodman, *Fact, Fiction, and Forecast,* chapter 4.
[22] J. J. Katz, *The Problem of Induction and Its Solution,* University
of Chicago Press, 1960.

without begging the question at issue. For such a presupposition would raise the question of how these extrapolations were made.

Finally, we may briefly mention another criticism of the empiricist hypothesis. The previously discussed difficulties of this hypothesis stem from the fact that associationist principles fail to place constraints on what can qualify as a simple idea. The difficulty we will now consider arises because such principles do not place any constraints on the nature of the bonds that link ideas together to form complex ideas. That is, there is just one notion of connection between ideas, that of a pure association between them. The fact that there is only one way in which ideas can be connected to one another means that different conceptual relations must be expressed in terms of differences in the strength of the associative bonds connecting component ideas (together with differences in the component ideas and differences with respect to which components are connected with which other components in each particular case). However, such different conceptual relations as sameness of meaning, meaning inclusion, difference in meaning, incompatibility of meaning, and so on are wholly unexpressable in these terms. Given that two ideas are associated, each with a certain strength of association, we cannot decide whether one has the same meaning as the other, whether the meaning of one is included in that of the other, whether they are different in meaning, whether they are incompatible in meaning, etc. Strongly associated expressions like 'ham' and 'eggs' or 'one' and 'two' are not for that reason strongly related in meaning, and weakly associated expressions like 'eye-doctor' and 'oculist' or 'natatorium' and 'indoor swimming pool' can be equivalent in meaning. Similarly, no invariant feature of association separates synonyms from antonyms or pairs of sentences exhibiting a logical entailment from pairs exhibiting a causal relation. The fact that such conceptual relations are unrepresentable in terms of associative connections means that the empiricist hypothesis provides no way to explain how the speaker's acquisition of language equips him to determine such relations. What is required is a wide variety of different kinds of connections not one type of connection with possible variations in the degree of its strength.

Of course, classical empiricists such as Hume were aware of this difficulty and thus posited relations between ideas, such as resemblance, contrariety, etc., which they made no effort to reduce to networks of associative connections. But such posits must be regarded as concessions to the rationalist's position, as Leibniz pointed out,[23] since they have to be construed as positing the existence of innate ideas. Thus, from the viewpoint of classical empiricism, Quine's doctrine that sentences are learned by the mechanism of conditioned response, together with its corollary that relations such as logical connections and causal connections are differentiated in terms of different conditioning of sentences as responses to sentences as stimuli, is a purer version of empiricism, although, from the viewpoint of adequacy, Quine's is far less defensi-

[23] Leibniz, *New Essays Concerning Human Understanding.*

ble.[24] The complete inadequacy of the empiricist hypothesis becomes quite obvious once we realize that speakers can detect such conceptual relations between linguistic constructions even when they have not heard either of the constructions before.

The above arguments show that the empiricist hypothesis attributes far too little internal structure to the language acquisition device (D). The obvious moral to draw is that we need a stronger hypothesis if we are to successfully explain the output of (D) in terms of its input. This hypothesis must be strong enough to fully determine the output, given the input, but not so strong that it determines an output having properties that conflict with what is known about the ways in which natural languages can diverge. For example, the internal structure attributed to (D) by the hypothesis cannot be so rich that it incorporates the rules for English phonological structure, since, then, the hypothesis would predict that every natural language sounds like English. Within the known limits of richness, we wish to find a hypothesis that is rich enough as an explanatory hypothesis, rather than to find a hypothesis that is weak enough to satisfy empiricist preconceptions about the insignificance of innate contributions to knowledge. The empiricist falsely identifies his preconceptions about the paucity of the innate contribution with simplicity as a methodological canon and then argues that simplicity considerations favor his hypothesis. He overlooks the fact that simplicity is a consideration in choosing between competing hypotheses

[24] Quine, *Word and Object*, section 3.

only when the hypotheses can afford an equally plausible basis cn which to explain the available evidence.

A hypothesis strong enough to account for what we know about the product of language acquisition will be rationalistic in that it will be designed to introduce into the language acquisition device, as part of its internal constitution, all those facets of natural languages which must be taken as innate equipment to explain how a child's earliest linguistic experience enable him to arrive at an internalization of the rules of a linguistic description. The hypothesis we suggest (to be referred to as the 'rationalist hypothesis') is this: *the language acquisition device contains, as innate structure, each of the principles stated within the theory of language.* That is, the language acquisition device contains,

(i)   the linguistic universals which define the form of a linguistic description,

(ii)   the form of the phonological, syntactic, and semantic components of a linguistic description,

(iii)   the formal character of the rules in each of these components,

(iv)   the set of universal phonological, syntactic, and semantic constructs out of which particular rules in particular descriptions are formulated,

(v)   a methodology for choosing optimal linguistic descriptions,

as described in Chapter 4.

It should be noted that this hypothesis is open-ended in the sense that it asserts that anything which, for good empirical reasons, is found to be part of the theory of language is *ipso facto* part of the language acquisition

device, and hence part of the child's native language-
forming apparatus, his innate ideas about language. But,
even with this open-endedness, there is no indefiniteness
about what is thus given the status of innate ideas. What
the hypothesis asserts to be part of the language acquisition device is just what the theory of language specifies
as universals, and these are established on the basis of
definite empirical evidence from the analysis of natural
languages. Hence, any particular claim that something
is or is not an innate idea can be justified or refuted
within the same methodological framework that serves
this purpose in other sciences. The theory of language
formulates its principles with scientific precision, so that
the characterization of the set of innate ideas is itself explicitly specified. This makes up for the vagueness of
classical rationalist attempts to put forth their doctrine.
Thus, the principal defect of the rationalist position is
removed. Note, finally, that innate ideas are conceived
of as components of a device for internally representing
linguistic rules and as constituents of the particular rules
acquired by the operation of this device. Accordingly, the
question as to what are innate ideas can be answered by
saying that innate ideas are parts of a system of principles for organizing experience whose existence has been
hypothetically inferred from the linguistic performance
of speakers in their acquisition and use of language.

Adopting the rationalist hypothesis enables us to explain why every natural language has the features attributed to it by the principles of the theory of language.
Why, that is, natural languages that have been investi-

gated and those that will be investigated conform to the linguistic universals in the theory of language. We may assume that the generalizations in the theory of language which formulate the linguistic universals are true over the set of natural languages and ask, with respect to this assumption, why these generalizations hold. We are thus asking why the facts that they express are the way these generalizations say they are. We are seeking a more comprehensive and deeper explanation for the facts than is provided by laws that express them. We seek an explanation of those laws.[25] The explanatory power of the rationalist hypothesis lies in its ability to provide such an explanation.

We cannot assume that the presence of some feature in every natural language is merely an accidental correlation, such as the proverbial correlation between rum sales and preacher's salaries. We must provide a more scientifically plausible account. We must find something in the context in which natural languages are acquired which is invariant from one such context to another and can be plausibly regarded as the *causal antecedent* for the existence of common features in different natural languages. (Accordingly, we ignore such invariants as the fact that all speakers of a natural language live close to the earth's surface, that all breathe air, that all walk on two legs, etc., since these invariants cannot plausibly count as causally sufficient for the acquisition of a natural language.) This context includes, besides a

[25] In the sense in which N. Campbell, *What is Science?* Dover Publications, New York, 1952, speaks of the explanation of laws.

nonverbal infant and fluent speakers of a natural language speaking their language, geographical, cultural, psychological, and sociological factors. When we compare communities in which languages such as English, Chinese, Croatian, Urdu, Mohawk, Norwegian, Arabic, Hebrew, Greek, etc., are spoken to determine if any environmental factors are invariably present in contexts where natural languages are acquired, it is obvious that no such factors qualify. The psychology, sociology, and anthropology differ from case to case as much as does the geography and climate. In child rearing patterns, mores, traditions, properties, rituals, artifacts, political and social structure, etc., there is no sufficiently strong cross-community regularity that could account for the impressive fact, that all languages which human children acquire have those features which the generalizations in the theory of language prescribe. Moreover, we must also rule out every aspect of the psychology of infants and adult speakers which constitutes a respect in which one individual can differ normally from another, i.e., unique past experience, system of beliefs, morals, attitudes, emotional make-up, intelligence, disposition toward special ability or talent, etc. For, even within a given language community, children and adult speakers differ markedly from one another in these respects and yet normal children acquire essentially the same linguistic fluency so long as they are exposed to an adequate sample of speech. Hence, by this process of elimination, the only thing left that can provide the invariant condition that we want to connect with the universal features of language as their causal antecedent is the common innate endowment of human language learners, i.e., some component of their specifically human nature. This is not only the one constant feature amid all the differences among the participants in language acquisition situations and between the behavioral and contextual aspects of these situations, but it is also the differentia between language at the human level and its absence at lower levels of the animal kingdom. We thus conclude that the genetic endowment of a human being *qua* human being is the only invariant feature of language acquisition contexts which can causally account for nonverbal infants achieving a successful internalization of languages having the universal properties described in the theory of language. This gives us the regularity that whenever such languages are acquired there is the antecedent condition that the language learner possessed the genetic endowment of a member of the human species.

Now, if we bring in the rationalist hypothesis, we can obtain an explanation of this regularity. This hypothesis says that part of the genetic endowment of a human being is the full set of linguistic universals (i)–(v) and that these universals constitute the internal structure of the device which the nonverbal infant utilizes to become a fluent speaker on exposure to a sample of the utterances of a language. Since the innately given language acquisition device incorporates the linguistic universals, we can explain why the linguistic universals are necessary features of any language that is spoken by a human being. Namely, the linguistic universals are found in each and every natural language because, in acquiring a language, they are emplanted in the speaker's internalization of the rules of his language by the device that accomplishes its acquisition. The very mechanism which the child uses to acquire fluency in a natural language introduces them as the framework in which his linguistic experience is organized in the form of linguistic rules.

This explanation, it should be noted, is neither vacuous nor a *petitio principii*. To say that the language spoken by any human has the universal features of natural languages because the rules that define his linguistic competence are modeled on inborn archetypical representations of these features would be vacuous if there were no independently arrived at formal statement of these archetypical representations. But there is such a statement. Thus, this explanation is not vacuous because it is formulated in terms of the independently arrived at specification of the linguistic universals given in the theory of language. On the other hand, this explanation is not circular because the justification of the theory of language nowhere presupposes it. Note also that, although no account of the origin of such innate ideas is given, there is no question to be begged because there is no account of the origin of the principles of associative learning which the empiricist takes as inborn.

To exhibit the explanatory power of the rationalist hypothesis, we must describe a model which specifies just how the universal features of language are imparted to speakers' internal representation of the rules of particular languages. Such a model will be the alternative to the empiricist model in which such rules are conceived of as acquired by inductive generalization and association, and it will provide an account, not provided by classical rationalist discussions, of the steps by which these rules become part of a person's linguistic competence.

Chomsky has offered a conception of such a model.[26] He conceives of language acquisition as a process of implicit theory construction similar in character to theory construction in science but without the explicit intellectual operations of the latter. According to Chomsky's conception, the child formulates hypotheses about the rules of the linguistic description of the language whose sentences he is hearing, derives predictions from such hypotheses about the linguistic structure of sentences he will hear in the future, checks these predictions against the new sentences he encounters, eliminates those hypotheses that are contrary to the evidence, and evaluates those that are not eliminated by a simplicity principle which selects the simplest as the best hypothesis concerning the rules underlying the sentences he has heard and will hear. This process of hypothesis construction, verification, and evaluation repeats itself until the child matures past the point where the language acquisition device operates.[27]

[26] N. Chomsky, "A Review of B. F. Skinner's *Verbal Behavior*" in Fodor and Katz (eds.), *The Structure of Language: Readings in the Philosophy of Language*.

[27] The ability to acquire a language in the effortless, natural way in which children do appears to terminate at about puberty, after which the more rote-like method of learning familiar to those who have to learn a second language as an adult is required to produce fluency. Thus,

Chomsky's conception can be combined with the rationalist hypothesis to yield the model of language acquisition we require. The theory of language contains essentially four types of universals, as we indicated above. First, there are *formal universals*. These specify the form of the system of rules that comprise a linguistic description, the form of the rules of the phonological, syntactic, and semantic components, and the form of the rules within each of these components. Second, there are *substantive universals*. These specify the theoretical vocabulary to be employed in formulating particular rules of the form prescribed by the formal universals. The formal and substantive universals together permit the construction of a set of possible hypotheses about the linguistic description of a language. This set contains the systems of rules for each actual, natural language as well as systems for indefinitely many possible, but not actual, natural languages. Thus, we can regard this set of hypotheses, which we may refer to as 'initial hypotheses,' as those from which the child selects in arriving at his internalization of the rules of his language. But, so far, we have provided no conception of the mechanism by which the utterances in the input to the language acquisition device are utilized to produce a system of rules of the prescribed form and employing the prescribed constructs, i.e., no way to select among the initial hypotheses. To accomplish this, we

---

this ability of the child's is much like the abilities of various animals described as 'imprinting' with respect to the existence of a 'critical period.' Cf. C. Schiller (ed.), *Instinctive Behavior*, International Universities Press, New York, 1957, especially the papers by Lorenz and Tinbergen.

must consider the other two types of principles in the theory of language. In the methodology for choosing optimal linguistic descriptions is a *simplicity metric* which evaluates alternative systems of rules of the proper kind to determine which is preferable on the basis of the sort of methodological considerations appropriate to the choice of one hypothesis as the best of those equally well supported by a body of evidence. This metric is a function F such that the value $F(H_i)$, where H_i is one of the initial hypotheses, is an integer assigned to H_i determining its preference ranking with respect to $H_1, H_2, \ldots, H_{i-1}, H_{i+1}, \ldots$, where the lower the integer, the higher the position of H_i on the ranking. Since the rationalist hypothesis states that each principle in the theory of language is represented in the structure of the language acquisition device, this simplicity metric is also part of the innate language forming equipment of the child. With this metric the child can rank the set of initial hypotheses prior to any linguistic experience, and thus can obtain a best hypothesis or set of best hypotheses given no evidence about the language community he is in. Fourth, and finally there is, also in the methodology for choosing an optimal linguistic description, a *structure assignment algorithm* which converts the derivations of sentences that can be constructed from syntactic rules into phrase markers. The structure assignment algorithm provides the language acquisition device with a means of deriving predictions about sentences from the highest ranked initial hypotheses: each such hypothesis contains syntactic rules which generate derivations and these can be converted into phrase markers by the algorithm. If the device also has a method by which it can decide whether the observable structure of input sentences verifies or refutes the predictions made by the phrase markers constructed by the algorithm, it can eliminate initial hypotheses that do not predict correctly.[28] Note that the predictions about an input sentence are not confined to syntactic predictions, any more than the syntactic predictions are confined to those made by the final derived phrase markers. For, given the underlying and final derived phrase marker for a sentence, predictions about its semantic and phonological properties can be obtained without the aid of a further algorithm because the rules of the semantic and phonological components operate directly on the phrase markers that result from the application of the structure assignment algorithm. The child's internalization of the rules of a language *at any given time* is the maximally simplest hypothesis all of whose predictions are compatible with the facts about the linguistic structure of the sentences available to him from his experience *up to that time.*

We are now in a position to comment briefly on two connected philosophical matters. Unfortunately, I cannot go into them very deeply, but, on the other hand, I cannot avoid discussion of them, since the foregoing bears

---

[28] Thus, the role of experience is primarily to provide the data against which predictions and thus hypotheses are judged. Experience serves not to provide the things to be copied by the mind, as in the empiricist's account, but to help eliminate false hypotheses about the rules of a language.

directly on them. First, there is the question left open in my treatment of categories of language, as to why such categories are a necessary feature of any language that it is possible for humans to acquire in the normal fashion. This, it will be recalled, was the question Kant raised when he asked why "each language has just this and no other formal constitution." I think we can now give a plausible answer to Kant in terms of the above theory of language acquisition. If we assume that the categories of language are, like other substantive universals in the theory of language, parts of the language acquisition device, then the reason why each language has just these categories as the highest concept types in its semantic structure is that linguistic experience is organized in the form of rules on the basis of these categories. This is an appropriately Kantian answer to Kant's question.

Second, there is the question of synthetic a priori knowledge. If our case for the existence of a rich system of innate principles for language acquisition and use is a sound one, then, given that the principles are indeed synthetic, it follows that in some sense we can have synthetic a priori knowledge, since we can have knowledge of these innate principles. Now, the question arises of whether we can correctly assert that some P which formulates one of the innately determined features of language is a priori. That is, granting the truth of P, what sense does it make to assert that it is a priori if P requires evidence for us to accept it, and if the evidence might have shown P to be false? Here is where the concept of a priori splits into the idea *that what is described by P is antecedent to and the formal determiner of some range of experience* and the idea *that P itself is necessary, not merely contingently true.* In the sense of the first of these component ideas, we can, without adding anything further, say that *P* is a priori because our theory of language accords it the appropriate status. But, in the sense of the second, it might be argued that no such assertion can be made because something is necessary just in case there can be no possible empirical evidence that would count against its truth. It is clear from the appeals to empirical evidence in the above discussion of language acquisition that the truths that formulate the innate ideas of language cannot count as necessary in this sense. For to establish such principles as that of transformational grammar as an innate idea, we had to depend on a considerable body of empirical evidence concerning the character of the input sentences to (D) and the fluent speaker's linguistic competence. It is certainly logically possible that these facts we relied on could have been otherwise than they are—in which case the empiricist hypothesis might have been right.

Let us, therefore, admit at the outset that in this overly strict sense of necessary no such principle, even if it is known to formulate correctly one of the innately determined features of language, is necessary. However, to insist that this sense of necessity is the only one that philosophers should accept, and that everything which is not necessary in this sense must be lumped together as contingent, serves only to cover up real differences between the things so lumped together. There is obviously no point to quibbling about the word 'necessary'; rather, we should look at the class of principles that are not necessary in the strict sense to see if we can find an appropriate difference, one that will give content to the claim that some P is necessary in some important sense, even though it could have evidence against it.

The difference that is relevant is between those truths in the complement of the class of strictly necessary truths which are just empirical generalizations from a sample and can, accordingly, be overthrown by finding cases outside the sample that run counter to them, and those truths in this class that serve as successful explanatory principles and cannot be overthrown by such counter-examples without a new explanatory principle to serve as a replacement for them. Some explanatory principles can be overthrown without replacement, but what is unique about the principles that comprise a hypothesis concerning the inborn capacity for language acquisition is that they describe a device that determines what can count as genuine linguistic experience. Thus, if such principles are true, they are not merely contingently true in the way inductive extrapolations from empirical regularities are. Rather, they are necessarily true because, in principle, they cannot meet with counter-examples. Counter-examples cannot appear in linguistic experience because they would not count as linguistic experience.

With this distinction, which, of course, requires considerably more philosophical clarification, we can say that the principles of the theory of language are a priori principles about language, for we mean thereby, not only that what they describe is antecedent to and the formal determiner of linguistic experience, but that they are necessary in this less strict sense. That any particular one of the principles in the theory of language is a priori is, then, a consequence of the empirical success of the explanation of language acquisition which employs it and so accords it the status of an innate principle. On this account, the principles in the theory of language determine what can count as a possible natural language for human beings and so prescribe the general form of anything that humans can interpret as linguistic communication.

These principles provide the framework within which humans are able to interpret a portion of their experience as linguistic. The fact that we can imagine 'languages' which do not conform to these principles shows only that we have a faculty of imagination. Nothing more, unless what we thus imagine enters into a new explanation of language acquisition that replaces the old one. In short, we can hold that these principles are a priori and admit, nevertheless, that there could be evidence about linguistic communication that contradicts them, for admitting this is only admitting the possibility that these principles might be replaced by others that better explain the facts about language acquisition and linguistic universals.

LINGUISTIC ANALYSIS

The last philosophical problem to be treated is of a different sort from the previous three. It is a problem in metaphilosophy, a problem about the nature of philosophical analysis. In the most general terms, this problem is how to formulate the meaning of a philosophically significant word so as to clearly exhibit every facet of its meaning that might be involved in those epistemological questions in whose statement the word enters essentially. In other words, how should we go about analyzing the meanings of words, and with what kind of representation should we express the results of such analysis. This problem is thus a crucial part of the broader problem of what role linguistic analysis plays in philosophical investigation.

Logical empiricists and ordinary language philosophers were both much concerned with this problem, but neither faced it squarely. As we have seen, logical empiricists presupposed its solution by assuming that natural languages are too incongruous, too amorphous, and too irregular for sheer description of them to reveal anything very much in the way of solutions to philosophical problems. They embodied this presupposition in their doctrine that philosophers should cultivate the development of a theory of ideal, artificial languages which permit such great latitude for "improving" on natural languages that the individual philosopher is given virtually a free hand in deciding what is to be understood by the words in which a philosophical question is posed. As we have seen, on the other hand, the ordinary language philosopher also presupposed the solution to this problem, on what can be regarded as the opposite assumption. He assumed that informal description of the use of words in a natural language provides practically everything required for the solution of philosophical problems. Only in very rare cases did an ordinary language philosopher question the ultimate success of sheer case-by-case description or reflect on the possibility that without a theory of language to guide in the organization and generalization of his results such description might reach a terminus far short of what would be required to deal successfully with philosophical issues.

The position we wish to defend is that the proper assumption lies somewhere between the one extreme of disregarding the facts about the meaning of words in natural language and the other of disregarding the construction of a theory of language in which such facts can be organized, generalized, and empirically motivated. But we do not want just to make this assumption with no more by way of support for it than logical empiricists and ordinary language philosophers offered on behalf on their assumptions. Rather, we want to proceed the other way around, and try to present evidence and reasons for the acceptance of the assumption that descriptive inquiry into the meanings of words must go hand in hand with theory construction if philosophy is to obtain fruitful insights from language.

We can put this another way. Whether or not the meaning of a word in a natural language can help to solve a philosophical problem depends in the first place on just what its meaning is. We cannot find out its meaning unless we have an adequate conception of how to formulate the meanings of words in a natural language, and, therefore, the problem of how to represent the meanings of words is logically prior to the question of whether, and to what extent, linguistic analysis serves philosophical goals. The logical empiricist thus put the cart before the horse: he tried to formulate a theory which permits philosophers to improve on natural languages before he knew whether such improvements are required. He is, therefore, open to the charge that the incongruity, amorphousness, and irregularity that he claims to find in natural languages is nothing more than a mere artifact of his own inadequate tools for describing natural languages. The ordinary language philosopher, to extend the metaphor, uncritically chose a horse when he might have had a truck pull the cart. He is thus open to the charge that, without a theory of language which determines the formulation of the meanings of words in such a fashion that we can empirically evaluate the success of particular analyses of the meanings of words on the basis of how well they predict semantic properties that the theory of language requires them to predict, his particular analyses of the meanings of words cannot provide a secure foundation on which to rest the solution to a philosophical problem.

If the conceptual distinctions embodied in the meanings of philosophically significant words were all as clearly manifest to us as the distinction between 'spinster' and 'bachelor' with respect to the concepts of female and male, there might not be any problem for the ordinary language philosopher. Then, the security of the foundation on which he rests his solutions to philosophical problems would be guaranteed him by general agreement on intuitively obvious cases. However, it is just the philosophically significant words that are most unclear. Part of the reason why philosophy has been puzzling about such words for over two thousand years is that the conceptual distinctions embodied in their meanings are in some sense hidden from our unaided linguistic intuition. Perhaps this is because these distinctions are very complex, or subtle, or abstract. Whatever it is, the fact remains that these cases are among the least clear cases upon which we might have to make intuitive judgements. Given that this is so, the disagreements about their treatment will be reflected in disagreements about the adequacy of a solution to a philosophical problem that rests upon simple intuitive judgments about the conceptual distinctions embodied in the meanings of words. But if this is the case, the only way to resolve such disagreements is to start with clear cases and construct a theory to cover them which also provides a treatment of the unclear cases. The theory must extrapolate from the clear cases in such a fashion as to extend its generalizations to the unclear cases, thereby utilizing our strong intuitions about clear cases to compensate for our weak intuitions about unclear ones. In this way, the empirical support for the claim that a certain philosophically significant word embodies a certain conceptual distinction can be the same as the support for the clearest cases we have, even though the word itself is among the most unclear cases in the language. However, such an approach presupposes a theory of language in which the form of the generalizations from clear to unclear cases is described. That is, it presupposes a general conception of the nature of the formulation of the meaning of a word and of the rules that connect particular descriptions written in this form with predictions about the various semantic properties and relations found in languages. It is true that ordinary language philosophers have at times talked about such notions as 'rule of language,' 'oddity,' etc., but they relied on what is, from the linguist's viewpoint, a rather vague, intuitive, unexplicated conception of these concepts. And they never sought to construct a theory of language which offered a satisfactory formal definition of the proper formulation for the meaning of a word.

In Chapter 4 a theory of language that contained a general, formal definition of the formulation of the meaning of a word in a natural language was presented. This definition was framed within a theory of semantics that relates the meanings of words to the meanings of the constituents and sentences that are made up from them and that formally defines the semantic properties and relations of sentences in terms of the semantic characterizations of their constituents. Thus, the theory determines the predictions that are made about these semantic properties and relations on the basis of the manner in which the meanings of the words in a sentence are formulated. This semantic theory, then, provides a way of handling philosophically significant unclear cases in terms of generalizations from clear cases whose consequences imply their treatment. How successful this theory is cannot be decided without extensive investigation of the semantic structure of natural languages carried out in terms of the theory. A final decision on how successful the theory is at handling philosophically significant unclear cases must thus await such extensive investigation.

However, we can begin this investigation and thus offer evidence for the claim that this semantic theory is successful. We shall take the English word 'good' as an example of a philosophically significant unclear case. We choose this word because the difficulties encountered in previous attempts to describe its meaning are at least as severe as those encountered in connection with any other philosophically significant word. We hope to show that much progress can be made toward a formulation of the meaning of 'good' within the framework of semantic theory as described above. We do not pretend to give a completely exhaustive treatment, but we do desire to handle most of the central uses of this word.

Within a semantic component of a linguistic description, the task of characterizing the meaning of 'good' is that of providing an acceptable dictionary entry. Acceptability is here a matter of how well the entry serves as a basis from which the meanings of the infinitely many sentences containing 'good' can be projected by the rules of the semantic component. Thus, to formulate such an entry, we must first ask what semantic information should be included in this entry in order that an otherwise empirically successful semantic component for a linguistic description of English may be able to mark the semantic properties and relations in sentences in which 'good' appears, i.e., their semantic anomaly, semantic ambiguity, paraphrase relations, and so forth. Once we have included the semantic information we believe should be included in this entry, we can test our hypothesis about the meaning of 'good' by determining how well the semantic interpretations based upon our putative entry for 'good' succeed in marking the semantic properties and relations in larger and larger classes of sentences in which 'good' occurs. We may have to revise our initial hypothesis, but the direction of such revisions will be indicated by the sentences where our predictions fail.

We can easily state the essential features of the syntactic portion of the entry for 'good': 'good' occurs as an adjective, as a noun, as an interjection, and as an adverb. Thus, there will be lexical readings for each of these types of occurrence. However, we will be concerned here only with its adjectival and adverbial meanings, since they are the philosophically most interesting cases. We thus ignore occurrences of 'good' as an interjection, e.g., 'Good!,' and occurrences of 'good' as a noun, e.g., "The farmer sold his goods at market." Furthermore, we shall ignore occurrences of 'good' in idioms, such as 'Good grief!,' 'The Good Book,' and 'goody-goody.' But, even among the cases where 'good' occurs as an adjective or adverb, we cannot be exhaustive. We shall ignore such cases as "That he came on time is good.' 'What we heard about her is good,' etc.

Fortunately, there is only one type of sentence that needs to be considered to arrive at a lexical reading for the occurrences of 'good' as an adjectival modifier of a noun. These are the simple copula sentences of the form *Article – Noun – is – good.*

Any syntactically compound sentence containing an occurrence of 'good' as an adjectival modifier of a noun is derived transformationally from an underlying phrase marker such as (44) of Chapter 4 which contains as a constituent a phrase marker for a copula sentence in which both 'good' and the noun it modifies in the compound sentence appear with the same grammatical relation of modification holding between them. In general, compound sentences of the form $X – Noun – (who, which) – is – Adjective – Y$ or $X – Adjective – Noun – Y$, where 'X' and 'Y' are variables for strings of words one of which may be null, are syntactically constructed from an underlying phrase marker that has the subconfiguration,

(k)

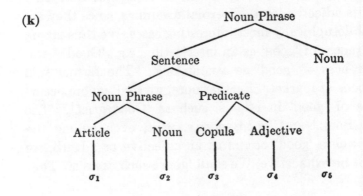

just in case the nouns σ_2 and σ_5 are identical, by a transformational process in which, first, the σ_5 is wh-ed in the form of 'who' or 'which' and moved between σ_2 and σ_3, yielding a sentence structure $X - Noun - (who, which) - is - Adjective - Y$, and second, the relative pronoun is deleted along with the copula σ_3 and α_4 is preposed in front of σ_2 but behind σ_1, yielding a sentence structure $X - Adjective - Noun - Y$. The reason we can restrict our attention to the meaning of 'good' in simple copula sentences is that this pattern of syntactic construction leaves the semantic relations among the words involved unchanged.[29] Given that expressions of the form $Article - Noun - is - Adjective, Article - Noun - (who, which) - is - Adjective$, and $Article - Adjective - Noun$, where the same words appear under the same category marker, e.g., 'the watch is good,' 'the watch which is good,' and 'the good watch,' have the same semantic content, we have the motivation we need for confining our attention to occurrences of 'good' in simple copula sentences, for given that we have successfully characterized the meaning of 'good' for these cases, we can automatically extend our characterization to the infinite set of compound sentences which correspond to them. Moreover, we can regard the empirical correctness of predictions about the semantic properties of either simple copula sentences or compound sentences as evidence for the adequacy of the dictionary entry for the adjectival sense of 'good.'

[29] This claim follows from the more general principle that syntactic transformations do not affect meaning, which is established in Katz and Postal, *An Integrated Theory of Linguistic Descriptions*.

Since, on the basis of the syntactic component's description of the syntax of simple copula sentences, we know that when 'good' is the adjective in such sentences it modifies the word or sequence of words that is the noun subject, the projection rule (R1), discussed above, applies in forming a derived reading for the sentence. Narrowing our attention now to combinations of readings for 'good' and its head noun, we may start by looking at some of the semantic facts about simple predicate-adjective sentences in which 'good' appears that a semantic component must predict on the basis of such combinations of readings. Some of the facts against which predictions concerning the semantic anomalousness or non-anomalousness of such sentences must be verified may be stated as follows. Nouns in English divide into two exclusive categories. In one we find 'knife,' 'anesthetic,' 'money,' 'razor blade,' 'torture,' 'citizen,' 'meat,' 'poker hand,' 'jewelry,' 'mother,' 'lung,' 'watch,' 'hammer,' etc., and in the other we find 'liquid,' 'electricity,' 'planet,' 'molecule,' 'scribble,' 'truth,' 'speck,' 'mote,' 'noun,' 'amoeba,' 'integer,' 'grain of sand,' etc. If the noun in a sentence of the form *Art – Noun – is – good* is from the first of these lists, the sentence is not semantically anomalous, whereas, if the noun is from the second, the sentence is semantically anomalous. Compare 'The razor blade is good' with 'The grain of sand is good.' Of course, one could concoct special circumstances in which to attach an interpretation to an utterance of 'The grain of sand is good'—e.g., we are trying to erect a geology exhibit and need a certain kind of grain of sand for a specimen—but, then, the utterance is best regarded as a reduced version of the sentence 'The grain of sand is good for a specimen of the kind we need' rather than as an occurrence of the anomalous sentence. We shall return to this matter at a later point in this chapter.

A minimum condition for predicting these facts is that the dictionary contain a generalization expressing the respect in which the members of the first lists are semantically similar and in which they are semantically dissimilar to each member of the second list. Such a generalization can be formulated within a dictionary by introducing a specific semantic marker into a lexical reading for every noun on the first list and excluding this semantic marker from readings for nouns on the second. We shall differentiate the nouns that belong to the first of these two categories from those which belong to the second by introducing what we call an *evaluation semantic marker* into the lexical readings of the former nouns but not the latter. Roughly, the inclusion or exclusion of this semantic marker indicates whether or not things covered by the meaning of the noun are evaluable in terms of good and bad. In a reading, the evaluation semantic marker functions to represent that component of the meaning of a noun which has to do with the particular respect in which evaluations are made, within the language, of things in the extension of the noun.

Evaluation semantic markers are to be so represented in the notation of a semantic theory that it will be possible to determine from the way in which a semantic marker is written whether it is an evaluation semantic marker. Thus, we write an evaluation semantic marker in the form '(Eval: (   )),' where the inner parentheses indicate the presence of a semantic marker that specifies the particular aspect of the meaning of the noun which serves as the standard of evaluation. A noun whose meaning is represented by a reading containing an evaluation semantic marker may have other components of its meaning that cannot be represented by such a marker. In this case the reading will contain as well semantic markers that are not evaluation semantic markers. Examples of this case include: 'knife,' 'watch,' 'lung,' 'meat,' etc. The lexical reading for 'knife,' might be *knife* → Noun, Common Noun, . . . , Count Noun; (Physical Object), (Nonliving), (With Blade), (With Handle), (Eval: (ease of dividing substances softer than its blade)); <SR>. In the reading for 'knife' the semantic markers that represent the information that a knife has a blade and handle, for example, are not evaluation semantic markers, whereas the semantic marker that represents the information that a knife is used for cutting is. On the other hand, just as there are words whose readings do not contain evaluation semantic markers, there are words whose readings contain only evaluation semantic markers. For example, the reading for 'anesthetic' contains only the evaluation semantic marker '(Eval: (Effective in producing a temporary loss of feeling in a part of a body)).'[30]

The respects in which evaluations of things can be made differ with differences in the other semantic fea-

---

[30] Among other things, hypnosis is an anesthetic.

tures of the words that refer to those things. Nouns whose readings contain the semantic marker (Artifact), such as 'knife,' 'torpedo,' 'watch,' etc. and nouns whose readings contain the semantic marker (Natural Substance), such as 'coal,' 'wood,' 'iron,' etc., permit evaluation of their referents in terms of the uses normally made of them. Alternatively, nouns whose readings contain the semantic marker (Component of a System) or the semantic marker (Member of a Team), such as 'heart,' 'camshaft,' 'eye,' 'quarterback,' etc. permit evaluations of their referents in terms of *functions* performed by them in their positions. A noun that has the semantic marker (Role) in its reading, such as 'mother,' 'teacher,' 'foreman,' etc., permits evaluation in terms of the performance of *duties* to which someone occupying such a role is obligated. A noun such as 'jewelry' which has the semantic marker (Ornamentation) in its reading permits evaluation in terms of the purposes, decorative and symbolic, that its referents serve. A noun that has the semantic marker (Food) in its reading, such as 'meat,' 'apples,' 'cheese,' etc. permits evaluation in terms of *pleasurability* and perhaps *healthfulness*. There are, of course, many other respects in which things or persons can be evaluated by uttering appropriate sentences, but such further cases must be by-passed as matters of detail.

Such differences in type of evaluation suggest that the evaluation semantic markers in readings be subcategorized in order that nouns may be grouped into subclasses according to the specific different respects in which their referents are evaluated. We may accomplish

such subcategorization by subscripting the evaluation semantic markers with symbols representing the concepts
of *use, function, duty, purpose,* etc. For example, the
evaluation semantic marker in the reading for 'knife' will
have a subscript symbol that expresses the fact that a
knife is evaluated in terms of its use, whereas the evaluation semantic marker in the reading for 'mother' will
have a subscript symbol that expresses the fact that
someone who is evaluated as a mother is judged in terms
of the performance of duties associated with this role.
Employing the abbreviations 'us' for 'use,' 'fn' for 'function,' 'pu' for 'purpose,' 'du' for 'duty,' and so on, we can
formulate evaluation semantic markers of the types:
$(Eval_{us}: (\quad))$, $(Eval_{fn}: (\quad))$, $(Eval_{pu}: (\quad))$, $(Eval_{du}:$
$(\quad))$, and so on. With these differentiated evaluation
semantic markers we can express generalizations to the
effect that artifacts are evaluated on the same basis,
that foods are evaluated on the same basis, and so forth.
Later we will be able to say something more by way of
justifying this set of distinctions.

We can now state the lexical reading for 'good' as an
adjectival modifier: *good* → Adjective, further syntactic
markers; $(+)$ $<(Eval_x: (\quad))>$, where the semantic
marker $(+)$ is contextually defined as follows:

$$(M_1), (M_2), \ldots, (M_i), \ldots, (M_k), (+)<SR>$$
is by definition equivalent to
$$(M_1), (M_2), \ldots, (+M_i), \ldots, (M_k)<SR>,$$

where 'x' is a variable over the subscripts 'us,' 'fn,' 'pu,'
'du,' etc., and where (M_i) is an evaluation semantic

marker. The left-hand side of this contextual definition is a reading-schema that represents a derived reading formed from the combination of the above reading for 'good'—hence the presence of the semantic marker (+)—and a reading for a noun. The right-hand side is a reading schema that represents the reading into which such a derived reading is converted by the operation of (+), i.e., by the application of this contextual definition. The selection restriction in the reading for 'good,' namely, $<(\text{Eval}_x: (\quad))>$, imposes the requirement that a derived reading formed from the reading for 'good' and a reading for a noun can result only if the reading for this noun contains an occurrence of an evaluation semantic marker.

We can now show how a semantic component of English can predict the aforementioned facts about the semantic anomaly of sentences such as 'The grain of sand is good,' 'The liquid is good,' 'The scribble is good,' 'The planet is good,' etc. and the nonanomalousness of sentences such as 'The razor blade is good,' 'The watch is good,' 'The meat is good,' 'The poker hand is good,' etc. Sentences of the former type have subject nouns whose reading contains no occurrence of an evaluation semantic marker and thus, in their semantic interpretation, these sentences receive no readings because the readings of their subjects do not satisfy the selection restriction in the reading for 'good.' Therefore, these sentences are marked as semantically anomalous. On the other hand, sentences of the latter type, because their subject nouns have readings containing an evaluation semantic marker, and so satisfy the selection restriction in the reading for 'good,' receive readings and are thus marked as nonanomalous.

($+$Eval$_{us}$: ( )) is to be construed as specifying that the object concerned has the ability to perform the task indicated in ( ); ($+$Eval$_{fn}$: ( )) is to be construed as specifying that the object concerned has the ability to perform the function indicated in ( ); ($+$Eval$_{pu}$: ( )) is to be construed as specifying that the object concerned has the ability to serve the purpose indicated in ( ); ($+$Eval$_{du}$: ( )) is to be construed as specifying that the person concerned has successfully carried out the duties indicated in ( ); and so forth. ($+$Eval$_{us}$: (Reliability in keeping accurate time under normal conditions), which is the evaluation semantic marker in the reading for the sentence 'The watch is good,' specifies that the timepiece concerned has the ability to reliably keep accurate time under normal conditions. Alternatively, an unplused occurrence of an evaluation semantic marker specifies only the relevant standard of evaluation. It does not specify any specific evaluation that can be made on the basis of the standard. Thus, the evaluation semantic marker in the reading for the sentence 'The watch was found in his pocket' implies no actual evaluation of the watch.

This mode of construing the plus immediately suggests a lexical reading for 'bad.' The reading for adjectival occurrences of 'bad' should be identical with the reading for 'good' except that, where ($+$) appears in the reading for 'good,' ($-$) appears in the reading for 'bad.' The contextual definition for (—), which specifies the operation of this semantic marker, is, then, to be the same as that for (+) except that wherever '+' appears in the above contextual definition '—' appears in the equivalence defining (—). (—) is thus regarded as the opposite of (+) in the sense that (—Eval$_x$: ( )) specifies the inability of the object concerned to perform the task indicated in ( ) in case 'x' has the value 'us,' the inadequacy of the object to perform the function indicated in ( ) in case 'x' has the value 'fn,' and similarly in the case of other kinds of evaluation semantic markers.[31] With this lexical reading for 'bad,' we can account for the further facts that the sentences 'The grain of sand is bad,' 'The liquid is bad,' 'The scribble is bad,' and so forth are also semantically anomalous. The reading for 'bad' has the same selection restriction as the reading for 'good' and so such sentences receive no readings and are consequently marked as semantically anomalous.

Besides enabling us to predict the semantically anoma-

[31] Note that the actual features a thing must have to enable a certain use to be made of it, to enable it to perform a certain function, to permit it to serve a certain purpose, etc., are not, and should not be, determined by the dictionary entry for the word that refers to such a thing. Thus, what actual features watches, hearts, quarterbacks, stock-market consultants, etc., must possess in order to be good watches, hearts, quarterbacks, stock-market consultants, etc., are not something a person knows qua speaker of the language, but, rather, are something he knows qua specialist or expert of some sort, i.e., qua watchmaker, physiologist, football coach, stock-market expert, etc. One who knows English knows that a good watch is reliable in keeping accurate time under normal conditions, but, unless one is also a watchmaker, he need not know anything at all about the physical properties of watch mechanisms—mainsprings, jewels, etc.—that enable watches to perform properly.

lous and nonanomalous sentences containing an adjectival
occurrence of 'good,' these dictionary entries for 'good'
and 'bad' in conjunction with suitably formulated entries
for the nouns of the language enable us to represent the
intuitively acceptable senses of the nonanomalous cases.
Roughly, the derived reading for the sentence 'The knife
is good' will be: (Some contextually definite), (Physical
Object), (Nonliving), (With Blade), (With Handle),
($+$Eval$_{us}$: (ease of dividing substances softer than its
blade)). The derived reading for 'The knife is bad' will be
the same except for the apropriate change of sign. The
former reading represents the fact that 'The knife is good'
means the knife cuts easily what it is supposed to cut
while the latter represents the fact that 'The knife is bad'
means the knife is not a satisfactory tool to use in
cutting. In addition, the theoretical machinery introduced to enable us to represent the meaning of 'good'
and 'bad' also enables us to represent the meaning of
certain nouns whose meaning has a certain form of
goodness, or badness, built into it. Thus, we can propose
the following lexical reading for 'bonanza': noun; (Ore
Deposit), (Excavated), ($+$Eval$_{cd}$: (Abundant in valuable ore)), where 'cd' indicates a subclass of standards
having to do with evaluation in terms of condition. If
we define the word 'mine' with the lexical reading: noun;
(Ore Deposit), (Excavated), (Eval$_{cd}$: (Abundant in
valuable ore)), we will have successfully distinguished
between the meanings of these two semantically similar
nouns in terms of the presence or absence of a plus on
their evaluation semantic marker. Given the interpreta-

tion of the presence and absence of a plus, this appears to be just the right semantic difference between them.[32] Moreover, there are cases of triplets of nouns whose meanings are the same except for plused, nonsigned, and minused evaluation semantic markers, e.g., respectively, 'gusher,' 'oil well,' and 'dry hole.' Now, important predictions about the semantic properties of sentences can be obtained from such lexical readings. The sentence 'The bonanza is good' will be marked as analytic because the reading for its subject noun 'bonanza' already contains the semantic marker ($+$) which is in the reading for the verb phrase, which contains the reading for 'good.' 'The mine is good' will, correspondingly, be marked as nonanalytic because the combination of the reading for 'mine' and the reading for 'good' involves a nonredundant addition of the semantic marker ($+$). Also, since the noun 'mine' has at least the additional lexical reading: Noun; (Physical Object), (Explosive Charge), ($Eval_{pu}$: destruction of enemy personnel, vehicles, or vessels)), the sentence 'The mine is good' is marked as at least two ways semantically ambiguous. Furthermore, just as 'The bonanza is good' and 'The gusher is good' are both marked as analytic sentences, the sentence 'The dry hole is bad' will be marked as analytic. Finally, we note that 'The mine is good,' 'The oil well is good,' and similar cases are marked as synthetic and that, be-

---

[32] I am aware that this treatment of 'bonanza' and 'gusher' is somewhat of an understatement, that a bonanza is more than a good mine. But this point, though it involves only minor adjustments in the treatment of these words, leads to complications that are better left out of a discussion of this nature.

cause the semantic markers (+) and (—) are antonymous semantic markers, the sentences 'The bonanza is
bad,' 'The gusher is bad,' and 'The dry hole is good'
are each marked as contradictory and the sentence which
results from just the replacement of 'good' for 'bad' or
'bad' for 'good' in any sentence of the kind we are considering is inconsistent with the original sentence.

We now return to a previous point. Even though 'The
scribble is good,' 'The liquid is good,' and 'The planet
is good' are semantically anomalous, sentences such as
'The scribble is good for diagnosing the patient's neurosis,'
'The liquid is good to drink,' and 'The planet is good as
a subject for class discussion' are not. Moreover,
sentences such as 'The knife is good to pry open jars
with,' 'The knife is good for picking teeth,' 'The knife
is good because it has a grip handle,' etc., express evaluations different from that expressed by 'The knife is good,'
and these evaluations are not predictable from the dictionary entries for 'good' and 'knife' alone. However,
none of these facts, including, in particular, the fact that
the meaning of the last triplet of sentences is not predictable from the dictionary entries of 'good' and 'knife' as
presented above, is a basis for criticizing our account so
far. Constructions such as 'X is good for Y-ing,' 'X is
good to Y,' 'X is good as a Y,' 'X is good because it is
a Y,' etc. can easily have their meaning described as a
compositional function of the meanings of their parts, as
long as the meaning of *all* their parts is taken into account. Such constructions play a very special role in language: they permit speakers to depart from standard

forms of evaluation and to make evaluations that are suitable to special occasions, to specific needs and motives, to idiosyncratic jobs, etc. In these constructions, we can variably supply the semantic information that functions as the standard of evaluation by filling in 'Y' with an appropriate expression of the language, as in the above cases, 'diagnosing the patient's neurosis,' 'prying open jars,' 'picking teeth,' etc. A semantic component of the kind we have been describing can correctly interpret sentences based on such constructions by including in its dictionary entries for the words 'for,' 'to,' 'as,' 'because,' etc. semantic markers which formalize an instruction to the effect that, when one of these words appears in such a construction, the reading of the expression that it introduces either institutes an evaluation semantic marker where there was none before or replaces the semantic marker content of the evaluation semantic marker of the sentence's subject noun. In the case of 'The knife is good for picking teeth,' the reading for 'picking teeth' replaces (ease of dividing substances softer than its blade) in the evaluation semantic marker (Eval$_{us}$: (ease of dividing substances softer than its blade)). Thus, cases of the kind treated in this paragraph are not exceptions to our account but rather provide further confirmation for it.

Notice that in the case of *Article – Noun – is – good* sentences in which *Noun* has a reading which contains, besides an evaluation semantic marker, semantic markers that are not evaluation semantic markers, ($+$) and ($-$) do not operate on any of them. This is the formal explication of the English speaker's intuition that an evaluation of the goodness or badness of a thing has nothing *per se* to do with its having any one or another of the properties whose presence is, as it were, guaranteed definitionally. This explains, for example, why a knife is not evaluated as good by virtue of its being a physical object, having a handle, or having a blade.

Next, we turn to the prediction of paraphrase relations between sentences containing 'good.' To provide an exhaustive treatment of both these relations and the dictionary entry for 'good,' we must consider the lexical reading for adverbial occurrences of 'good.' As an adverb, 'good' occurs in sentences of two types: those of the form *Noun Phrase – Auxiliary – Verb*$_{tr}$ *– Noun Phrase – Adverb* and those of the form *Noun Phrase – Auxiliary – Verb*$_{intr}$ *– Adverb*. In both, 'good' occurs phonologically or orthographically as 'well.' Since in both types 'good' is a modifier of the verb, the grammatical relation here is the same as in the case where 'good' is an adjectival modifier and so (R1) is the projection rule which provides derived readings for verb-phrases in which 'good' occurs adverbially. The same is, of course, true for 'bad' as an adverb, which appears as 'badly.' Thus, the simplest and most uniform treatment of the meaning of 'good' and 'bad' is one in which their adverbial occurrences are interpreted on the basis of the same lexical readings as their adjectival occurrences. We may carry over the semantic constructions we found successful in the case of their adjectival forms by including alternate adverbial markers with the adjective markers in the syntactic portion of their lexical readings. These lexical readings are thus: $good \to A, A_1, A_2, \ldots, A_n$ or Adv, Adv$_1$, Adv$_2$, $\ldots$, Adv$_m$; $(+)$; $<$(Eval$_x$: ( ))$>$, and $bad \to A, A_1$, $A_2, \ldots, A_n$ or Adv, Adv$_1$ Adv$_2$, $\ldots$, Adv$_m$; $(-)$; $<$(Eval$_x$: ( ))$>$.[33] This treatment is possible because the syntactic structure of 'well' and 'badly' are, respectively, 'good $+$ ly' and 'bad $+$ ly.' 'well' and 'badly' are simply the pronunciations or orthographic realizations of these underlying syntactic forms.

Now, consider the fact that the sentences 'The knife is good' and 'The knife is bad' are paraphrases of 'The knife cuts well' and 'The knife cuts badly,' which accounts for whatever humor there is in such 'joke' sentences as 'The knife is good except that it cuts badly.'[34] In order to be able to predict this fact, we must construct a lexical reading for the intransitive verb 'cuts' so that these sentences in which it occurs have the same reading as their copula-sentence paraphrases. Thus, we give: $cuts \to V$, V_{intr}, further syntactic markers; (Process), $\ldots$, (Eval$_{us}$: (Ease of dividing substances softer than blade of X)); $<$Subject/(Physical Object)$>$, where 'X' is the reading of the subject of 'cuts.' By the application of (R1), this evaluation semantic marker will be appropriately plused or minused to yield derived readings that are the same as those for the corresponding copula-sentence paraphrases. In this way, these paraphrase relations, and

---

[33] There seems to be some prospect of deriving adverbial occurrences of 'good' and 'bad' from adjectival occurrences. If this is so, these new readings will be unnecessary.

[34] More precisely, they are paraphrases on a reading. 'The knife cuts badly' is, of course, semantically ambiguous, having both the sense that it cuts poorly and the sense that it inflicts severe wounds.

others like them, can be predicted on the basis of the semantic interpretations of the sentences between which they hold.

The treatment of paraphrase relations between copula-sentences and sentences with transitive main verbs, though essentially the same, is slightly more complicated because account must be taken of the fact that in the latter type of sentence the goodness or badness of the process, action, etc. expressed by the verb is restricted by the meaning of the verb's nominal object. Thus, the sentences 'The knife cuts meat well' and 'The knife cuts meat badly,' which are paraphrases, respectively, of 'The knife is good for cutting meat' and 'The knife is bad for cutting meat,' make far less comprehensive evaluations concerning the knife than do their corresponding intransitive sentences 'The knife cuts well' and 'the knife cuts badly.' The first of these two sentences says that the knife is suitably adapted to cutting meat, but it does not imply that it is also suitable for cutting wood, metal, cloth, or other substances. Likewise, the second does not imply that the knife is not suitably adapted to cutting wood, metal, cloth, or other substances. In order to take account of this semantic relation to the meaning of the nominal object, it is necessary only to capitalize on a general feature of the readings of transitive verbs. Just as the readings for intransitive verbs contain a slot which takes the reading of their subjects, so the readings of transitive verbs contain two slots which fix the places at which the readings of their subjects and objects are embedded by the projection rule that combines a reading of a transitive verb with a reading of its subject and the projection rule that combines a reading of a transitive verb with a reading of its object. For example, the reading for 'eats' might be: $eats \rightarrow V, V_{tr}$; (Process), (Physiological), . . . , (X takes in through mouth and swallows Y); <Subject/(Physical Object) and Object/(Physical Object)>, where the 'X' is the slot for the reading of the subject of 'eats' in a particular sentence and the 'Y' is the slot for the reading of its object. Accordingly, the reading for a transitive occurrence of 'cuts' might be: $cuts \rightarrow V, V_{tr}$; (Process), . . . , ($Eval_{us}$: (Ease of X dividing Y)); <Subject/(Physical Object) and Object/(Physical Object)>. In both of our examples, the slot 'X' is filled by the reading for 'knife' and the slot 'Y' is filled by the reading for 'meat.' Given this reading for 'cuts' as a transitive verb, not only can a semantic component reveal how the evaluation of the thing referred to by the subject in a sentence of the form *Noun Phrase – Auxiliary – cuts – Noun Phrase – Adverb* (Adv = 'well' or Adv = 'badly') is appropriately restricted by the meaning of the object, but it can also corrrectly mark the paraphrase relations between such sentences and others of different syntactic form. A similar treatment of the lexical readings of other transitive and intransitive verbs will enable us to obtain correct predictions about the paraphrase relations in different sentences of the types we have been considering.[35]

---

[35] The selection restriction in the readings for both intransitive and transitive occurrrences of 'cuts' requires that the readings with which the verb phrase that contains 'cuts' can combine, namely, those for its subject, include the semantic marker (Physical Object). This enables

Adverbial occurrences of 'good' and 'bad' can also modify adjectives, as in 'She likes a good green hat,' where this means a hat colored a good green. But these cases deserve no special comment. An adjective that can be modified by 'good' or 'bad' will receive a lexical reading containing an evaluation semantic marker which expresses the respect in which the attribute concerned is evaluated within the language.

We should briefly comment on the further problem of providing semantic interpretations for comparative and superlative sentences with 'good' and 'bad.' In order to semantically interpret such sentences, we need dictionary entries for the forms *as Adjective as, Adjective er than,* and *Adjective est.* On the basis of the previous discussion, the general lines along which such entries are to be constructed are clear, even if the specific details are not. We require a semantic marker which functions as an operator on the plus or minus attached to an evaluation semantic marker. This operator expresses the relation between the degrees of different signs. *As Adjective as,* where Adjective = 'good' or 'bad,' specifies that the degree of the signs in the readings for the two nouns compared is equal, e.g., that the degree of the plus in the reading

---

a semantic component to predict the semantic anomaly of a sentence such as 'The belief cut the meat.' Likewise, the selection restriction in the reading for 'well' and 'badly' requires that the readings for verbs must include an evaluation semantic marker. Thus, the sentences 'The man knows well' and 'The man believes John well' are both marked as semantically anomalous because 'knows' and 'believes,' in the appropriate senses, do not have an evaluation semantic marker in their readings. Sentences such as 'The man knows John well' involve both a different sense of 'knows' and a different sense of 'well.'

for 'knife' is equal to the degree of the plus in the reading for 'shovel' in the sentence 'The knife is as good as the shovel.' *Noun₁ is better (worse) than N₂* specifies that the degree of the sign in the reading for Noun₁ is higher than the degree of the sign in the reading for Noun₂, e.g., that the degree of the plus in the reading for 'knife' is higher than the degree of the plus in the reading for 'razor' in the sentence 'The knife is better than the razor.' *Noun₁ is the best (worst) of the Noun₂s* specifies that the degree of the sign in the reading for Noun₁ is higher than that in the reading for any Noun that is one of the Noun₂s, e.g., that the plus in the reading for 'knife' in 'The knife is the best of the tools' is higher than the plus in the reading for 'the saw I bought yesterday,' 'the screwdriver,' 'the solid steel hammer,' 'my rusty chisel,' etc., where these Nouns refer to things belonging to the collection referred to previously by 'the tools.' However, the problem of constructing the actual dictionary entries for *as Adjective as, Adjective er than, and Adjective est* is further complicated because the lexical readings for these forms must make suitable provision for the semantic effect of any adjective (or adverb) that can enter into comparative or superlative constructions. Hence, a full analysis of these forms is beyond our scope here.

Earlier we introduced a subcategorization of the evaluation semantic marker. We can now further justify the subcategories of *use, function, purpose, duty*, etc., on the grounds that they are necessary in order for a semantic theory to mark the semantic anomalousness of certain comparative constructions. Consider the semantically anomalous sentences 'The knife is as good as my mother' and 'The teacher is better than the jewelry,' and compare them, respectively, with the nonanomalous sentences 'The knife is as good as the screwdriver' and 'The teacher is better than the lawyer.' Roughly speaking, the former cases are semantically anomalous because they involve a comparison of things that are not capable of being evaluated by the same type of standard of goodness and badness, while the latter cases are nonanomalous because they compare things on the basis of a common type of standard of evaluation. Thus, in 'The knife is as good as the screwdriver' we have an evaluation to the effect that the knife performs the use normally made of knives as efficiently as the screwdriver does the use normally made of screwdrivers, and in 'The teacher is better than the lawyer' we have an evaluation to the effect that the teacher performs his duties as a teacher better than the lawyer does his as a lawyer. These anomalous and non-anomalous cases can be predicted if we introduce in the lexical readings for the forms *as Adjective as, Adjective er than*, and *Adjective est* a selection restriction that requires the readings of the nouns compared to have the same subcategory of evaluation semantic marker. Suitable formulations of the lexical readings of these comparative and superlative forms will also enable us to represent the meaning of nonanomalous sentences of the type under consideration. The need to have such subcategorization for these purposes is, then, further justification for the subcategorization of evaluation semantic markers.

This completes the discussion of how the meaning of a philosophically significant word can be represented in the general form for dictionary entries provided by the theory of language and how such a representation can be empirically supported on the basis of clear cases about which it, together with the rest of the dictionary and the projection rules of a semantic component, makes correct predictions. I shall not try to draw any philosophical implications from the dictionary entries given above for 'good' and 'bad.' In the first place, it has not been my objective to argue that there are such implications. Perhaps the best linguistic analysis of the meanings of these words would show that the implications are nonexistent or trivial as far as the substantive issues of moral philosophy are concerned. Rather, I have argued for a way of formulating the meanings of words in a natural language, one which avoids the logical empiricist's linguistic libertinism, on the one hand, and the ordinary language philosopher's sterile antitheoretical orientation, on the other. In the second place, I do not regard the above analysis of the meaning of 'good' as complete. For example, we have given no treatment of such philosophically important constructions as 'good man.' These cases are especially difficult because this treatment presupposes the explication of some very complex matters, e.g., the anomaly of sentences such as 'He is a good man because he has at least one hair on his head.' Therefore, since, as I have already said, a complete and successful linguistic treatment is logically prior to a discussion of philosophical implications, it is best to avoid speculations based on an incomplete treatment.

However, it is worthwhile to compare briefly the theory of meaning put forth in Chapter 4 with other theories with respect to the above treatment of the meaning of 'good.' Such a comparison will bring out some of the advantages of semantic theory in my sense and also clarify some of the features of the treatment of the meaning of 'good.'

The meaning of 'good,' as we have seen, does not have the kind of structure that the meanings of most other English words do. Whereas the meaning of words such as 'bachelor,' 'honest,' 'hard,' 'cuts,' 'liquid,' etc., is made up of component elements that are attributes in their own right, the meaning of 'good' is a function which operates on other meanings, not an independent attribute. Apart from combination with the conceptual content of other words and expressions, the meaning of 'good' does not make sense. Since the meaning of 'good' cannot stand alone as a complete concept, we shall say that the meaning of 'good' is *syncategorematic*.

The semantic marker (+) provides the theoretical machinery required to handle this syncategorematicity. In conjunction with the system of evaluation semantic markers and the selection restriction in the lexical reading for 'good,' (+) enables a semantic component to formally reconstruct the dependency of the meaning of 'good' on certain semantic properties of the words and expressions that 'good' can modify. Thus, this semantic marker has significance only within a reading that contains an evaluation semantic marker and its significance lies in the way in which it operates on that evaluation semantic marker to produce a correct representation of the meaning of the constituent to which the reading is assigned.

Therefore, for a semantic component to be able to represent the meaning of 'good,' it must be designed to do more than simply characterize the meanings of words and expressions individually. No theory of meaning can give the meaning of 'good' in the form of some unique specification for this word because, since the meaning of 'good' is syncategorematic, it cannot be given in such terms. This observation suffices to show that a number of different types of semantic theories are empirically inadequate. Included in this category are Platonic theories of meaning, Osgood's theory based on his Semantic Differential,[36] reference or designation theories of meaning,[37] stimulus-response theories of meaning such as Skinner's and Quine's,[38] and theories that identify meaning with information content (in the communication engineer's sense).[39] The basic idea underlying each of these conceptions of meaning would limit a semantic

[36] C. E. Osgood, G. J. Suci, and P. H. Tannenbaum. *The Measurement of Meaning,* University of Illinois Press, 1957.

[37] An example of such a theory is one of Carnap's early conceptions of meaning in which the semantic interpretation for the descriptive symbols of a system was given solely in terms of rules of designation.

[38] B. F. Skinner, *Verbal Behavior,* Appleton-Century-Crofts, 1957, and particularly chapter 2 of W. Quine, *Word and Object,* M. I. T. Press, 1960.

[39] Cf. any of the wide variety of approaches to meaning based on C. E. Shannon and W. Weaver, *The Mathematical Theory of Communication,* University of Illinois Press, 1949.

component to the task of trying to state the meanings of words individually.

Another serious defect of such theories is that the meaning of expressions and sentences in which 'good' appears cannot be given by listing them and pairing each with some sort of semantic characterization. In principle, such a procedure, which is the only one ever offered by the proponents of these theories, would leave infinitely many expressions and sentences containing 'good' uncharacterized, since any finite list would necessarily leave off infinitely many cases. 'good' occurs in noun-phrases and also in verb-phrases that have noun-phrase objects. Because of the recursive nature of the syntactic mechanism for forming noun-phrases, there is no longest noun-phrase, and hence no longest expression or sentence that contains 'good.' The length of a noun-phrase can always be increased by adding another modifier such as a relative clause, or another modifier within a relative clause, and such additions can always affect the contribution that the meaning of an occurrence of 'good' makes to the whole. To appreciate this, it is only necessary to recall that in sentences of the form $Noun\ Phrase_1 - Verb_{tr} - Noun\ Phrase_2 - well$ the evaluation expressed is limited in scope by the meaning of Noun Phrase$_2$. For example, if the sentence 'The knife cuts meat well' is expanded by adding a relative clause to the noun 'meat,' thus forming the sentence 'The knife cuts meat which is tenderized well,' then the evaluation, the claim about the knife's performance, made by this newly formed sentence is restricted as compared with that made by the original sentence. Such an evaluation can be fur-

ther and further restricted by adding other components
to the relative clause, e.g., 'by a new process,' or other
relative clauses, e.g., 'and which is boiled for six days.'

Thus, besides the syncategorematic feature of the meaning of 'good,' there are other features that make it an adequate basis from which to project the meaning of
infinitely many syntactically compound expressions and
sentences containing 'good,' as a compositional function
of the meanings of their components. This *compositional
potentiality* makes the dependency resulting from the
syncategorematic feature a part of the system of interrelations whereby the meaning of 'good' contributes to the
meaning of expressions and sentences. In terms of this
compositional potentiality, we may criticize certain theories of meaning whose conception of the meaning of a
word is too loosely formulated to be criticized on the
grounds that it cannot account for syncategorematicity.
These theories are ones that characterize meaning in such
a manner that there is no way for them to relate the
meaning of a word to the meanings of other words in an
infinite variety of syntactic constructions. An example of
one such theory is the conception of meaning according
to which the meaning of a word is construed as its distribu-
tion in a set of linguistic frames, where occurrence in the
same set of frames, holding constant some such parame-
ter as truth or oddity, is the test of synonymy. Another
example is the pure version of the emotive theory of
meaning proposed by certain positivists.[40] Still other examples can be found in the various 'use' theories of mean-

---

[40] For example, in Carnap's earliest writings or in C. L. Stevenson,
Ethics and Language, Yale University Press, 1945.

ing propounded by Ordinary Language philosophers.[41] None of these theories have the conceptual machinery for relating meanings to one another that it necessary to reconstruct the way that the compositional potentiality of word-meanings is realized at the expression and sentence level.

Among the theories of meaning that do provide some conceptual machinery for interrelating meanings, only the one described in Chapter 4 provides the kind of machinery needed to handle the syncategorematic and compositional potentiality aspects of the meaning of 'good.' The other theories, two examples of which are Wittgenstein's picture theory of meaning[42] and various intensionalist accounts such as Carnap's *Meaning and Necessity*,[43] fail to extend their compositional analysis of meaning down to the level of the minimally syntactically functioning elements of the language, i.e., down to the semantic structure of the meaning of words, or whatever unit is the syntactically minimal one. Because these theories do not decompose the meanings of words into their component semantic elements, they provide no basis for dividing such elements into those that are and those that are not affected by the meaning of 'good.' For example, the meaning of 'good' in constructions such as 'good knife,' 'good lung,' 'good citizen,' etc., affects only the

[41] For example, Wittgenstein, *Philosophical Investigations*. Other examples are too numerous to mention.

[42] L. Wittgenstein, *Tractatus Logico-Philosophicus*, Routledge & Kegan Paul, London, 1922.

[43] R. Carnap, *Meaning and Necessity*, University of Chicago Press, 1956.

evaluational component in the meaning of 'knife,' 'lung,' 'citizen,' etc. It does not affect those components, such as the concept of having a handle, being a physical object, being human, etc., which have to do with the physical characteristics that are part of the meaning of 'knife,' 'lung,' 'citizen,' etc. Thus, on these theories there is no possibility for a contextual definition of the meaning of 'good' that is selective in the appropriate sense. As we have seen, for such a contextual definition, it is necessary to break down the meanings of words that 'good' can modify into at least two kinds of semantic elements, those that are related to the meaning of 'good' and those that are not, since such a definition connects the meaning of 'good' with the meanings of nouns, verbs, and adjectives only in terms of such a division into semantic elements. Furthermore, such theories will be unable to formulate selection restrictions on semantically acceptable combinations without such a division. This means that they will be unable to predict the semantically anomalous sentences whose anomaly has to do with the meaning of 'good,' the semantic ambiguities in sentences where the meaning of 'good' influences the degree of semantic ambiguity, and the other semantic properties and relations of sentences in which such properties and relations are, in part, determined by the semantic contribution of 'good.'

BIBLIOGRAPHY

Alston, W. *The Philosophy of Language.* Englewood Cliffs, N. J.: Prentice-Hall, Inc., 1964.

Aristotle. *Organon,* in Richard P. McKeon (ed.), *The Basic Works of Aristotle.* New York: Random House, Inc., 1941.

Arnauld, A. *The Art of Thinking.* Indianapolis: Bobbs-Merrill Company, Inc., 1964.

Austin, J. L. *How to Do Things with Words.* Cambridge: Harvard University Press, 1962.

Austin, J. L. "A Plea for Excuses," *Proceedings of the Aristotelian Society,* vol. 57, 1956–1957. Reprinted in J. L. Austin, *Philosophical Papers.* Oxford: Clarendon Press, 1961.

Campbell, N. *What Is Science?* New York: Dover Publications, Inc., 1952.

Carnap, R. "The Elimination of Metaphysics Through the Logical Analysis of Language," in A. J. Ayer (ed.), *Logical Positivism.* New York: Macmillan Company, 1959.

Carnap, R. *Introduction to Semantics.* Cambridge: Harvard University Press, 1946.

Carnap, R. *The Logical Syntax of Language.* London: Routledge & Kegan Paul, Ltd., 1937.

Carnap, R. *Meaning and Necessity.* Chicago: University of Chicago Press (2nd edition), 1956.

Carnap, R. "Meaning Postulates" and "Meaning and Synonymy in Natural Languages." Supplements to 2nd edition of *Meaning and Necessity.*

Carnap, R. *The Philosophy of Rudolph Carnap.* La Salle, Ill.: Open Court Publishing Company, 1963.

Chomsky, N. *Aspects of the Theory of Syntax.* Cambridge: M. I. T. Press, 1965.

Chomsky, N. *Cartesian Linguistics* (in preparation).

Chomsky, N. "On Certain Formal Properties of Grammars," *Information and Control*, vol. 2, 1959.

Chomsky, N. "Current Issues in Linguistic Theory," in J. A. Fodor and J. J. Katz (eds.), *The Structure of Language: Readings in the Philosophy of Language.* Englewood Cliffs, N. J.: Prentice-Hall, Inc., 1964.

Chomsky, N. "On the Notion 'Rule of Grammar,'" in J. A. Fodor and J. J. Katz (eds.), *op. cit.*

Chomsky, N. "A Review of B. F. Skinner's *Verbal Behavior*," in J. A. Fodor and J. J. Katz (eds.), *op. cit.*

Chomsky, N. *Syntactic Structures.* The Hague: Mouton & Company, 1957.

Chomsky, N. "Topics in the Theory of Generative Grammar," in T. A. Sebeok (ed.), *Current Trends in Linguistics,* vol. 3, Indiana University Press (to appear).

Chomsky, N. "A Transformational Approach to Syntax," in J. A. Fodor and J. J. Katz (eds.), *op. cit.*

Estes, W. K., *et al. Modern Learning Theory.* New York: Appleton-Century-Crofts, Inc., 1954.

Ferster, C. B., and B. F. Skinner. *Schedules of Reinforcement.* New York: Appleton-Century-Crofts, Inc., 1957.

Fodor, J. A., and J. J. Katz. "The Availability of What We Say," *Philosophical Review,* vol. 72, no. 1, January, 1963.

Fodor, J. A., and J. J. Katz (eds). *The Structure of Language: Readings in the Philosophy of Language.* Englewood Cliffs, N. J.: Prentice-Hall, Inc., 1964.

Frege, G. *The Foundations of Arithmetic* (J. L. Austin, trans.). Oxford: Basil Blackwell & Mott, Ltd., 1963.

Frege, G. *Translations from the Philosophical Writings of Gottlob Frege* (P. Geach and M. Black, eds.). Oxford: Basil Blackwell & Mott, Ltd., 1952.

Goodman, N. *Fact, Fiction, Forecast.* Cambridge: Harvard University Press, 1955).

Goodman, N. "On Infirmities of Confirmation Theory," *Philosophy and Phenomenological Research* vol. 8, no. 1, 1947.

Goodman, N. "Positionality and Pictures," *Philosophical Review*, vol. 69, no. 4, 1960.

Goodman, N. "A World of Individuals," in *The Problem of Universals.* South Bend, Ind.: University of Notre Dame Press, 1956.

Halle, M. "On the Bases of Phonology," in J. A. Fodor and J. J. Katz (eds.), *op. cit.*

Halle, M. "Phonology in Generative Grammar," *Word*, vol. 18, pp. 54–72, 1962. Reprinted in J. A. Fodor and J. J. Katz (eds.), *op. cit.*

Halle, M., and N. Chomsky. *The Sound Pattern of English.* New York: Harper & Row, Inc., (in preparation).

Hampshire, S. "The Interpretation of Language: Words and Concepts," in C. A. Mace (ed.), *British Philosophy in the Mid-Century.* New York: Macmillan Company, 1957.

Hempel, C. G. "The Concept of Cognitive Significance: A Reconsideration," *Contributions to the Analysis and Synthesis of Knowledge, Proceedings of the American Academy of Arts and Sciences,* vol. 80, 1951.

Hempel, C. G. "On the Nature of Mathematical Truth," *American Mathematical Monthly,* vol. 52, 1945. Reprinted in *Readings in Philosophical Analysis* H. Feigll and W. Sellars (eds.). New York: Appleton-Century-Crofts, Inc., 1949.

Hempel, C. G. "Problems and Changes in the Empiricist Criterion of Meaning," *Revue Internationale de Philosophie,* vol. 11, 1950. Reprinted in L. Linsky (ed.), *Semantics and the Philosophy of Language.* Urbana: University of Illinois Press, 1952.

Heyting, A. *Intuitionism*. Amsterdam: North-Holland Publishing Company, 1956.

Hume, D. *An Inquiry Concerning Human Understanding*. Indianapolis: Bobbs-Merrill Company, Inc., 1955.

Kant, I. *The Critique of Pure Reason* (N. K. Smith, trans.). New York: Humanities Press, 1929.

Kant, I. *A Prolegomena to Any Future Metaphysic* (L. W. Beck, trans.). Indianapolis: Bobbs-Merrill Company, Inc., 1950.

Katz, J. J. "Analyticity and Contradiction in Natural Language," in J. A. Fodor and J. J. Katz (ed.), *op. cit.*

Katz, J. J. *The Problem of Induction and its Solution*. Chicago: University of Chicago Press, 1960.

Katz, J. J. "Semantic Theory and the Meaning of 'Good,' " *Journal of Philosophy*, vol. 61, no. 235, December 10, 1964.

Katz, J. J., and J. A. Fodor. "The Structure of a Semantic Theory," *Language*, vol. 39, 1963. Reprinted in J. A. Fodor and J. J. Katz (eds.), *op. cit.*

Katz, J. J., and J. A. Fodor. "What's Wrong with the Philosophy of Language?" *Inquiry*, vol. 5, 1962.

Katz, J. J., and P. Postal. *An Integrated Theory of Linguistic Descriptions*. Cambridge: M. I. T. Press, 1964.

Kleene, S. C. *Introduction to Metamathematics*, Princeton, N. J.: D. Van Nostrand Company, Inc., 1952.

Klima, E. "Negation," in J. A. Fodor and J. J. Katz (eds.), *op. cit.*

Lees, R. B., and E. Klima. "Rules for English Pronominalization," *Language*, vol. 39, 1963.

Leibniz, G. W. *New Essays Concerning Human Understanding* (A. C. Langley, trans. and ed.), La Salle, Ill.: Open Court Publishing Company, 1949.

Miller, G. A., K. Pribram, and E. Galenter. *Plans and the Structure of Behavior.* New York: Holt, Rinehart and Winston, Inc., 1960.

Osgood, C. E., G. J. Suci, and P. H. Tannenbaum. *The Measurement of Meaning.* Urbana: University of Illinois Press, 1957.

Passmore, J. *A Hundred Years of Philosophy.* London: Gerald Duckworth & Company, Ltd., 1957.

Postal, P. *Constituent Structure.* Bloomington: Indiana University Press and The Hague: Mouton & Company, 1964.

Postal, P. "Underlying and Superficial Linguistic Structures," *Harvard Educational Review,* vol. 34, no. 2, 1964.

Quine, W. V. "Notes on the Theory of Reference," in *From a Logical Point of View.* Cambridge: Harvard University Press, 1953.

Quine, W. V. "The Problem of Meaning in Linguistics," in *From a Logical Point of View.* Reprinted in J. A. Fodor and J. J. Katz (eds.), *op. cit.*

Quine, W. V. "Two Dogmas of Empiricism," *Philosophical Review,* vol. 60, 1951.

Quine, W. V. *Word and Object.* Cambridge: M. I. T. Press, 1960.

Ryle, G. "Categories," in A. G. N. Flew (ed.), *Logic and Language,* vol. 2, Oxford: Basil Blackwell & Mott, Ltd., 1955.

Ryle, G. *The Concept of Mind.* London: Hutchinson & Company, Ltd., 1949.

Schiller, C. (ed.). *Instinctive Behavior.* New York: International Universities Press, Inc., 1957.

Shannon, C. E., and W. Weaver. *The Mathematical Theory of Communication.* Urbana: University of Illinois Press, 1949.

Skinner, B. F. *Verbal Behavior*. New York: Appleton-Century-Crofts, Inc., 1957.

Stevenson, C. L. *Ethics and Language*. New Haven: Yale University Press, 1945.

Strawson, P. F. *Introduction to Logical Theory*. New York: John Wiley & Sons, Inc., 1952.

Tarski, A. "The Semantic Conception of Truth," *Philosophy and Phenomenological Research*, vol. 4, 1944.

Urmson, J. O. "On Grading," in A. G. N. Flew (ed.), *Logic and Language*, vol. 2. Oxford: Basil Blackwell & Mott, Ltd., 1955.

Urmson, J. O. "Parenthetical Verbs," in A. G. N. Flew (ed.), *Essays in Conceptual Analysis*. London: Macmillan & Company, Ltd., 1956.

Vendler, Z. "Verbs and Times," *Philosophical Review*, vol. 66, no. 2, April, 1957.

Wittgenstein, L. *Philosophical Investigations*. Oxford: Basil Blackwell & Mott, Ltd., 1953.

Wittgenstein, L. *Tractatus Logico-Philosophicus*. London: Routledge & Kegan Paul, Ltd., 1922.

INDEX OF NAMES

Hilbert, David, 18, 23–24, 26–27, 35
Hobbes, Thomas, 240
Hume, David, 5, 18, 81, 93, 240, 267
Husserl, Edmund, 5

Kant, Immanuel, 189–194, 221, 226–227, 237, 239–240, 279
Katz, J. J., 58 n., 93 n., 95 n., 110 n., 126 n., 129 n., 131 n., 138 n., 142 n., 150–151 n., 162 n., 172 n., 184 n., 185, 200 n., 247 n., 265 n., 275 n., 291 n.
Kleene, S. C., 24 n., 122
Klima, E., 138 n., 200 n.

Lees, R. B., 138 n.
Leibniz, G. W., 5, 187, 240, 244, 267
Locke, John, 5, 178, 180, 240
Lorenz, K., 276

Mach, Ernst, 18
Mill, J. S., 5
Miller, G. A., 261 n.

Newton, Isaac, 65, 106, 115

Osgood, C. E., 313 n.

Passmore, J., 79
Plato, 5, 93, 240, 313

Postal, P., 110 n., 130–131 n., 138 n., 151 n., 172 n., 184 n., 200 n., 291 n.
Pribram, K., 261 n.

Quine, W. V., 48 n., 53–54, 56–59, 94, 173, 267–268, 313

Reichenbach, Hans, 18
Russell, Bertrand, 5, 19
Ryle, G., 5, 79, 82–88, 90, 238

Schlick, M., 18
Shannon, C. E., 313 n.
Skinner, B. F., 242 n., 275 n., 313
Stevenson, C. L., 315 n.
Strawson, P. F., 81–82
Suci, G. J., 313 n.

Tannenbaum, P. H., 313 n.
Tarski, A., 44
Tinbergen, N., 276

Urmson, J. O., 88

Vendler, Z., 88

Weaver, W., 313 n.
Whitehead, A. N., 19
Wittgenstein, L., 5, 69–81, 83, 85–86, 89–90, 316